"*Mothers Are Leaders* offers testimonials of women in senior leadership positions using their management and leadership skills, not only in their professional but also in their personal lives. As a single mother of two with a career in university management, I could very well relate to the stories that are shared. They do not pretend combining a career and family life is easy, but show how skills from professional life can enhance the personal life, and vice versa. The mild irony with which some of the stories are written brought a smile to my face. Humour and perspective are also important tools for career mums. Indeed, you can have it all, but perhaps not all at the same time. That is okay, since setting priorities and adapting to the environment is exactly what we do as leaders. This is a must read for young women struggling with life decisions. I wish I could have read it ten years ago."

—**Machteld Verbruggen,** PhD, President, Thomas More University College, Antwerp, Belgium

"Kimberly Battle-Walters Denu and Janet S. Walters have gathered a diverse group of women whose essays offer compelling personal stories and wise advice for mothers in a variety of leadership positions, from business to the ministry. We've all read about 'leaning in,' but here we read about the benefits of leaning back, zooming in, and zooming out for perspective, too. An important contribution to the growing library on women, work, and family."

—**Caroline M. Grant,** Associate Director, The Sustainable Arts Foundation; co-editor of *Mama, PhD: Women Write About Motherhood and Academic Life*

"The women who share their stories did not have roadmaps to navigate their lives or even literature that validated their journeys. And yet, as women of faith, there is a continuous message of God's provision. The writers remind women of faith that God knows us intimately and calls us by our name, and thus are with us on the journey of life. Further, their stories provide strategies for new mothers to employ as they consider how to balance their personal and professional lives, and as they live a God-centered life."

—**Barbara Dickerson,** Executive Director, Our Neighborhood Homework House

"The life of a working mother is personally challenging, complex, and rewarding. The authors of *Mothers Are Leaders* take the joys of motherhood, the conviction of faith, and the rewards of work and intertwine them into a fabric of graceful understanding and encouragement. This book provides insight both to women and the men who work with them."

—**Dr. Deana L. Porterfield,** President, Roberts Wesleyan College

"Research on leadership is incomplete when confined to the business world, for throughout human history, women—and men—have practiced the values and skills of leadership in their family roles. *Mothers Are Leaders* offers a valuable contribution to the literature on work/family balance by exploring the vital proposition that leadership begins at home."

—**Lorrie Greenhouse Gardella,** JD, MSW, ACSW, Vice President, Professional and Graduate Studies, Professor of Human Services, Albertus Magnus College; co-author of *A Dream and A Plan: A Woman's Path to Leadership in Human Services*

"If you are a mother, you will see your own story in *Mothers Are Leaders*, a compilation of wise, insightful, and thought-provoking essays by women who have made a remarkable difference in their workplaces, their communities, their churches, and their homes. As a professional woman with three daughters of my own, I found inspiration in the genuineness and openness of the authors. I saw, too, true beauty in the deep wisdom shared. Above all, I found peace in the revealing of lives so marked by unpredictable journeys, and yet lives so well-lived. These are the authors' stories, but they are ours, too. Above all, they must be celebrated."

—**Debra Pozega Osburn,** PhD, Vice President of University Relations, University of Alberta Edmonton, Alberta, Canada

"This gift from Denu and Walters is an invaluable bird's-eye view into the lives of nine dynamic and successful women leaders who share their wisdom on how they developed strategies and negotiated life, love, motherhood, and their work lives. These women teach us, by example, how to overcome any obstacle and triumph in the face of adversity. Through their passion, communication ethic, collaboration, and leadership principles, they model the courage and strength for all women to face each day anew and overcome individual challenges to meet success in their personal and professional lives."

—**Sheila T. Gregory,** PhD, Executive Director, The Institute of Scholarly Writing & Critical Thinking; Editor, *The Journal of Invitational Theory and Practice*

"As a mother of a three year-old and as one expecting our second child later this year, I was eager to dive into *Mothers Are Leaders*, and found myself immersed in each chapter. The outstanding contributors of the book shared their personal stories and leadership lessons in an engaging style, grounded in research and theory. Each of these mothers told her story and captured motherhood across the years—from their pregnancy to their children's infancy, college years, and adulthood. For all of us who are seeking that elusive balance of the roles of mother and leader at home and in the workplace, it was satisfying to be reminded that they are interconnected roles, and the lessons learned in these places have a profound effect on us and our children."

—**Carol McLaughlin Kennedy,** Director, Office of the President and University Secretary, Bucknell University

"This book puts into words what I know to be true. Learning to become a good mother wasn't easy, but it gave me the opportunity to learn what I needed to know to be a strong leader. Each chapter highlights the different ways women hone their leadership, management, communication, and other critical skills by loving and caring for their children."

—**Mary Adams,** President, American Sentinel University

"I grew up with a mother who was a leader. In our single-parent home, I watched her exhibit crisis-management skills, make wise work/home choices, be a wise spiritual leader, and have a strategy for raising three boys in a very difficult situation. *Finally,* here's a book that celebrates all those ways I saw my mother lead, as well as the countless mothers today who lead in their homes, careers, ministries, and workplaces. In this "must read" book from a select group of scholars and leaders, you'll find the research, the heart-grabbing stories, and the life-changing principles that mark mothers as leaders. It's a book that needs to be handed to every mother who leads."

—**John Trent**, PhD, Gary D. Chapman Chair of Marriage and Family Ministry and Therapy, Moody Theological Seminary, Chicago, Illinois

MOTHERS ARE LEADERS

MOTHERS ARE LEADERS

Editors Kimberly Battle-Walters Denu, PhD,
and Janet S. Walters

Abilene Christian University Press

MOTHERS ARE LEADERS

ACU PRESS

LIBRARY OF CONGRESS CATALOGING-IN-PUBLICATION DATA
Denu, Kimberly Battle-Walters, 1967-
Mothers are leaders / Kimberly Battle-Walters Denu, PhD and Janet S. Walters.
  pages cm
Includes bibliographical references.
ISBN 978-0-89112-580-8
1. Working mothers--United States. 2. Working mothers--Religious life. 3. Work and family--United States. I. Walters, Janet S., 1950- II. Title.
HQ759.48.D46 2014
306.874'3--dc23

2014029827

Cover and interior text design by Sandy Armstrong, Strong Design

Cover images from left to right:

"A Mother Cares for Her Infant," c. 1940, Library of Congress, Children's Bureau Centennial, public domain.

"Present Day Mother and Child . . . Not Pure Negro," Library of Congress Prints and Photographs Division, public domain.

Image of U.S. congresswoman Barbara Jordan speech, public domain.

For information contact:
Abilene Christian University Press
ACU Box 29138, Abilene, Texas, 79699

1-877-816-4455 toll free | www.acupressbooks.com

To mothers around the world who do so much with so little, as they steward families, callings, and leadership. To my own mother Janet, who has modeled good leadership and good motherhood. To my dear husband Yohannes and my precious children Joshua, Mahlet, and Kylee, who have provided support, patience, and love during this seminal project. Thank you!

—Kimberly

To my mother Estella, who exemplifies the philosophy of mothers as leaders and has demonstrated resilience in mothering, while performing numerous leadership roles for over sixty years. A special thanks to my husband Randall for his encouragement, thoughtfulness, and patience. To my daughter Kimberly; it has been great working with you. And to my daughters Tessla, Ericka, and Rhandi, who have learned firsthand and have somehow embraced the daunting task of "doing it all."

—Janet

ACKNOWLEDGMENTS

Special thanks to Dr. Mignon Jacobs, who first introduced the idea for this project. To our contributors for their transparency and hard work to produce such meaningful chapters. To Robyn Burwell for her amazing support during multiple drafts, edits, and reviews. Thanks to Maleea, Sharon, Brenda, Marguerite, and Gloria, who had amazing stories to tell, but cheered us on instead. To the Harvard Institute for Educational Management 2014 group for its support and patience during my many comments about "the book." To Dr. John Trent for his mentoring and helpful feedback. To Azusa Pacific University for providing the space for us to write. To our church families, many encouragers, and a host of colleagues and friends. Thank you!

CONTENTS

INTRODUCTION

KIMBERLY BATTLE-WALTERS DENU, PhD,
AND JANET S. WALTERS

"There is something you must always remember.
You are braver than you believe,
stronger than you seem, and smarter than you think."
—Pooh's Grand Adventure

Every mother is a leader. In fact, the act of parenting is one of the most important leadership positions that a person can ever fulfill. In the 1800s, poet William Ross Wallace wrote, "the hand the rocks the cradle / Is the hand that rules the world."[1] While some believe that this poem was originally intended to confine women and women's roles to the home, the prominence of this quote is a starting point for us to re-conceptualize mothers as leaders.

Mothers, also known as the Chief Everything Officers (CEOs),[2] are daily leading both in their homes and in the global community. Dr. Roberta Hestenes, former president of Eastern University, said, "Leadership is the ability to make a difference through influencing others."[3] Mothers do this every day, all day, for twenty-plus years of their children's lives. The complex and multifaceted role of motherhood thrusts mothers into a leadership position. If a leader is one who influences, leads, motivates, instructs, and trains, then mothers are in fact the first leaders that each of us encounters from the time of birth until young adulthood.

While many might agree that mothers are leaders within the home, they may not make the connection between motherhood and leadership outside of the home. In this book we assert that the instincts and skills that are indigenous and necessary for motherhood are the same, or as crucial, as those needed in professional leadership roles. In essence, motherhood forces one to be adaptable, to make challenging decisions quickly, and to move fluidly among multiple roles and tasks. On any given day the average mother moves seamlessly through a surplus of jobs: counselor, chef, chauffer, educator, doctor, and accountant, just to name a few. It is a demanding job that requires strategic planning, prioritizing, management, constant change, adaptability, nurturing, and training, all while building a team of competent and compassionate future leaders. This being said, very few books acknowledge mothers as leaders or the inherent leadership skills that are a part of mothering, yet in the corporate world, these skill sets are championed daily.

The women leaders in this book, all from the academic, church, and business arenas, will share how they provide leadership both within and outside of their homes, how they balance family and work, and how their roles as mothers prepared them for or made them more effective in leadership in the workplace.

Mothers in the Workplace

In the United States, over 71 percent of women with children under the age of eighteen work outside of the home.[4] The number of women with children in the workplace has increased substantially from the mid-1900s.[5] With more and more women working outside of the home, fewer American homes fit the model of traditional nuclear families, families in which the father is the primary breadwinner and the mother cares for the family at home. In fact, 41 percent of mothers are the primary breadwinners in their families, and another 23 percent are co-breadwinners.[6]

There are three major factors that have contributed to the increase of mothers in the workplace. First, there has been an increase in the levels of education among women, and with it, a greater acceptance of women in the workplace. Many universities across the U.S. are seeing student enrollments that are roughly 60 percent female or higher.[7] As a result of the women's movement, policy changes, and changes in social mores, more women than ever are encouraged to get an education and to use it. By the time many women get ready to start their families, many have established careers, are accustomed to working, and continue to work after they have children.

Second, with career and educational opportunities, more women are delaying the age at which they first marry and have children. Today the median age for first time marriages is twenty-seven years of age for men and twenty-five for women, and women are having children well into their forties.[8] While there may be educational, professional, and social benefits to delaying marriage and children, it must also be noted that there may be implications for a woman's health, fecundity, and selection of marriageable partners later in life.[9]

Third, more women are working due to financial necessity. With lagging economies, underemployment, and rising expenses, more families are dependent on two or more incomes. Each of these factors, in addition to personal choice and a sense of calling and passion, have contributed to the number of mothers today who work outside of the home.

Limited Options

In the past there were limited options for working women and their decision to have children. During both world wars, women were only expected to work in the absence of men and to fill in the workforce gaps while men were at war.[10] Following the wars, women were expected to care for their families. If a woman was single and without children, it was socially acceptable for her to work, traditionally in what was seen as "women's work" such as secretarial support, domestic service, the garment industry, and teaching; the moment she married and had a child, she was expected to leave her career and raise her children. This was because traditionally a woman's employment was considered secondary to the caring of her family and a man's family role was considered secondary to his role as provider.[11] This further endorsed the notion that men were breadwinners and women were bread bakers.[12] So the first option was for women to stop working when children arrived.

There was another option for successful career women. If a woman was highly successful in her field, then it was assumed that she would probably not marry, or if she did and chose to continue to work, that she would not have children and would focus strictly on her career. This was the "either-or" option. If a woman *chose* a career, people expected her to sacrifice her choice of a family. She was made to choose either "baby or briefcase."[13]

Still another option was related to women who chose to work *and* have children. It was expected, albeit often unspoken, that these women would work in less competitive occupational tracks that were more time flexible, sometimes referred to as the "mommy track."[14] Perceived as trying to "have it all," working mothers have been socially ostracized and taunted. When they have striven for more ambitious roles, they have encountered roadblocks by both men and women.[15]

While many mothers have been confined to this "either-or" work-family paradigm since the 1950s, mothers today are expanding the boundaries and moving to an inclusive "both-and" approach when it comes to their careers and families. The women leaders in this book will discuss how they manage to balance both successful careers and thriving families.

The Mommy Factor: The Unique Contributions of Working Mothers

In *The Mommy Brain*, Katherine Ellison highlights fascinating neuroscience research that looks at how motherhood in fact changes a woman's brain for the better. She examines research that highlights five *attributes* of a mother's baby-boosted brain: (1) efficiency—as mothers learn multitasking and resilience; (2) resilience—as motherhood helps with stress reduction; (3) emotional intelligence—motherhood facilitates street smarts and social mores; (4) perception—motherhood provides an expansion of the senses; and (5) motivation—mothers gain mental agility and strength to do all they must do.[16] In one lab experiment on rats, researchers found that mother rats outperformed bachelorette rats in both learning and memory tests.[17] While such findings may be flattering to mothers, it does not imply that mothers are smarter than others; however, it does propose that there are certain cognitive, social, and physiological advantages that mothers experience and can use for good.

These five attributes can be applied to the workplace and translate to unique leadership skills that working mothers bring to professional milieus. First, an analogy could be made that mothers lead like they cook.[18] Mothers have the ability to multitask. Being a mother forces a woman to be aware of and do multiple things simultaneously. Just as a chef coordinates the timing and preparation of various dishes, working mothers have a sense of timing, order, and how to do several projects at the same time. Second, they have intuition or perception, a subjective sense of knowing about things. This comes in the form of perceptive impressions. This intuitive skill can help them navigate difficult or challenging leadership situations. Third, working mothers have the ability to provide care, which allows them to be sensitive to the needs of others. Ellison's work ties this to emotional intelligence. They have a unique ability to balance nurturance with governance, which is not an easy task. Fourth, they have the ability to share power. Mothers, in their daily lived experiences, practice being more inclusive and relational, thus making it easier for them to work collaboratively rather than competitively. Since mothers look out for the well-being of their entire families, they learn to gather feedback and input from everyone. Feminists have long heralded how women leaders, including mothers, tend to empower others rather than derogate them. Finally, working mothers often have a fierce protectiveness and loyalty for their organizations and areas of stewardship, much like a mother would for her child. This protectiveness and sense of loyalty is often evident in the hours and years of service that they give to the organizations in which they serve.

Opening the Door for Mothers as Leaders

In 2013, two women—Sheryl Sandberg and Marissa Mayer—mothers, created a fire storm around the topic of mothers as leaders. Sheryl Sandberg, Chief Operating Officer of Facebook, wrote a book called *Lean In*, which quickly became a topic of debate in the workplace and in homes. Why? Because her book challenged women to lean into leadership opportunities, to not hold themselves back professionally, and to make their partners true partners at home so that women could pursue unique career endeavors. Marissa Mayer, the Chief Executive Officer at Yahoo, stirred controversy when she revoked an established telecommuting option for employees in the tech industry, which lends itself to creative flexibility. This alone was enough to fuel the news fires for a few weeks, but in addition, she vowed to only take two weeks of maternity leave, as a soon-to-be mother, and reportedly spent thousands of dollars to build a nursery onto her Yahoo office.[19] Whether or not people agreed with these two women is not the point. The issue is that these women resurfaced an age-old question: Can women really have it all? Following these events, women debated not only *can* they have it all, but whether or not they *wanted* it all, and whether or not having a prominent career was really the apex of their existence? The writers of this book will discuss having it all, juggling it all, and seasons when it may be wise to step away from *some* of it all.

The Sandberg and Mayer media explosions inadvertently raised attention to some of the "external barriers" in the workplace that need to be addressed in order for women to have better access to leadership positions in a variety of settings. Such things as child care options in the workplace, better maternity/paternity policies, flex time, telecommuting, women mentors (e.g., leanin.org), and added support in the home (where women do the majority of child care and housework, even when they work) are greatly needed.[20]

Mothers Who Lead

The mothers in this book come from a variety of backgrounds. They are new mothers and veteran mothers. Mothers from diverse racial, ethnic, and socioeconomic backgrounds. They represent women who are in cabinet-level positions in academe, pastors of large churches, campus pastors, and professionals in business. They are respected leaders in the professional world, but also beloved mothers and spouses. They are known for excellence in the workplace, as well as prioritizing their families first. How do they balance work and family in busy careers that could easily consume the margins of their lives? In the following chapters they will tell you their stories—including the challenges, victories, and concessions. And how does their faith play a part in their lives? Each of these mothers is a Christian. Their faith is not quietly left on a shelf but actively lived out each day in the care of their spouses and children, the care of those they lead in the workplace, and in the ways that they live out their true callings unapologetically.

Each mother will also highlight a leadership principle that she has applied in the workplace and in her home. While these principles are largely recognized for their application in professional settings, each chapter will depict how these same leadership principles are used by mothers in the home every day.

In conclusion, every mother is a leader—whether she is in the workplace or at home. However, those mothers who also lead outside of the home have an opportunity to provide a unique perspective of leadership in the workplace, due to their roles as mothers, and the distinctive attributes and skills that mothers bring. But just as there are no perfect leaders, there are no perfect mothers. At times, mothers make mistakes—super heroes they are not! However, the mothers in this book choose to keep moving forward, knowing that tomorrow is another opportunity to love better, learn more, live more richly, and lead. So buckle up and enjoy the ride as the women in the following chapters transparently discuss the rewards and challenges of leading, balancing work and family, and much, much more.

Notes

[1] William Ross Wallace, "What Rules the World," in J. K. Hoyt's *Cyclopedia of Practical Quotations* (New York: Funk & Wagnalls, 1896), 402.

[2] Kathryn Sansone, *Woman First, Family Always: Real-Life Wisdom from a Mother of Ten* (Des Moines, Iowa: Meredith Books, 2006), 23.

[3] Karen Longman, *Thriving in Leadership* (Abilene, Texas: Abilene Christian University Press, 2012), 21.

[4] U.S. Department of Labor: Bureau of Labor Statistics, "Women in the Labor Force: A Data Book," Report 1011 (December 2008), accessed July 16, 2009, http://www.bls.gov/cps/wlf-table7-2008.pdf ; National Women's Law Center, "The Reality of the Workforce: Mothers Are Working Outside the Home" (February 2008), accessed August 6, 2008, http://www.nwlc.org; Sheryl Sandberg, *Lean In* (New York: Alfred A. Knopf, 2013).

[5] Ibid.

[6] Sandberg, 23.

[7] Daniel Borzelleca, "The Male-Female Ratio in College," *Forbes*, February 16, 2012, accessed May 20, 2014, http://www.forbes.com/sites/ccap/2012/02/16/the-male-female-ratio-in-college/; Alex Williams, "The New Math on Campus," *The New York Times*, February 5, 2010, accessed May 20, 2014, http://www.nytimes.com/2010/02/07/fashion/07campus.html.

[8] U.S. Census Bureau, "Fertility of American Women: 2008," accessed August 6, 2009, www.census.gov/population/www/socdemo/fertility/mer-fert-slides.htm; U.S. Census Bureau American FactFinder, "Selected Social Characteristics in the United States: 2005–2007," accessed July 17, 2009, http://factfinder.census.gov/servlet/ADPTable?_bm=y&-geo_id=01000US&-qr_name=AC; Pamela Ferrara, "Women in the Labor Force," *Oregon Labor Market Information System*, April 2008, accessed August 6, 2008, http://www.qualityinfo.org/olmisj.

[9] Linda Waite and Maggie Gallagher, *The Case for Marriage: Why Married People Are Happier, Healthier, and Better Off Financially* (New York: Doubleday, 2000). In the *Case for Marriage*, authors Waite and Gallagher outline research that highlights a plethora of benefits that are associated with marriage. They say that married people are physically healthier, financially stronger, and emotionally happier than singles. While some scholars may refute this, the data are substantiated in the literature.

[10] Maurine W. Greenwald, "The Woman's Part," in *Women, War, and Work: The Impact of World War I on Women Workers in the United States* (Ithaca, New York: Cornell University Press, 1990); R. J. Q. Adams, *Arms and the Wizard: Lloyd George and the Ministry of Munitions 1915–1916* (West Sussex, United Kingdom: Littlehampton Books), 1978.

[11] Sampson L. Blair, "Employment, Family, and Perceptions of Marital Quality among Husbands and Wives," *Journal of Family Issues* 14.2 (1993): 189–212; Bryan Strong and Christine DeVault, *The Marriage and Family Experience*, sixth edition (St. Paul, Minnesota: West Publishing Company, 1995).

[12] Diane Halpern and Fanny Cheung, *Women at the Top: Powerful Leaders Tell Us How to Combine Work and Family* (Malden, Massachusetts: Wiley-Blackwell, 2008), 9.

[13] Ibid, 5, 95.

[14] Felice Schwartz, "Management Women and the New Facts of Life." *Harvard Business Review* 89.1 (Jan.–Feb. 1989): 65–76, cited in James Henslin, *Sociology* , seventh edition (Boston: Allyn and Bacon, 2005), 314.

[15] Halpern and Cheung, *Women at the Top*, 118.

[16] Katherine Ellison, *The Mommy Brain: How Motherhood Makes Us Smarter* (New York: Basic Books, 2005).

[17] Ibid, 8.

[18] T. D. Jakes, "Maximize the Moment," *Time Life Video* series (Alexandria, Virginia, 2001), noting a woman's ability to multitask.

[19] Bonnie Fuller, "Marissa Mayer Shouldn't Be Criticized for Building an Office Nursery," *The Huffington Post* (Feb. 26, 2013), accessed May 25, 2014, www.huffingtonpost.com/bonnie-fuller/marissa-mayer-office-nursery.

[20] Sarah Gibbard Cook, "Research Universities Work to Increase Faculty Flexibility," *Women in Higher Education* 17 (July 2008): 6–7; Gibbard Cook, "Mama, PhD: A Companion for Mothers and Scholars," *Women in Higher Education* 17 (Aug. 2008): 21; E. Elrena Evans and Caroline Grant, *Mama, PhD: Women Write about Motherhood and Academic Life* (Piscataway, New Jersey: Rutgers University Press, 2008); Kimberly Battle-Walters Denu, "Sheroes: Mothers Make Great Leaders, Naturally," *Women in Higher Education* 18 (2009).

1

STRATEGIC LEADERS

DORETHA A. O'QUINN, PhD

"I know God will not give me anything I cannot handle.
I just wish that he didn't trust me so much."

—Mother Teresa

As he held my baby's head in his hand, the doctor who delivered my first son cheered loudly, "I just delivered the next linebacker for the L.A. Rams!" He was a nine pound baby boy. My husband and I were excited young parents, working two jobs and beginning new careers. Eleven months later, at only seven months along (because she could not wait to join her brother), my daughter arrived—through extensive toil and a life-threatening delivery for both her and me—at just five pounds, six ounces. With her soft whimpers, her safe and healthy delivery brought much joy to all in the room. I was tired but I had the perfect family—a boy and a girl.

Two years later, after starting my new teaching career, I heard, "Congratulations, you're pregnant!" Totally unexpected, I was speechless, tearful, and in shock, not because of the baby but because I was worried about how I would handle a new baby, two small children, and a new career. I already had the perfect family. How could I tell my principal I could not finish the year because I was pregnant? After all, I was a new teacher who could not fulfill my ten-month contract. With many questions, fears, and worries, alongside three babies, a new career, and some experience with depression, I saw no way possible to handle both family and work.

"It's a ten-pound baby!" Those were the doctor's words about my third child. He arrived with no sound and his thumb in his mouth. I looked at my son and instantly all questions, fears, and worries, as well as the depression I had prior to his birth, were gone. I possessed deep faith that there would be provision for our family. My big baby boy became the center of my world alongside his other siblings. I pulled his thumb from his mouth because I just wanted to hear him cry. It was something about hearing that little voice that brought such joy to my experience as a mother.

I had a great family support system and returned to my career in teaching after six months. With three babies and a hard-working husband, we had enough numbers to be a small business organization. But unbeknownst to me, the business was not yet finished growing.

At my sixth-month check up, the doctor suggested I go to the lab that day, take a pregnancy test, and wait for the results. Since my doctor had a keen sense of humor and he had been with me through all of my pregnancies, I was sure he was playing a practical joke. It was no joke! I was pregnant with my fourth child. How would I tell my husband? I had actually convinced myself I had done this all by myself, and somehow it was my fault we were going to have our fourth child. I was twenty-seven, married, and had three children, a new teaching career, and major responsibilities in my church. What would I do with another baby?

Again, it had nothing to do with having the baby, because that was going to happen. I questioned whether I had the skills and resources to adequately take care of all the children. Again, the doctor's words confirmed the arrival of another child: "You have a nine pound baby boy." God really had a sense of humor. He weighed in at the exact same size as my first son. Those loud cries of new life replaced my feelings of inadequacy and uncertainty and affirmed my resilience and desire for the work ahead. Little did I dream or dare to hope that one day I would be invited to write a chapter on motherhood and strategic leadership.

The questions I asked as a new mother were those selfsame questions I asked myself as a school administrator. What am I supposed to do? Do I have the skills to be effective? What happens if something happens to me? How will I find resources to meet the needs? What can I do to ensure success? I came to realize that each of those questions focused directly on the skills of a strategic leader. Strategic leaders create a sense of purpose and direction, which guides strategy formulation and implementation within an organization.

I discovered that the bedrock of leadership is the ability to anticipate, envision, maintain flexibility, and empower others to create strategic changes. The components of strategic leadership described by Michael Hitt are determining the firm's purpose or vision, exploiting and maintaining core competencies, developing human capital, sustaining an effective organizational culture, emphasizing ethical practices, and establishing balanced organizational controls.[1] The family became my first organization to lead.

For the strategic leader, Paul Schoemaker, Samantha Howland, and Steve Krupp offer six essential skills which, when mastered and used simultaneously, allow leaders to think strategically and navigate the unknown effectively.[2] The six skills are the ability to anticipate, challenge, interpret, decide, align, and learn as a leader in the organization. The mothering skills I possessed to lead my family strategically were innate and arose as I needed them. Organizations and the environments in which they operate are increasingly complex and ambiguous, as is motherhood. Therefore, both leaders and mothers must navigate through these complexities and develop strategies, as Natalie Slawinski describes, that will allow their homes and their organizations to be successful.[3]

All organizations have a management structure that determines relationships between and among the different activities and members; it subdivides and assigns roles, responsibilities, and authority to carry out different tasks. An organization has been described as an "open system that affects and is affected by its environment,"[4] and it was no different with my family. It would become the first organization that fostered the beginning of my development in strategic leadership, even though I didn't have the academic and professional language to articulate it. This chapter will affirm that mothers are strategic leaders in their initial organization of family and will clarify how the academic or professional language and concepts of strategic leadership contribute to their effectiveness in the workplace.

Strategic Leadership and Personal Growth

Being the mother of four dynamic and diverse individuals is the greatest revolutionary and transformational experience of my life. It is, I believe, the greatest trust of leadership a woman can ever have. The birth of my first child began the journey of learning. My second child came eleven months and twenty-two days later. At that point, I was only twenty-three and a newlywed with two small children. A three-year space marked the difference between my second and third child, and the fourth was born nineteen months later. By twenty-seven, I had a five-year-old, a four-year-old, a one-year-old, and an infant.

Leading strategically, as a mother and in the workforce, is what L. R. Forcey describes as a socially constructed set of activities and relationships involved in nurturing and caring for people.[5] My role as a leader in the home and workforce required good organizational skills and time management. Leading in each of these areas involved fostering healthy relationships and conflict resolution skills, as well as the ability to discipline and balance both a personal and professional life. All these skills act as contributors for nurturing and caring for people. Kelly Starling in a 1999 article for *Ebony*, describes the role of an effective mother in the workforce as a "Power Mom."[6] Throughout my experiences as mother, I maintained my role as a wife, minister, director of Christian education, classroom teacher, school administrator, college professor, program director, and now as a senior-level administrator in higher education and a grandmother. Everything about my involvement in these roles has required the ability to lead. Motherhood had demands that affected lives and schedules, and the workforce had similar demands along with governing policies that added to the complexity of my effectiveness in both roles. Kim Oates, Elizabeth Hall, and Tamara Anderson describe these demands as a "benefit," my "pursuit of multiple callings" through balancing career and family.[7] As I reflect on the diverse experiences of motherhood and the workforce, I can attest to numerous experiences that have been beneficial for both professional development and for the pursuit of multiple callings.

During the earlier stages of motherhood, I had five different family members who required that I develop structures and put systems in place to be effective. As one example, bedtime for four young children, whether it was for a nap or for going to sleep for the evening, required structures and systems. We were in a two-bedroom apartment. One bedroom was for the three older children and one bedroom was for the baby alongside my husband and me. Putting my children to bed became the dreaded experience. My husband was quick to yell out "Go to bed!" or go in their room to discipline them. I realized, as I observed them watching *Sesame Street*, how much they loved music and listening to stories. I purchased several children's albums with songs from *Sesame Street*, *Dr. Seuss*, and other children's books. This became the strategic leadership structure I put in place for nap and bedtime success. Slawinski, in her article on strategic leadership, calls this developing human capital, referring to the components of knowledge, skills, and abilities of the firm's employees that are strategic to the organization's success.[8]

What I did not realize was the way my role as a mother would strengthen and enhance my ability to learn leadership skills for professional application. I divided my time between my leadership role and responsibilities of motherhood and those of my career, each setting acting as its own organization. Knowledge@Wharton calls this balancing act of family and career "the juggle struggle."[9] However, gaining professional skills in leading strategically offers an alternative to the juggle struggle. Strategic development skills provide mothers who are leaders with the ability to form a planned approach to the diverse responsibilities of motherhood and the workforce.

As a key strategy, I had to know my own personal capacity in order to be effective as a mother with church and school administration responsibilities. Samuel Rima's book, *Leading from the Inside Out,* states, "Before we can expect to exercise effective leadership that will withstand the hostile elements of our culture, serious preparatory work must be done in those areas of a leader's life that will provide a firm foundation on which an effective leadership career can be built. . . . All effective enduring leadership must be built on the foundation of effective self-leadership. It is our ability to successfully lead our own life that provides the firm foundation from which we can lead others."[10] Everything about the development as a leader in the workplace and as a mother requires a strategy.

The term *strategy* is not found in parenting manuals or offered to mothers as a skill needed to be a parent. Strategic planning is clearly the leadership skill that every mother develops automatically, one that becomes an effective skill for the workplace. A strategy is the well-defined roadmap of an organization to reach its goals.[11] Strategy, in short, bridges the gap between where we are and where we want to be. It is the knowledge of goals, the uncertainty of events, and the need to take into consideration the likely or actual behavior of others. The first time a woman hears "you are pregnant," and she is involved outside the home professionally, she starts out on the journey of strategic leadership. Strategies become the central focus of how life will function effectively. Everything she thinks about, wrapped in all its fear and excitement, revolves around understanding the need for developing a strategic plan. How does she manage a job in the workplace and at home?

Researchers for leaders or managers offer five essential steps to understanding how strategic plans are organized in professional businesses.[12] While mothers may not have the business language, they certainly do require and implement the skills. The first skill is the responsibility to understand and develop a strategic mission and vision. As a mother and leader of a family, I had a vision of what each child's future would be and how I would plan to make that happen. The second skill is setting objectives that indicate the leader's value to the organization. At the heart of this is the mother's style of leadership, knowing what she must do to assure that the children reach their goals and know their own worth and value. For a professional leader in the workplace, it is no different with the employees.

The third skill is knowledge of the target group (the niche market) so the strategy created is achievable. Professional organizations, such as those in higher education, often provide extensive training and development to ensure employees understand the intended customer. It may be clear the niche market is comprised of students, but the organization must know what type of student it wants to attract. In Christian higher education institutions, the niche is often students who are required to be of a specific religious denomination. Diverse expectations among departments within higher education institutions will result in variations in recruiting strategies to suit their particular niches. On the other hand, a mother's niche is her child. She is expected to have keen sensitivity and knowledge about strategies for learning each child's skills and abilities. One child might demand more personal attention and another may be quite independent. Mothers generally know their niche and know their children are able to achieve success, and they also have a special ability to discern how to make that happen. A mother's wit or wisdom will transfer into the professional workplace, just as it did for me as an administrator in personnel matters and student selection.

The fourth skill is implementing and executing strategy through clarifying aspirations or goals. Mothers are committed to making things happen for the family. Robert Kaplan and David Norton have designed a model for professional organizations called the "Balanced Scorecard," which other disciplines within higher education have adapted to better equip leaders in the institution to make things happen.[13] The family organization is where it all begins—where mothers are able to commit to the success of each one of their children.

The fifth skill is evaluating performance, monitoring new developments, and initiating corrective adjustments to assess organizational capacity. There is no doubt mothers leading families learn the importance of strategies for managing the family. Time management was very important when managing four children. We had to be at church each Sunday at 9:00 A.M. I laid everyone's clothes out the night before, including my own. I woke up at least two hours early, to prepare breakfast and prepare myself. Rather than wake each child up at once, the child who woke up first would get partially dressed and head to the breakfast table. My plan was always to finish a half-hour before we had to leave. This system worked well even though I did not associate it with time management. I am still conscious of being on time to events, meetings, work, and so forth; however, gaining the language, theories, and models for strategic leadership results in effective development skills as a practitioner in the home, as well as a navigator of professional organizations or institutions. These five steps contribute to effective leadership for mothers who lead.

Understand and Develop a Strategic Mission and Vision

An individual must begin with a clear understanding of the organization's mission and vision to be successful in leadership. It is all about looking toward the future. That vision is the leader's promise to those whom she or he will serve. This same principle applies to the organization of the family. The leadership role of the parents in the home should include a strategic mission and vision for the children, which include but are not limited to child care, education, discipline, etc.

The family is one of the oldest organizations in society and mothers usually have had the leadership role involving the children. While I worked for two professional organizations outside the home, my mission as a mother was clearly to ensure the welfare and care of my children. I was not just multitasking in developing plans for them in my absence, but according to Judith Bardwick in "Peacetime Management and Wartime Leadership," as a strategic leader I was taking responsibility and preparing followers to succeed when the leader was not present.[14] Ultimately, making good citizens would fulfill my vision and mission as a mother. Lesley Willcoxson describes this as developing the ability to integrate strategic insights into strategic choices.[15] Providing the children with clear behavioral expectations, such as showing respect for authority, treating everyone fairly, and demonstrating other positive character qualities outside of our presence, allowed them to integrate insights about proper family behavior in order to make choices that would not cause negative consequences.

Even though I believed the leader who achieved a balanced development with family and career would be an effective strategic leader, I did not necessarily know the right questions to ask to measure my leadership effectiveness. I found the mission of my workplace was often discovered through extensive training, literature, and orientation. I needed to know what the organization was about. Where was it going? How could it do what it said it would do? How could I be effective in supporting the mission? In some cases, the mission alignment and its conflicts with our family mission assisted me in knowing particular employment was not a professional fit for me and I could walk away in peace. It was during my first teaching position that I learned the importance of a coinciding organizational mission and family mission.

My husband was not quite ready for me to take a teaching job, but one came open. We had a major decision to make. The initial tension was the issue of childcare. I liked the idea of preschool, but he wanted the children to be cared for by his mother. The decision was a compromise. If they attended school it would have to be near my job, for only four hours each day, and they would get picked up and taken to his mother's until I finished work. My job was very close to the preschool and his mother's home. I faced the challenge of what Alonzo Strickland's and Arthur Thompson's strategic leadership research describes as my ability to develop networks and support systems that provided me with the people, materials, and resources to effectively manage my life as a professional.[16] I managed my work each day, as well as picking the children up from preschool, taking them to my mother-in-law's, and returning to work. It was a strategic approach that worked out for the first school term.

At the beginning of the second school term, however, I found out I was pregnant with my third child. This made it very difficult to keep up the pace. One afternoon, I picked up the two children, went back to the classroom, and laid my head on the desk thinking, "I can't do this anymore." I had a pressing feeling—I was not a mother called to work with twenty-eight other people's children and lose my own. Immediately, I wrote my resignation, to be effective at the end of the school year. I left the school, and, with extended time off, brought two sons into the world. Our family now had four small children.

It was evident that there were conflicts between the mission of the professional organization and the mission of my family. The organization's mission was to educate children, holding them to a high academic standard. The teaching responsibility was not only during the workday but also in the evening and, in some cases, on Saturdays. While I truly enjoyed teaching children, what I learned was the mission of the professional organization could be in conflict with the mission of my family. As a leader in the classroom and of the family, I discovered a key principle about the mission: where there is conflict, tensions will develop because of the desire to do both jobs well. I had decided to remain at the school and fulfill its mission until the end of the school year, which was my professional requirement. The mission and vision of the teaching profession and school leadership experience provided me with the language for understanding this phase of strategic planning and the importance of selecting the right organization for my career.

Set Objectives That Articulate the Organization's Value

The objectives for the development of the family were not explicitly stated and planned, but were deeply present, nonetheless. These objectives contributed to shaping the value system for the family. Each professional organization uses objectives to track its performance and progress, or take action to create a competitive advantage. I realized objectives would also shape my professional career. The strategic leadership research by Strickland and Thompson, as well as Rima and many others, bears this out.[17] Having professional language that offers direction for managing progress helps leaders remain focused on the purpose of the organization, as well as what it values, which is what builds a competitive advantage.

One of my objectives as a mother, which has had a direct influence on my professional career choice, is that I would never work in a job that prohibited me from leaving or responding to my family's needs. Professionally, I also never attended a function where my children were not welcome if there was no one to care for them. There would be no job or event priority that would pre-empt a legitimate family need. The objectives that led to identifying values in the family also became non-negotiables for my professional career. My outside or professional work was never to interfere with my ability to be available for my children. It was at that point of clearly defining my goals and values for my professional career that I returned to the education profession as a school administrator.

This position in education was a role both my husband and I were excited about as I returned to the field. However, it was leadership in an institution that would be challenging to the values I mentioned because that responsibility had its own non-negotiables. We began to utilize shared roles in the family, a strategic plan that we did not realize was developing. My charge as the administrator was to fulfill the institutional plan. This required extensive meetings with the school board, teachers, parents, staff, and students, along with occasional traveling, project management, excessive fundraising, and the list goes on. Suddenly, there was a conflict of value systems; however, the need for a second income heightened what Thomas Licona refers to as the need for the clarification of values, and making professional adjustments to fit with my stated objectives.[18]

As a mother, I was able to engage my husband in areas of family leadership that were new to him. Unlike his prior resistance with the younger children, he willingly took on the responsibility of assuring their safety and care in a school close to his job. Psychological and leadership research offers the term of this transition as a "role reversal."[19] Nothing is taken away from the people involved, but the roles are reversed or shared. Our mission, vision, and values of the children's welfare did not change, but our way of reaching our goals did. We made adjustments that would support me professionally, as well as sustain the family. I did experience inter-role conflicts in balancing multiple roles as a mother.[20] Through this experience, I learned the reality of how outside influences can alter one's objectives. Paul Schoemaker, Steve Krupp, and Beth Howland call this skill "interpreting."[21] To interpret is to reflexively see or hear what one expects and to synthesize all the input in order to make a wise decision.

Leading strategically may require the knowledge and clarification of organizational values. My experience as a school administrator assisted in my ability to clarify the objectives and value system for our family. These values are what the organization stands for and how it promotes itself using the principles that are generally non-negotiable. My husband and I are both from the Christian faith and are strongly influenced by it, which clarifies our responsibility in the home and the workplace. We were both from matriarchal homes and valued our mothers, but we were beginning our family with different values. Rima identifies values as "those things to which we attach a relative worth, utility, or importance."[22] He further explains that a leader with integrity has a unifying set of values that guide choices of action, regardless of the situation.

There were other values we learned from life experiences centered in character qualities and principles—trust, honesty, respect, obedience, love, justice, and friendship, to name a few—that would be important to our family as well as to my position as a school administrator. I was responsible for leading the institution by example, as well as teaching these values in special ways to my family. The institution did not influence the values of family, but the institution did benefit from having a strong leader who would embrace and promote its values. Many of the skills and principles applied to motherhood were the same principles I lived out and had to apply in the professional environment.

Knowledge of the Target Group
Creates an Achievable Strategy

In the midst of all the roles of leadership, the family is the most important organization I lead. Basic skills of leadership are applicable at home and in my professional world. I had to identify ways to create achievable goals for my target groups at school, which were the students, faculty, and staff. The children were my target group at home.

The role of school administrator presented a new challenge to our family values and my professional values. I then decided to get my master's degree in education in order to be more effectively prepared as a professional administrator. During this time, I became employed by the church part-time to develop the Christian education department. Simultaneously, I worked full-time as a school administrator, part-time in my church, and went to school to earn my master's degree. Involvement in each came alongside my role as a mother. The leadership of school administration, church, and some aspects of family became the subjects of my homework assignments, which contributed to understanding strategic leadership development. Throughout my studies, I applied skills and learned the language of strategic and organizational planning. These classes helped me acquire the language for leadership, but the concepts, terms, and examples used in the course clearly applied to my work as mother.

When I attended graduate courses, my children actually attended school with me and sat in the back of the classroom. Furthermore, they were always involved in the activities we planned for the church. It was during the latter part of our time serving in the youth department that our oldest son approached his dad with this comment: "Dad, you and Mom have a lot of time with the youth and they are always at our house. I feel left out and there is no time for me." That moment, my husband called for a family meeting and asked all the children how they felt. We discovered they were beginning to feel as if they were sharing us with the youth. My husband and I decided that very night that we would resign from the church positions. A new phase of life I had never anticipated in motherhood began. What was unique about that conversation with our oldest son was that it began a new approach to problem solving, described in leadership research as collaboration.[23]

Clarifying and Implementing Goals

My career as an administrator required continual application of the clarification strategy. Implementing plans based on objectives identified through a continuous clarification process allows an organization to retain a fluid, not static, state. This kept those who were working in the school aware of their investment and of my expectations for them as employees. When employees know where a leader is going and remain engaged in the process of implementing the organization's plan, they will support the endeavor. This style of strategic leadership is what Richard Hughes and Katherine Beatty describe as the greatest opportunity to observe and experience growth in the organization. A major outcome, according to Hughes and Beatty, is the ability to clarify the objectives so the organization has the ability to move in the right direction.[24]

At this time, the growth and development of the school I was leading would contribute to several transitions that would take place. One, I would leave school administration to work in higher education. Two, my husband's role in coaching sports would expand significantly. Three, the growth of the children from teen to young adulthood would require the clarification of family objectives. It was also a time in the family to observe the gifts of leadership my husband and I had as a team. My role in motherhood quickly shifted to carpooling mom and serving as a weekend hostess for my husband's teams while I prepared for doctoral studies and began the transition from school administrator to doctoral student and adjunct professor. The children became involved in swimming, baseball, and football teams. I would leave the gyms, head to the pool, then to cheerleading and the football field for practice throughout the week. It was exactly as Lydia Saad described as managing well through having less time and rest.[25] My role as doctoral student and adjunct professor allowed me to adjust my schedule, and there were times when I left my children at a practice in order to return to a class or teach while their dad met them for pick-up. I lived with a calendar and appointment book in hand, an effective strategy for time management. It was during that time I read the book by Gordon MacDonald called *Ordering Your Private World*.[26] Everything about leadership in the workplace and the family required executing strategies that would accomplish goals and would keep everyone aware of the plan.

Our children were committed to various outside activities alongside their schoolwork and church activities. Their involvement was a result of our intentional commitment to train and nurture our children based on our faith principle. Our mission and values never changed, but our aspirations were changing. I expanded my educational goals and, in doing so, my professional roles would undergo an exceptional change. My leadership expanded outside the school through workshops, presentations, and writings.

Our two younger sons entered high school, the oldest son was in his second year of college, and our daughter was in her first year of college. The youngest decided he only wanted to run track, while the other two boys remained in college and high school basketball. My involvement in these extracurricular activities meant the discovery of a new aspect of motherhood. Everyone at my office—faculty, staff, and friends—knew that my children's world was my world. The mission of leading my children effectively in order to ensure their success was my priority. Slawinski, in her research on components for strategic leadership, calls this sustaining an effective organizational culture.[27] As a strategic leader, the mother sustains an effective family culture by including everyone in the decision, which allows the shaping of the family's values and symbols, so they may become more competitive and navigate their way to success.

I want to digress and offer a perspective for my commitment to my family and my professional career. It was not because it was transmitted or handed down from our parents. It was the absence of my mother's presence in the extracurricular activities of my childhood and teen years that made me so certain of my need to be present with my children. I knew the pain of not having someone to applaud my accomplishments or walk home with me after an event where I had been recognized with an award. I never wanted my children to feel the absence of my presence. It is a painful experience that shapes the life, value, and worth of a child. My mission and vision for my children was to always support them. That shaped my focus and the value system of our family.

My mother was very involved with her faith but not with my activities. This left me feeling like I did not want to be a part of that same faith after age eighteen. However, I am thankful for the relationship with my mother and the faith in which she raised me, because I found a new life of restoration and an understanding of my true worth and value through that same Christian faith. This was what I wanted to implement and execute as an ongoing strategy for the family. The consistency in leadership as the children grew older with Christian values is what Slawinski characterizes as the ability to emphasize ethical practices. What is most important in this component is the use of honesty, trust, and integrity to create an organizational, or familial, culture that generates consistency.[28]

Evaluate, Monitor, and Initiate

My influence and presence in the life of my family did not eliminate the personal challenges the children would face when making decisions. My doctoral studies were advancing in the midst of acting as a part-time teacher and now part-time school administrator. My professional career went through an evaluation process that helped me determine it was time to make a transition. This was a slow process, as everything in my life as a leader in transition made it a difficult period for the family, my career, and other areas of leadership. This transition turned out to be a strategic leadership skill identified by Schoemaker, Krupp, and Howland as "learning."[29] According to these researchers, strategic leaders are the focal point for organizational learning. They promote a culture of inquiry, and they search for the lessons in both successful and unsuccessful outcomes.

Mothers naturally want to shelter their families from influences and choices, those outside of the desired value systems that don't align with those that they have taught. Thompson, et al. refers to this as initiating corrective adjustments.[30] While there was some preadolescent and teenage rebellion with my boys, I am thankful to say that our daughter did not venture too far. The transition to the university for my oldest son was a time for him to push the envelope as he began his learning experience. It was amazing to me that while he thought he was hurting us, he only hurt himself, which was so hard for me to handle. I cried, anchored myself in my faith, and initiated plans for corrective adjustments; but I tried hard never to equate his value with his behavior, so I remained present in his life, a process that Slawinski calls developing human capital.[31] My son was still important for me to invest in and train.

A transition was happening in my career as I resigned from my position as school administrator and moved to full-time teaching and part-time administrative responsibility in higher education. The strategy of monitoring new developments that would cause me to initiate corrective adjustments seemed to happen more as the family matured and my career advanced. A time of decision making for my oldest son is a good example of this strategy. Maternal instinct will always challenge decisions made on behalf of our children.

It was during our son's senior year of high school that we chose to allow him to live away from home to accommodate his sports career. I didn't feel good about it at all and in fact opposed it. He begged and pleaded. He expressed his strong desire to show us responsibility. It would involve my husband and me living apart from him for a few months, and he would be supervised minimally. I believe this decision changed his life and ours forever. His grades dropped, and he was exposed to drugs and alcohol, nightlife, and a hardening of his heart toward the Christian life. This was the beginning of several events that were heartbreaking for the children and me. The pressures of society contributed to his challenges, but my deep faith and hope would keep him out of serious trouble and even spare his life. Our plan to live separately to accommodate his desire to attend a school for basketball moved us away from our established mission and values for the family; we had succumbed to making a decision based on emotions.

Strategic leaders must have the courage of their convictions informed by a robust decision-making process. The teenage and young adult years, for our family, would test the courage of our parental convictions. My deep faith was a personal non-negotiable during my children's teen years and throughout their lives. The influence of peers is very difficult to overcome, even when the children are immersed in faith, values, and positive opportunities. Mothers must hold fast to their commitment of presence, faith, and praise for their children during this period of their lives. Mothers have to take time to get to know their children's friends, and the parents of those friends, and remain engaged in holding the children accountable for their responsibilities. Any compromise in what one views as a value or non-negotiable will begin the downward turn for the children.

It is during this period of time that motherhood has to emphasize a role that is relational and filled with active participation in children's lives. While my husband and I actively participated in their lives, our strict discipline had a negative effect on our relationship with them during their teen years. Though strict discipline is not in and of itself a bad thing, it made an impact on our ability to understand the challenges the children were facing. We needed to listen more, to allow them to express their internal challenges by open and honest communication. I believe, had we enacted these strategies, better outcomes and relationships during their teen years would have resulted.

In some way, my role as a school leader also had an impact on raising the discipline standard because it involved my "looking good" to others, which I now realize was a personal failing—one of false pride. It was the children's pain I believe I lost sight of. This period of time has always been a self-reflection time for me on my effectiveness and worth. This experience is what Rima entitles and refers to as *Leading from the Inside Out*. The leader's integrity, self-worth, basic values, and motivation are central to being effective.[32]

The tribulations of my children's teen years have caused me to reflect on the realities of motherhood and work being defined by stages embedded in the developmental process and experience of the child. My personal experience has gone through a developmental process as a direct result. Each stage that the children experienced caused my role as a mother leading the family to shift or transition. My workload, emotions, and responsibilities also went through adjustments. The diverse behaviors and actions of the children also required adaptations for how I approached each situation. It caused me to ask new questions and explore different answers that would not be just a "quick fix." I did not have the academic or professional language that explained all the various strategies I was implementing as the leader of the family. I had to stand strong on principles that broader culture resisted, which often caused my children to choose sides against my husband and me. This was very hard for me because something was going very wrong with my ability to lead strategically. I moved from being the leader in the family organization to the enemy.

Transitions in Motherhood: The Absence of Plans

The last transition seemed to be absent of the five key strategies. For the most part, it is evident there was some loss and dysfunction in the family. Multiple roles of leadership on my part without a clear plan also contributed to a lack of balance. Having to account for multiple target groups with diverse goals and objectives without a clear plan impacted each organization in different ways and each suffered during various periods of my leadership.

I am excited to say that education became a non-negotiable modeled message for my children. Even though the teen years were difficult for each of them—far too many experiences to include here—I can say they all chose to attend college. Two went on basketball scholarships and the other two went on financial aid, loans, and help from my husband and me. They went to four very prestigious universities. It was during my oldest son's first year of college that I began my doctoral studies. My personal goal was to finish when he graduated college. I completed my degree while he still had courses to finish. I worked as a school principal and managed a friend's office part time. I also began a private consulting business to conduct workshops and programs for schools.

During the college years of two of my children, another period of time came where I experienced clear godly direction. I was working on my doctoral studies, leading a school site, and trying to keep up with my children at their campuses. It was a difficult time for me because I had not set boundaries for myself. I would call their rooms at different hours of the night and, when they were not at home, they were close enough for me to get in the car to go and check on them. My husband challenged me to let go, to let them grow up. That was not a decision I was ready for until I was strengthened by my faith and an internal message. I sensed very strongly that, *My children were given to me to steward until adulthood, and I did well. Now I had to turn them over to their personal faith and trust they would be taken care of whether I was there or not. They had to possess their own personal faith.* It was a startling moment for me, but the sense of peace I felt made me not want to even relate to them as my children any more. It was amazing. I felt a freedom and peace regarding their lives that I never felt before. I was learning to trust less in my own plans and to trust God to take care of them. I slipped from time to time, but I was reminded that through my faith their lives had a destiny and purpose. This was a time when strategic leadership concepts challenged me to clarify and reassess my goals now that my children were no longer my target group. The role of leadership for the family was changing, I was losing one of my jobs, and I had to make a key transition. I became immersed in my doctoral studies. I began to set new goals and objectives. Self-assessment and plan development for my professional career became the priority.

My opportunities for frequent travel and conference presentations began to expand and, during the summer, my daughter would travel with me. I have spoken a lot about my sons, but my daughter is a jewel. She was far from perfect but observed many challenges faced by the boys. She was second in the order of the children. It was at one of the conferences where I spoke that I invited her to speak to young women in attendance. Her presentation about her personal identity caught me off guard at first. Our oldest and middle sons were well known for their basketball achievements. As close as my daughter was to me, I never connected that she was only known for being her older brother's "younger sister," the "coach's daughter," or the younger brother's "big sister." People didn't even know her name. I was heartbroken to hear how her identity had been impacted over the years.

She would often travel with me when I spoke at conferences or other events and she was also concerned about others expecting her to be in ministry leadership as I was, rather than allowing her to be herself and live out her own identity. I was devastated that she felt she lived in the shadows of each of us. How could I right this wrong? Once again my faith was what I reached for. This experience was very difficult. The poor balance of my multiple roles had resulted in what Oates, Hall, Anderson, and Michelle Willingham identify as a decreased sense of subjective well-being, including depression, anxiety, anger, stress, guilt, and other negative self-assessments.[33] I spent a lot of time with her, desperately wanting to affirm the value of who she was as a member of the family and being wonderfully unique. Motherhood does have its mysteries. This was one I sought to solve and we have moved forward from it.

This period for both leadership in the home and the move to university instruction and administration was filled with evaluating performances, monitoring new developments, and initiating corrective adjustments. Ironically, another professional change for me came in that transition to higher education. The position in higher education contributed to understanding the new language of evaluation, monitoring new developments, and adjustments. Each leadership role I filled at the university called for much of the leadership strategies already in place. The bureaucratic structure in higher education generally has mission, vision, values, and goals in place. Much of the leadership here involved my working solely with adults who chose the institution because of its mission and vision. My role at this stage was filled with evaluating the organization's performance of the goals presented and how effectively they were reached. Each professional organization I worked with seemed to provide language and strategies for what I was experiencing as a family leader.

Monitoring new developments is a unique leadership strategy because of the changes that occur within the culture of higher education learning. Most of my experience involved development of off-campus innovative initiatives. My work has always involved organizational culture change. This time, the work involved engaging the current organizational structures and leadership styles that proved to be uncomfortable for the traditional campus. Just as I experienced watching teen and young adult peer pressure influence the effectiveness of strategies that had to be monitored in leading the family, so it was that program development became part of my leadership in higher education, which required monitoring the effectiveness of new programs designed by faculty. As new research develops, these new developments must be monitored in order to assess whether new program requests align with the earlier strategies of the vision. My strategic leadership abilities were growing both as a mother and a professional.

The culture change for a mother with adult children, some with families of their own, is to wait until you are asked before offering your thoughts, and if not asked, to keep silent. This is never easy, but I do respect them as adults. My children often say to me, "Mom, you are so much fun now that we are adults." The first time I heard that I took it personally and was insulted. But then I realized I valued their lives enough to see them as my friends, with mutual respect. I will always be Mom and they will always be my children. However, now they are responsible for themselves and I am responsible for myself. I experienced a paradigm shift that allowed me to see and respect my children as adults.

Mothers are indeed leaders. When I think about the thirty-eight years of motherhood—the learning and growing the family has experienced—I realize that it was strategic leadership that made my role as mother most effective. I did not possess the language or knowledge of what it meant to be a strategic leader—it was my ability to own my faith that directed my life in the early years. My faith informed how I would work with my four children. It also informed me of what it meant to lead my family and my home, and to be a wife to one man for over forty years.

Now, as an administrator in higher education, these same skills inform my strategic leadership in the organization. While research defines the essential skills along with a diverse set of components that create success and effectiveness, my faith remains a strong contributor to my strategic leadership both in the family and in the workplace. Leading in the home can never be underestimated as easy work or taken for granted. A mother who takes the innate strategies gained through leading her children can exert great influence on organizational development.

Mothers are strategic leaders. The leadership begins at the moment the words "you're pregnant" are spoken. Everything becomes focused on the new responsibilities that require the strategic leadership of another life. Those responsibilities, though they may experience transition and transformation, cross over into the roles of community and workplace throughout all the seasons of life.

Discussion Questions

1. How do the essential skills of strategic leadership compare with a mother's role of leading family?
2. Identify the mission, vision, and values of your family. How do they align or conflict with those of your workplace?
3. How are your family and professional objectives supportive of one another, or how do they conflict?
4. What about leadership can a mother anticipate if there is no strategic plan in place? How can you transition your effectiveness without a strategic leadership plan?
5. List the essential skills and components of strategic leadership in a chart. Analyze your roles and experiences as a mother to identify constructs at work in your life.

Notes

[1] Michael Hitt and Duane Ireland, "The Essence of Strategic Leadership: Managing Human and Social Capital," *Journal of Leadership and Organizational Studies* 9 (Summer 2002): 3–14.

[2] Paul Schoemaker, Samantha Howland, and Steve Krupp, "Strategic Leadership: The Essential Skills," *Harvard Business Review* (Jan.–Feb. 2013): 2–5.

[3] Natalie Slawinski, "Strategic Leadership," in *Cases in Leadership*, eds. W. Glenn Rowe and Laura Guerrero (Los Angeles: Sage Publications, 2010), 297–99.

[4] Paraphrased from the *Business Dictionary*, which also describes an organization as a "social unit of people that is structured and managed to meet a need or to pursue collective goals." See "Organization," *Business Dictionary*, WebFinance. Inc., accessed July 12, 2014, http://www.businessdictionary.com/definition/organization.html.

[5] Linda Renny Forcey, "Feminist Perspectives on Mothering and Peace," in E. Nakano Glenn, Grace Chang, and Linda Renny Forcey, eds., *Mothering: Ideology, Experience, and Agency* (New York: Routledge, 1994), 357.

[6] Kelly Starling, "Power Moms," *Ebony* (July 1999), 52-58.

[7] Kim Oates, Elizabeth Hall, and Tamara Anderson, "Pursuing Multiple Callings: The Implication of Balancing Career and Motherhood for Women and the Church," *Journal of Psychology and Christianity* 27. 3 (2005): 227–37.

[8] Slawinski, "Strategic Leadership," 298–99.

[9] "The Juggle Struggle: Strategies for Balancing Work and Family," Knowledge@Wharton, University of Pennsylvania (December 2010), accessed August 17, 2014, http://knowledge-stage.wharton.upenn.edu/10000women/article.cfm?articleid=6223.

[10] Samuel Rima, *Leading from the Inside Out* (Grand Rapids, Michigan: Baker Books, 2000), 17.

[11] Gregory Dess, Thomas Lumpkin, and Marilyn Taylor, *Strategic Management: Creating Competitive Advantages* (New York: McGraw-Hill, 2004).

[12] Alonzo Strickland and Arthur Thompson, *Strategic Management: Concepts and Cases* (Boston: McGraw-Hill, 2003), 1–25.

[13] Robert Kaplan and David Norton, "The Balanced Scorecard-Measures that Drive Performance," *Harvard Business Review* (1992), 71–79.

[14] Judith Bardwick, "Peacetime Management and Wartime Leadership," in *The Leaders of the Future* (New York: Jossey-Bass, 1996), 131–39.

[15] Leslie Willcoxson, "Leading Strategically," *International Journal of Organizational Behavior* 2.2 (2002), 30–36.

[16] Strickland and Thompson, *Strategic Management*, 319–24.

[17] Ibid.

[18] Thomas Licona, *Educating for Character* (New York: Banton Doubleday Dell Publishing, 1991), 23–26.

[19] Jeanne Stevenson, *In Her Own Time: Women and Developmental Issues in Pastoral Care* (Minneapolis: Augsburg Fortress, 2000), 75–78.

[20] See Oates, Hall, and Anderson, "Pursuing Multiple Callings," 227–35.

[21] Schoemaker, Howland, and Krupp, "Strategic Leadership," 3.

[22] Rima, *Leading from the Inside Out*, 38.

[23] Jim Kouzes and Barry Posner, "Seven Lessons for Leading the Voyage to the Future" in Francis Hesselbein, Marshall Goldsmith, and Richard Beckhard, eds., *The Leader of the Future* (San Francisco: Jossey Bass, 1996), 99–110.

[24] Richard Hughes and Katherine Beatty, "Five Steps to Leading Strategically," *Glendale College of Law Journals* 12 (2005), 59.

[25] Lydia Saad, "Despite Less Time and Rest, Working Moms Managing Well," Gallup Well-Being (May 2010), accessed July 12, 2014, http://www.gallup.com/poll/127745/despite-less-time-rest-working-moms-managing.aspx.

[26] Gordon MacDonald, *Ordering Your Private World* (Nashville: Thomas Nelson, 2003).

[27] Slawinski, *Strategic Leadership*, 298.

[28] Ibid.

[29] Schoemaker, Howland, and Krupp, "Strategic Leadership," 2–5.

[30] Strickland and Thompson, *Strategic Management*, 1–25.

[31] Slawinski, "Strategic Leadership," 298–99.

[32] Rima, *Leading from the Inside Out*, 129–30.

[33] Kim Oates, Elizabeth Hall, Tamara Anderson, and Michelle Willingham, "Calling and Conflict: The Sanctification of Work in Working Mothers," *Psychology of Religion and Spirituality* 4.1 (Feb. 2012): 71–83.

2

MANAGED CHAOS
Confessions of a Wife, Mother, Business Woman, and Dean

ILENE L. BEZJIAN, DBA

"Chaos is rejecting all you have learned.
Chaos is being yourself."

—Emile M. Cioran

To anyone looking in from the outside, my life seems organized and well planned. Truth be told, I live in managed chaos. From early in my life to the day the final period was placed on this chapter, chaos has always been an integral part of each day's activities. I don't create it; it is just there. Some background information may help in understanding the context of my opening statement. I am a devout Christian. It is the core of everything in my life and has been since my late teens. I was raised in a Christian home; my parents were the pastors of a small community church and worked full-time, as well. This would affect my life's choices forever. It was normal seeing people devoted to a calling and living out an apostolic life. My parents were clear about getting a college education. It was not an option; it was required. I was a dutiful child and stepped into the world of higher education in 1970, majoring in business with an emphasis in marketing.

Graduating in the spring of 1975 brought a few challenges. Women weren't hired in marketing, and the end of the Vietnam War brought a new supply of ready workers to the marketplace, mostly men. Competition for sales jobs was fierce and after a few months of searching for a job, I decided to start my own consulting business, hoping to change the world. It never occurred to me that I needed real-world experience. I landed a part-time teaching assignment at a local university that kept a steady flow of income while building my business. Entering my late twenties, it seemed normal to be free and single, yet friends constantly reminded me I was behind—no husband or children. I was labeled *odd, non-compliant,* and *abnormal* in the midst of the 1970s when the hippie generation was espousing, "Do your own thing," just don't be a woman in business.

People of Influence

There were a handful of people encouraging my endeavor, and one in particular would never know the impact of her words. I had attended a seminar in my mid-twenties, conducted by Natasha Josefowitz. Her book, *Paths to Power,* completely altered my career and led me to believe I could be a change-maker.[1] Josefowitz explained that women were unwilling to be like men, and yet had no idea what they wanted to be or where they wanted to go, therefore they must consider the seven A's: authority, assertiveness, accountability, accessibility, affiliation, approval, and affability.[2] It was true; we all wanted something more but failed to define exactly what that meant. We couldn't define what we didn't know. We observed men in positions of power and it seemed interesting, but without feminine insight, it was just observation, not fact.

Josefowitz peaked my curiosity in the section of her book titled "Accessibility." The first three traits surrounding accessibility I learned from being a pastor's daughter, although from a skewed perspective—the traditional male-dominated church perspective:

> The issue here is in the difficulty that most women have in setting boundaries. Women are so accustomed to meeting the needs of other people—husbands, children, family, and friends. Society has always said that this was woman's most fulfilling role. But what about our own needs? Do we fulfill them by meeting everyone else's needs, or do we neglect them by doing so? Often the boundaries are fuzzy and hard to define. This dilemma becomes apparent in every aspect of

work as we have the tendency to be available to anyone who wants to come and talk. We listen, try to help, find some time. We are more available than men to employees, to students, to clients, or to patients. We must learn to close our doors and say, "No, I'm too busy now," so as to pursue other tasks.[3]

This was the first time I had heard the word *boundaries*. Traditionally, women worked until the job was complete. Somewhere in the back of my mind, I remember my mother wearing an apron, stating, "A woman's work is never done!" My business was relational, as were my connections with family and friends. Saying no to a meeting or conversation never entered my mind. As a side note, thirty-five years later, I still have time to stop and talk to people who need a moment. It is the diamond bracelet of relationships. I am never too busy to meet for a few minutes.

Josefowitz's book was packed with advice on the benefits and costs of maintaining boundaries noting two examples—having power would cost you a family and garnering influence would cost you the benefit of "being taken care of."[4] Statements concerning information on resumes were direct and to the point: "Legally, you do not have to mention family. However, if a man writes that he has a family, he is seen as stable; if you do, you may be seen as having too much responsibility outside of work."[5]

Tips on how to succeed in a man's world were plentiful, even down to the point of eliminating family pictures and flowers from one's desk. Refraining from looking too feminine was also suggested. You were there to work, not find a husband or cause any men to drift from their corporate duties. Out of the 281 pages written, less than 15 were dedicated to personal life outside the company, including marriage and family. What was emphasized stated that both marriage and family were detrimental to success and climbing the organizational ladder—for women. I had no reason to give up my dream of accomplishing the goal of a corporate job.

When I attended Josefowitz's seminar, I wasn't married, nor did I have any children. It would be full speed ahead for the next thirty years. Now was the time to act on the advice she poured out to more than one thousand women that day. This would be the primary source of information for young women pursuing careers in business. There were no CEOs or high-profile VPs running Fortune 500 companies. We sought information about future options from those who were brave enough to conduct seminars or write books.

A second book hit the stands and the title would be discussed in organizations and universities alike. Jo Foxworth's *Boss Lady* raised eyebrows with her opening sentence: "Boss is a four-letter word, and 'Boss Lady' is two of them—double jeopardy and almost a contradiction in terms."[6] Her proclamation felt slightly ridiculous, but addressed the issues business women struggled to answer. Why would anyone believe a woman was any less capable than a man? Yet in the late 1970s, little had been achieved in terms of equality in the workplace. Foxworth was an advertising executive, a woman in a man's world. Her book exposed many of the problems faced by women in the 1970s, including lower wages, fewer promotion opportunities, and the lack of enculturation in the business world. Unlike Josephowitz, Foxworth warned women leaders about the complexity of power. She cautioned both men and women not to take the cookie-cutter advice from new books in the marketplace: "The books contain pointers that work brilliantly in some instances and bomb resoundingly in others. There are, of course, no foolproof recipes or fail-safe methods for achieving that Nirvana, success."[7]

Forty years later, I personally think little has changed. Jo Foxworth's book could be updated for today's market and still be relevant. Current books still caution or *coach* women on game playing, actions in the office, personal branding, and the sound of one's voice. Emphasis is still placed on appearances.[8] The message is nearly the same, but the words have been updated to reflect the contemporary culture. Women still need to learn how to encourage and support one another even when mistakes are made. We need to work as a team instead of competing and take to heart the five final suggestions made by Foxworth: 1) Don't try to be one of the boys, 2) Try to understand male bonding, 3) Don't fall for a male sob story, 4) Give the other women in your outfit a break, and 5) Do not assign jobs on a gender basis.[9]

Life Changes

I eventually found my soul mate and we married just after my thirtieth birthday and the completion of his first year of military duty. At the time, I was bordering on "old maid" status and shocked my friends and family when I finally tied the knot. We chose to delay having children and pursue doctorate degrees together in the field of business. Each of us worked two jobs and attended school on weekends, ninety miles from our home. Thus began the chaos. It was the best of times, and yes, it was the worst of times, but neither of us would change our decision to this day.

Did we have everything needed for work that day and perhaps the lecture material for the class we were attending that evening? Was the gas tank filled and did we have a few dollars in our pockets for coffee or a snack? I repeatedly checked as lack of these essentials constituted a disaster. Would we have time to eat before heading up to the home office, trying to grind out a few more words on a paper or the dreaded dissertation? What time would either of us even be home that night? We didn't always know. I felt like someone in an Alcoholic Anonymous program. My motto was, one day at a time. I couldn't live for the weekends since they were spent listening to lengthy lectures, albeit with interesting faculty.

I found it difficult to sleep after attending a weekend class, as there were so many ideas worthy of expansion rolling around in my head. I was consulting for large corporations during the day and teaching at several universities four nights a week until 10 P.M. I still found time to spend an hour or two reading or writing, preparing for the weekend classes. Dominos was on the automatic dialing system.

Years of Growth and Change

As a new graduate, I was ready to take my freshly minted degree and the small amount of advice from a few sages and make the steep step into the corporate arena. Again, I searched for someone who would render guidance, warnings, or just opinions on how to navigate the chaotic waters. Things were going well, but control within my life was still illusive. My consulting business was earning six figures and teaching provided a place to experiment with new ideas. Everything was falling into place as I found the chaos a bit more manageable.

In September of 1986, while teaching an evening MBA class, I experienced a bout of severe dizziness. It passed and I thought it may have been too much caffeine or another episode of low blood pressure, until it happened a second time. I arranged to meet with my doctor, and after a few tests, he came in the room and quietly handed me a prescription to see a specialist. I was terrified to look. Could this be a bad joke? Did I have an incurable disease? What if I died? How would Vic pay off the student loans? Did we have life insurance? It seemed as if extreme chaos had entered the scene. I had taken the piece of paper and turned it into a death sentence. It was not uncommon for me to make even the smallest problems a huge crisis. Looking down, I saw the name of a local obstetrician. I was pregnant, not dying. I was also thirty-six years of age. How could this be?

At the time, I was considered too old and too high risk for anything connected to birthing or raising a child. My friends' children were in middle school, some hitting the age of puberty. They questioned my decision, much like the ones to marry late and major in business. I refused to conform even when it came to having a child late in life. I was given a pamphlet on Downs Syndrome and genetic testing. I needed an amniocentesis test after the third month of pregnancy to determine the health of the baby. My doctor would not deliver a child with birth defects, so another specialist was assigned my case. What would happen to my business and the new doctorate degree tagged onto the end of my name if there were complications during delivery or after? The last thing I thought I wanted was a family, but my husband was thrilled, and secretly, I was as well. A new title would soon be added to my calling card, *Mom*.

Everyone was looking to understand strategy and I had just earned a degree in the field. This twist in my life was not strategic. Josephowitz and Foxworth had said the combination of marriage and family was the kiss of death to any woman pursuing a top spot in business. Preparations began for the unknown. Neither of us had much experience with babies, but how difficult could this be? We were both educated, working adults, and, given enough time and assets, we were sure a baby would fit into the mix. I worked until the last few days of my pregnancy, presenting six-hour seminars and teaching at night, often standing on my feet for twelve hours a day. My greatest worry was timing. Would my son be born on his due date, giving me opportunity to jump back into work as soon as possible, or would he be late, bringing chaos to my business timeline? Even in Lamaze classes I found myself thinking about making everything fit. Emotions needed minimizing since it was all about managing chaos.

Once again, this all changed the night before Mother's Day in 1987. I had just seen my doctor, who assured me I was a couple of weeks away from delivery. I went into labor not knowing what to expect, and just after midnight on Mother's Day, James was born. A little hand reached for mine and held it tightly. This was a different handshake than those from business clients. It was the sealing of a permanent relationship. At that moment, the chaos stopped. I wasn't in a hurry any longer. Someone needed me in a different way. My sense of purpose was jolted into a new direction. This client wouldn't be leaving for quite some time, and I loved it. My life had changed forever; it wasn't merely amended.

This new venture would be different and require all the skills obtained throughout my years in business. I also realized the advice from others may not work for me. Finding my personal rhythm would be imperative. Not comparing my life to the lives of others would be vital. God had given me unique opportunities and gifts. It was time to reassess who I was and where I was going. I was now a working wife and mother. Handing off this responsibility to someone else seemed cruel to both the baby and me. My career, which began as a means of support, now changed to one of security for my child if anything should happen to my husband.

Leadership Perspectives and Culture Shift

At this point in my life, conflict and chaos were everyday occurrences. Reference points were needed, but again, none were available. I had been raised in a strict Christian home and my father was a part-time minister of a small independent community church. He worked as a salesman to support our family while my mother worked most of my formative years for the State of California. Societal changes were vast during the late 1960s and all through the 1970s. While the culture shouted free will, the conventional church continued to teach and expect traditional values from the faithful.

Women were entering the workforce at record numbers, still relegated to more traditional roles. Those who had protested the Vietnam War and experimented with drugs and sex were the new establishment. The church held fast to the teachings of Jesus Christ. A young pastor, Chuck Smith, welcomed the hippy generation to a new, casual church, calling them to leave the fatalistic lifestyle and commit their lives to Christ. I found difficulty in relating to those who reveled in their hedonistic ways during the '70s but criticized my personal walk and labeled my choices as selfish. They were now the CEOs of organizations in Silicon Valley, carrying the same attitude toward women in business as their predecessors.

The popularity of Gloria Steinem and Helen Gurley Brown brought new chaos to my world. Were we really in control of our destinies or must we follow the traditional tenets of society? And, if we followed our destinies, would we be chastised for opting into a new combination of responsibilities? Would we always be trapped in the effort to be all things to all people or would we learn to follow our own hearts? Everyone had an opinion and most people were happy to share it, particularly if you were in violation of their standards. The established church pressed wives and mothers to make the traditional choice: stay home; don't work. How could we serve our husbands and children if we were engaged in the workforce? Often the husband was questioned about his ability to provide for the family if his wife was employed. This carried an emasculating stigma into the marriage and also into other social relationships, forcing couples to justify the decision of the wife to work and have a family. Movies such as *Mr. Mom* portrayed helping husbands as buffoons incapable of serving as an active parent.[10] I loved my husband too much to have him seen as a poor provider. I rarely mentioned my work when attending social events.

The next months were spent trying to manage a newborn and a business at the same time. I was gifted with a sleepless infant who was also lactose intolerant. My management skills taught me to investigate all issues until the root of the problem was found. The pediatrician admired my list of questions brought to every visit. Soon we found a rhythm, and while James was napping, I was on the phone talking to clients and preparing research for an upcoming visit. My mother and mother-in-law were a tremendous help on those days I needed to be away. I loved and trusted them both. They would tell me of small milestones or problems each time I would pick up James. I had traded a fantastic briefcase for a diaper bag that looked like a briefcase. I didn't know anyone who was in the same situation and often felt as if people judged my actions as stupid and unrealistic, particularly at those times when I reached for a pen and inadvertently pulled out a pacifier. I knew others had walked this path, but few were willing to talk about the ambiguity each day presented. I loved being a mom, but I also thrived when solving business problems or creating new ideas. Would I have to give up one or the other to realize my purpose? I had already encountered a few issues regarding late evening meetings. As I excused myself from an informal, after-hours get-together with one of my clients, they pleaded for me to stay just a little longer. I begged off, saying I had an infant at home waiting for me. The looks of disdain were obvious. Why was I trying to be something I was not? They let me know I should make a choice, work or children. Yet, I found both worlds to be enriching and unique from one another.

There were some similarities, but often my management skills were non-transferable. Male counterparts would be congratulated for attending an important football game and seeing a son make the winning touchdown. The same individuals spilling out the praise would later publically criticize me for taking time to attend my son's school events. I found myself walking a tightrope trying to decide if it was worth the effort to reach the other side or just turn back and settle for a one-dimensional world. Should I quit work or succumb to daycare? Would I ever reduce the amount of personal chaos?

I investigated a high-end daycare center located near our home and marveled at the computer center for toddlers, game room, and incredibly clean lunch room. Guilt engulfed my spirit knowing my own house could use some organization and a thorough vacuuming. I was impressed with the young women teaching children the art of potty training and eating with a spoon. All the children in attendance seemed calm and happy. This was quite different from our organized chaos at home. I know, more than once, I had dropped a bottle or a pacifier and chosen not to rinse them. The thought of walking across the room with a screaming child just to wash the nipple seemed ridiculous when faced with the instant comfort at hand.

As I walked toward the supervisor's office, convinced this was the right place for James, I heard her say, "If you bring James tomorrow, I won't be here. I am going to Las Vegas to marry my baby's daddy." Something inside me snapped. What was I doing? How could I leave this precious child with a stranger who would raise him and instill her values in his life? I handed back the papers I held. It was clear, I needed to rearrange my schedule and invest in the greater priority, a little boy named James. I cried all the way home. My husband was more than understanding and even agreed we could and would make changes.

Once again our training as managers and leaders led us to developing strategies. How could I stay home and still be engaged in the work world? We spent several nights mapping out ideas, and finally arrived at what seemed a suitable arrangement: a few clients and a couple of evening classes. Doors would need to open for the plan to be effective. The three of us would meet at a local restaurant for dinner on my teaching nights and Vic would take James home, enjoying playtime and bedtime. For me, there was a constant need to discover, and the field of marketing had opened up an insatiable appetite to create new things. Finding balance would, hopefully, minimize the chaos and sustain a reasonably happy environment.

Losing the Sharp Edge

New books on leadership were hitting the stands and Stephen Covey topped the charts.[11] His suggestions on trying to be proactive with a personal vision for your life lasted about three days for me. No one could predict what would happen with a baby, a job, and a husband who was working two jobs and attempting to finish his doctorate degree, traveling internationally and often away two or three weeks at a time. This was mission impossible, until our parents stepped in to help. The chaos allowed personal time and an opportunity to plan beyond the weekend. I never would have held it together physically, mentally, or spiritually without their assistance. Covey's advice was fine for those who had normal schedules, but couldn't help a new mother being stretched in different directions.

Covey's second habit was having an end in mind.[12] Finding a beginning seemed to be the most difficult daily process, and putting first things first was almost an irritating thought. I was lucky to get a shower and press my blouse before strapping James into the car and heading off to my parents', then hitting the freeway to meet a client or teach a class. I jumped to the seventh habit titled "sharpening the saw."[13] There was no use even reading this portion of the book. I had lost my edge weeks ago. Sleepless nights and days on the go had given way to bouts of memory loss. Was I tired or losing my ability to make quick and accurate decisions? My mind was at work when I was home with my son, and my mind was at home when working with clients. I was unable to shut down what I soon called "the second shift." Some kind of work was always waiting for me.

One of the most difficult circumstances I faced during the first few years of motherhood occurred when my son was sick. Who would stay home with him? How could I leave him with Grandmother or my husband when his arms reached for me and the tears would flow? Truthfully, I didn't leave him. My maternal instinct took over and unless it was a national emergency for my client, I rescheduled appointments. Did I lose clients? The answer is yes, I did. Those who understood my desire to parent my own child graciously allowed me a second and often a third opportunity to rearrange engagements. I realized my son would not remember how well I served my clients, but would remember the days I sat on the couch holding him when he was ill. He probably wouldn't remember the times I attended his events at school, but he would remember if I was a no-show.

We had just arrived at a reasonable rhythm balancing family as James began preschool. He thrived in the school environment and this allowed me to work undisturbed during the day. Once again, I felt the joy of working through problems and opportunities with clients and teaching two nights a week. Vic's parents had moved down the street and often my mother-in-law would often prepare dinner for us. She enjoyed having James come to visit. My parents picked James up from school on the days my work extended beyond the three o'clock pickup time. Life was beginning to run smoother. Work was incredibly rewarding, seeing companies grow because of marketing and strategy decisions I helped to facilitate. I enjoyed reading journals containing information on new trends and ideas and seeing innovation at its best. The most worthwhile part of work was meeting new people—the interaction with bright minds, the conversations about the future, and how the field of marketing was changing and growing. Textbooks remained the same; however, with the introduction of the Internet, there would definitely be a change not only in the field of marketing, but in the delivery of information to consumers and students. There would be a demand for those who understood the revolution about to take place. I loved all my jobs, and felt a high level of personal and professional satisfaction.

God continued to instill the joy of work in my heart, and my relationship with Vic was incredible. We would talk over issues and complex ideas in the evenings. One of those evenings began with a new conversation. Should we have a second child? I loved being a mother, sharing the world with my son. Participating in school events and helping him learn new skills were reward-ing beyond explanation. The thought of another baby made my heart swell with anticipation. Within the year, I found myself pregnant, this time at the age of forty.

It was 1992 and more women had entered the workforce, changing the dynamics of organizations across the nation. The ratio of men to women employees in the labor force was predicted to change in favor of women.[14] Many women were now in lower management positions and pushing their way into middle management. There was still an absence of female CEOs. The brave new world opened up for women who were strong enough to start their own businesses and appoint themselves the leader, but traditional orga-nizations remained skeptical. I believed a second child could be brought into my personal world while still running a successful business, but doubt crept into my mind every day. The glass ceiling was getting more difficult to break through as I climbed the ladder of success. Being pregnant did not help my image. Again, the literature favored women who worked like men and diminished the importance of their families at home. The Equal Employment Opportunity Title VII of the Civil Rights Act of 1964 (as amended by the Equal Employment Opportunity Act of 1972) stated that it was forbidden to discriminate in all areas of the employment relationship. This included the Pregnancy Discrimination Act. While it was law, it didn't keep organi-zations from hiring male competitors who could work without taking time off. I needed more time in the day. I struggled to keep my business profitable.

In the summer of 1992, I received a phone call from the dean of a local Christian university, asking if I would apply for a full-time teaching position. I politely declined, knowing I couldn't meet the start date in September. A second phone call prompted an interesting exchange concerning my hesitation to join the team. After divulging my condition, the dean responded with an approving laugh. Probing a little deeper, I asked about the gender makeup in the school. There were no women teaching full-time, yet half of their students were female. Again, I politely declined, adding I was disinterested in breaking through the glass ceiling in a new work environment.

A third call gave way to a meeting over lunch and this would turn into a formal interview before the end of the day. I was tempted, but not convinced. A young woman stopped me in the parking lot just as I was ready to leave. Her comment stirred a new feeling in my soul: "Are you the woman who is coming to teach us in the School of Business? We have prayed for you. We knew God would answer our prayers. Thank you so much for helping us." Still unsure about the decision, I drove home to talk with the two men in my life. What did they think? The pay was 60 percent less than my current income, but I would be working two days a week for only nine months out of the year. The grandmothers were willing to babysit two days a week, and it would be great to have summers free with the kids.

Two weeks later, I accepted the teaching position starting in January 1993. I should have considered the chaos factor with a five-year-old and an infant. My fear of timing once again raised a feeling of trepidation. Would she be born on the due date or come late? Would I be ready to return to work with two children needing me? Was changing my career a wise decision or would it add to the chaos that had diminished ever so slightly? My mind was in constant disorder as I weighed options, and at times, wished for the days when work was my singular focus.

In the fall months, the shift to a new lifestyle ensued. My business wound down and preparation for the new arrival began. At the same time, I put together lesson plans and syllabi and envisioned classrooms full of eager young people. Would this be part of the destiny God prepared for me? Could I make the shift to a new environment? Full-time teaching would be a new experience, one that could never take the place of the fast-paced corporate career. I was unaccustomed to teaching undergraduate students since most of my experience was in evening classes filled with graduate students or adults returning to school.

I searched the literature again to see if there were any women willing to share their secrets on work-life balance during transitions. There were random sentences in lengthy articles concerning women in the work environment. Kenneth Labich wrote an article for *Fortune* titled "Take Control of Your Career."[15] Out of the ten pages of advice, one statement referred to women: " . . . advice to ambitious female executives: Tone down the makeup and go for a look of simple elegance. Says [Phyllis Macklin, an outplacement specialist], 'You don't see a lot of women with big hair get senior positions. You've got to remember you are a product, and you need to be packaged.'"[16] These were infuriating words. Where were the articles and studies helping those of us who combed our hair on the way to work hoping it didn't look as if the leftover cereal from breakfast was the newest gel? How could I explain away the greasy handprints at the bottom of my suit skirt? Was I the only person willing to talk about the difficulties of motherhood and work?

The Feminist Movement of the 1970s opened up dialogue concerning choices for women. Much of it focused more on the right to control our bodies than on educating women in the workforce and trying to stabilize personal chaos. At times it seemed too radical, but I would be lying if I said their deliberate attempt to receive attention concerning promotions and salaries failed to begin the conversation to level the corporate playing field. Women's magazines printed superficial advice on how to dress for success and dug deeper into solving the difficulties of keeping a marriage together, yet the simple issues such as sharing responsibilities with your spouse were ignored.

Anxiety set in as I realized I was leaving the corporate world, quarterly results, and the adrenalin rush of life-and-death decisions. They would soon be distant memories. My hope was to return as soon as my daughter started kindergarten. I promised myself this would all be temporary and the five years would pass quickly. Little did I know it would be twenty years before the door would open and my primary career would once again lead back to the corporate world.

On November 2, 1992, we welcomed Laurie into our home. I was two days short of being six months past my fortieth birthday. I had exactly nine weeks to once again bring order to this new chaotic environment. God blessed me with a baby who loved to sleep. My days were spent completing class outlines and trying to squeeze back into a normal size suit. Juggling a kindergartener and a newborn proved much more difficult than I anticipated. Each day I longed to speak to individuals in the working environment, read the *Wall Street Journal*, and discuss the next new marketing idea. Work would be a welcomed relief. I think Sylvia LaFair stated it correctly in her book titled *Don't Bring It to Work*: "Few things seem more different than the worlds of work and home. We talk of 'work life balance' as if work and life were chunks of matter on opposite sides of a balance scale."[17] Guilt swept over me as the first day of work approached. This wouldn't be a balancing act; it was managing the chaos yet again. Would my children see me as mom or someone in a dark business suit that inhabited part of their lives? I asked God to help me notice the times my children saw me as mom.

The first event came fairly quickly. As I stood in the kitchen cooking dinner with an infant in my arms, James screamed for me to come outside. "Jesus is coming, Mom." Turning off the burner and sprinting out to the front yard, I saw him sitting on the steps looking up at the sky. A burst of light shown through the clouds, and if Jesus had been coming, it would have looked exactly like the sky did at that moment. We waited for quite some time and then my son announced, "I guess he changed his mind. But I am glad you were with me, Mom." At that moment I was a mom, not a business professional or professor. There were countless numbers of times I was awarded the title mom by my children. This was an internal promotion, one no organization could grant.

I recall the week our entire family had the stomach flu. My only desire was a hot shower and an hour without someone moaning or needing the sheets changed. In an act of bravery, I put the children in the older of our two cars for a quick outing to the grocery store. With soup, gelatin, and crackers ready for check out, I carefully counted out the exact change. As we retreated to the car, a kind gentleman stopped and asked if I needed assistance. He knew of a church who was reaching out to the homeless. I was mortified. Where were the articles on this type of humiliation? I thanked him and cried the remainder of the afternoon. I had a doctorate degree and was financially stable. Somehow, the thought of donning a suit, pantyhose, and high heels the next day seemed cruel. What appealed to me at the moment was a pair of warm pajamas, a cup of tea, and a down comforter. It didn't matter. Tomorrow was my first day of work. There would be four classrooms full of students expecting information regarding the next test.

Pushing the limits physically and mentally had become the norm. It was much like switching the channels on the television remote. At this time and place, I responded as a professor to students' needs, and an hour later, I switched to the needs of my family. It was imperative to stay on the tightrope and not look down—not worry about a gust of wind blowing the rope back and forth and knocking me over, but keeping my eyes on the next goal, which may have been only an hour away. My *lives* could not be separated as they were completely intertwined.

Input from the Sages

In my humble opinion, most of the articles on women in the workforce or in leadership positions were written by men casting a biased perspective. It still brings a smile to my face. Women just conduct themselves differently than men. What appears to be a life that is harmonious is nothing more than managed chaos. We are criticized if we say too much about our family at work and ostracized by non-working women when wanting to discuss business or world affairs. Working mothers have been displaced by both worlds. Each of us must find what works personally and professionally and stay the course. Comparing ourselves to one another or even to cultural standards will always bring a sense of deficiency. If someone objects or criticizes our methods, it is time to focus on results and hope the goals we are attempting to accomplish are in line with our personal life plans and purposes.

Shortly after arriving at the university, I was greeted with a note from an anonymous individual critical of my decision to live a dualistic life: "How could a woman suitably serve and usurp the authority of male faculty members?" How much time would someone have to spend thinking about a note, writing it, and sending it to an individual? One's calling is so personal; to have others judge it is extremely hurtful. I had learned in a sales class during my undergraduate program that a thick skin was necessary. Sales and marketing were difficult career options for men and almost impossible for women.

Ignoring personal comments and attacks was a necessity, not an option. I also learned labels and titles would be assigned by those in the corporate environment as well as in the Christian higher education community. Neither hid their contempt for women hoping to achieve leadership positions.

Just months after being hired, an appointment to the chair position would create a new form of chaos in my life. More hours, more days, and more responsibilities were added to the schedule; however, I loved working at the university and felt there was opportunity to change and improve the situation. It would take a decision maker to create competitive curricula and open up opportunities for students to engage the world beyond the safety of the Christian community. It was never about the title or the prestige, but rather about continuous improvement. Often women were more critical than men. The wife of a former faculty member took time to meet me for coffee. After she told me I should resign from my position of authority and quoted Scripture to justify her point, I simply responded by saying I would gladly move aside allowing her husband to take the responsibility when she stopped dying her hair and wearing makeup. I graciously showed her the verses in the Bible to support my opinion.

I also found it interesting how many people felt it necessary to sign letters and emails with all titles and accolades acquired over the years. A title is only as good as the paper on which it is written. I learned to be myself even when the situation required a title, which for me included "Vic's wife," "the Colonel's wife," or "Laurie and James' mom"—all nameless titles, but with deep meaning. It was never important for others to address me as anything other than Ilene. The complexity of donning so many hats was chaotic in itself, but very fun and extremely rewarding.

During this period of time, Vic would be deployed, his father would fall ill and pass away, and his mother would begin a battle with cancer that would claim her life seven years later. These events would pull me in a different direction, and all needed attention at the same time. Again, I looked for those who were in the same dilemma and found no one, so I did the best I could at each moment I was needed and prayed it would all work out for the better. Sometimes there were successes, while others times I failed miserably.

Balance

Trying to balance all areas of my life with excellence was nearly impossible. I would often tell my students that juggling many different jobs at once would inevitably lead to failure in one or more areas. The trick was never to juggle the balls at one time, but leave them on the table and move them around strategically, with the assistance of other people, until control could be regained. Although there was never a huge disaster during my time as a dean, I faced many difficult decisions, both personally and professionally.

Problems arose from those with private issues that ultimately affected job performance. Many had never worked for a woman and some believed I would have a softer leadership approach than the previous dean. My approach was not so tough as to be labeled masculine, but was strong in conviction. Fairness and long-suffering were two traits ingrained from my father's teachings. At times, even exemplifying fairness was difficult; after all, life isn't fair. It was difficult to discipline individuals at the university where many felt they were free agents and could take their talents to another school or organization. Balance was touted as the key to success, but that meant managing the chaos. The needs of every constituent continually pressed upon me.

Finding spiritual joy became an important component to each day. Whether it was praise music in the car on the way to work or an online devotion from *Marketplace Leaders*, I tried to engage God every morning in prayer for all the constituents within my span of care and those who would cross my path. I left room every day for unexpected sacred encounters and watched God fill the time according to his purpose. I spoke with my children from work every day, on the phone and eventually through text messaging, calming tears and fears from a middle school bathroom or the parking lot of the local high school. This wasn't much different than calming fears of students with academic or behavioral problems or from faculty needing to overcome their anxiety about finishing a dissertation or writing an abstract for publication. The skills were transferable, but the people and investments were different.

I made every effort to leave my work at the office. As the job became more complex and accessibility via cells phones increased, this became more difficult. Emails, texts, and phone calls were sent at all times of the day and night. Disconnecting even during vacation was impossible, or it seemed impossible.

My first priority was always my family, yet the tug to perform at an excellent level at work would often overwhelm my day. I loved making school projects with the kids and took pride in my ability to put a great costume together. Learning games, tide pools, mission trips, and back-to-school nights were incredibly fun and brought me close to the children. I was involved enough to stay connected and sufficiently detached to give them the space needed for their development and growth. Wasn't this the method for growing new leaders? Often they would ask me about problems at work. I would suggest they come up with a method to solve the dilemma. We all learned from one another's perspective.

Again, the chaos began to build. Mentors would say it was important to separate my business self from family self and some even suggested I set aside my own spiritual convictions and assimilate into the university culture. Spending more than forty hours a week with a team of professionals was required, but being a wife and mother was now my preferred profession. There were times the family would ask if something was wrong. Yes, there was something wrong, but not with them. My short temper or anxiety from a situation at work often spilled over to the dinner table and into the latter part of the evening. And occasionally, the fallout would cause everyone to walk on eggshells, wondering why mom was so upset. It was during these episodes I found myself seeking answers through faith and asking my husband for feedback. Each part of my life was complicated, but rewarding. There were no mentors or friends in the same situation offering directional advice. Seeing each area grow and prosper was all the feedback I needed to step into the next day with unbridled enthusiasm. All areas were important, but some took precedence over others. Treating faith as a piece of clothing to be worn only on Sunday or at church festivities was inconceivable. It was interwoven in my DNA. It shaped the decisions regarding leadership throughout my career.

A Look Back and Forward

As the years have unfolded, there are a few characteristics I believe are essential to managing chaos, serving your family, and being an effective leader, regardless of the followership. First, a spiritual grounding is crucial. I can't imagine starting my day without engaging Jesus in prayer. Second, standing only on your authority or title is risky and often flawed. Being a leader, especially a female leader, opens up a vulnerability others will often use as a weapon to undermine your authority. You must be brave—know yourself and your purpose in life. Third, there must be an appearance of confidence even when you are unsure. I am not a supreme fan of the phrase "fake it until you make it," but, occasionally, taking a brief moment of time to check with a friend will bring clarity to a decision. Fourth, you need a mentor or partner for support during the tough times. It is lonely at the top and people are rarely thankful for anything you provide. Make no mistake, everyone expects you to go above and beyond, regardless of how difficult the task. Fifth, practice making decisions, casting visions, and creating goals. Learn to respect the individuals who create the infrastructure of the organization. These actions are openly evaluated, especially when women lead. Sixth, having joy and a deep sense of humor will keep you from wanting to run away every day.

Each day brings incredible opportunities of which others may only dream. Sheryl Sandberg's book, *Lean In: Women, Work, and the Will to Lead*, summarizes the current climate for women in leadership.

> For decades, we have focused on giving women the choice to work inside or outside the home. We have celebrated the fact that women have the right to make this decision, and rightly so. But we have to ask ourselves if we have become so focused on supporting personal choices that we're failing to encourage women to aspire to leadership. It is time to cheer on girls and women who want to sit at the table, seek challenges, and lean in to their careers.[18]

While chaos will continue to exist, we must be willing to share the unique talents and abilities given for the purpose of enriching society; whether at home or in the boardroom, we are all capable of adding value.

I have learned that life will never feel normal. "Normal" cannot be defined for the general population; it is an individual standard. Comparing your personal experiences to others will only lead to more confusion. Taking encouragement from those who have both succeeded and failed allows all of us to live into our purpose. Wife, mother, doctor, CEO, entrepreneur, whatever the title at any given moment, we must see ourselves as more than capable, more than able. We have been given all the tools and gifts to live into our destiny. The chaos is a gift from heaven reminding us that every day is a new day filled with adventure.

Balancing a home and full-time career is difficult but not impossible. At this time of my life, I look back and can say both roles have been incredibly rewarding. However, we must work to change how roles are assigned. Men need to support women and women need to support one another. With less and less physical contact in the workplace, it is imperative we find ways to connect and encourage all women to live out their potential. While I look back with some satisfaction, my greatest days are ahead. I am validated each day by family and friends, true friends, who push me to do greater deeds. There is much for each of us to accomplish, even in chaos.

Discussion Questions

1. When was the first time you felt chaos in your life?
2. Who and what caused the chaos?
3. What methods do you use to manage your chaotic times?
4. Is the chaos in your life causing you to make excuses when it comes to setting personal goals? Are you blaming others for your lack of success?
5. How has chaos helped your life?
6. If you have a family and career, what have you learned about managing your day, week, year, and decade?

Notes

[1] Natasha Josefowitz, *Paths to Power* (Philippines: Addison-Wesley, 1982).
[2] Ibid., 15–18.
[3] Ibid., 16.
[4] Ibid., 214.
[5] Ibid., 40.
[6] Jo Foxworth, *Boss Lady: An Executive Woman Talks about Making It* (New York: Warner Books, 1978), 11.
[7] Ibid., 75.

[8] Lois P. Frankel, *Nice Girls Don't Get the Corner Office: 101 Unconscious Mistakes Women Make that Sabotage their Careers* (New York: Hachette, 2004).

[9] Foxworth, *Boss Lady,* 249.

[10] Michael Keaton, Terri Garr, and Fred Koehler, *Mr. Mom,* DVD, directed by Stan Dragoti, Pasadena, California, Metro Goldwyn Mayer, 1983.

[11] Stephen R. Covey, *The 7 Habits of Highly Effective People* (New York: Free Press, 1989).

[12] Ibid., 95.

[13] Ibid., 287.

[14] *Occupational Outlook Handbook* (Washington DC: U.S. Bureau of Labor Statistics, 1990–1991), http://data.bls.gov/pdq/SurveyOutputServlet.

[15] Kenneth Labich, "Take Control of Your Career," *Fortune* (November 18, 1991), 87–96, http://money.cnn.com/magazines/fortune/fortune_archive/1991/11/18/75761/index.htm.

[16] Ibid., 89.

[17] Sylvia Lafair, *Don't Bring it to Work: Breaking the Family Patterns that Limit Success* (San Francisco, California: Jossey-Bass, 2009), 6.

[18] Sheryl Sandberg, *Lean In: Women, Work, and the Will to Lead* (New York: Alfred A. Knopf, 2013), 159.

3

LEANING BACK
When Purpose Supersedes Position

KIMBERLY BATTLE-WALTERS DENU, PhD

"There is a time and a season for everything under the sun."

—Ecclesiastes 3:1

I had it all! From a *professional* standpoint that is. My prominent position, respected name and title, comfortable salary, and coveted private parking place made my life seem enviable to many. Life was good. What some academicians work all of their professional careers for happened fortuitously and rather quickly for me. After teaching and doing research as a university professor for ten years, I inadvertently found myself in a volunteer position that would give me access to executive leadership and would catapult me to a cabinet-level leadership opportunity in academe. While most academic promotions are linear in succession, mine would be non-linear, bypassing mid-level management altogether. Although my journey was not without its challenges, it had been truly remarkable and exciting. But now life as I had known it would change. It was time for me to have a talk—a very important talk—with the provost, my boss. A talk that would change everything. I was *pregnant*! My husband and I had just learned that we were expecting our third child.

As a *young-enough* woman of color who was on the fast track to success, I had read some of the research and knew that the academy may indeed have a built-in bias toward female professors/administrators who had more than two children.[1] This aside, I needed to decide what would be the focal point or priority of my life during this season—my demanding and prolific career or my demanding and growing family. While for many women my age, having a child at this stage in life might have been cause to go into a deep depression, for me it was indeed joyful news. My husband and I both agreed with the saying, "There are no accidental babies, only accidental parents."[2] After experiencing some health challenges, I had accepted each pregnancy and each child as a gift from God. As a result of my protracted singleness, marrying later and having my first child in my late thirties—none of which was by choice—each child that my husband and I had was considered a bonus blessing, especially in light of my original medical diagnoses. I wondered what the doctor who originally discovered my abnormally large fibroid tumors would say to me today if she knew that I was expecting my third child! After telling me my chances of conceiving naturally were small and that even with medical intervention the odds were against me, my husband and I were thankful that this doctor and other experts were wrong. Each of our children was conceived naturally, without medical intervention. We had indeed witnessed God's faithfulness and sovereignty with the birth of our children.

Now, wearing multiple hats—a university administrator, professor, author, minister, speaker, wife, and mother of three young children—I would have to step back from something, and it was not going to be from my family. For me the decision was clear. I would step down from my leadership role in the university in order to have more time, mentally and physically, to care for my family and to fulfill my *calling* in every area of my life. While this decision was simple for me, I realize that I was privileged by the fact that I even had another option and that the decision was not so simple for many women with children around the world. In fact, globally most women don't get to choose. Their choices are made for them—work, or you and your children don't eat.[3]

The "feminization of poverty" is very real, largely due to lower wages for women, single-parent female households, and the economic effects of divorce on women and children.[4] Many women are also not in careers or positions where they have flexibility. For me, although I still needed to work like most women in the United States and around the world,[5] I was able to work with my supervisor to reconfigure my position so that the changes would result in a win-win situation for me, my family, and my employer. For this I was truly thankful!

Working with a sympathetic supervisor, who is also a family expert, worked to my advantage as well. He understood the challenges and dilemma that I faced and afforded me the time and the flexibility to do what was best for me and my family. I do not take this for granted, but understand that this was truly a gift. After a few months of contemplation and prayer, I was able to reconfigure my role, part administration and part faculty, so that I could be off contract during the summers and work more family-flexible hours during the academic year.

While purposeful negotiating was an important part of my freshly-minted hybrid position, the ability to *prioritize* what was important and urgent was a critical factor. In this chapter, I will discuss the important principle of prioritizing both professionally and personally, and how to discern the various seasons for putting family before career or advancing professionally to the next level. I will also look at the social and psychological shifts that must be made when stepping back from a high-powered and prestigious career in favor of family.

Making Prioritizing a Priority

Having an infant and two young children under the age of seven has given me a whole new appreciation for organization and prioritizing. Most mornings, just getting myself and three children to two different schools and a babysitter feels like a major achievement. By the time I get to work, I feel like I should be awarded a Nobel Peace Prize, or something, for keeping the peace and getting everyone to their proper destinations—intact. What I have learned is that in order to run a household smoothly, or semi-smoothly, I have to organize things in advance and prioritize my life according to what matters most.

Good leaders and effective mothers must be skillful at prioritizing. In corporate, nonprofit, academic, and religious settings, effective leaders have to determine what is of primal importance at any given time in order to be competitive and sustainable. If they do the right things but at the wrong time, they often cease to exist or they lose their competitive edge.[6] For mothers the stakes are much higher. When faced with the daily urgencies of the family, if a mother neglects to prioritize what is most important, such as taking an infant to the emergency room for a persistent fever, it can literally mean life or death. Few mothers give themselves credit for how frequently they prioritize and multitask important matters in a given day.

In his popular book *First Things First*, Stephen Covey talks about doing what is *important* and not just what is *urgent*. He notes that urgencies scream for our attention, while important things only whisper. Covey describes four types of priorities:

> Important and urgent—highest in priority
> Important but not urgent—vital but not pressing
> Urgent but not important—time sensitive
> Not urgent and not important—time consumers[7]

Each leader and each mother has to focus the main part of their time on the first three items, especially the first two. The least amount of time should be spent on matters that are neither important nor urgent. Both quality leaders and quality parents have a finite amount of time, so using their time in a maximum capacity is crucial for effectiveness and efficiency.

Every mother and leader lives between the tension of the urgent and the important. For mothers, sometimes it comes in the form of her small child asking her to read a story or to look at something on the television while the mother is feverishly working on a deadline for work. With the pressure of multiple urgencies, it is easy for a mom to justify missing that moment because she says to herself that she can always read a story to her child another day or see what's on the television later. While this is generally true, and we don't need to guilt mothers over not paying attention to the hundreds of things pertaining to their kids that happen in a given day, enough of these missed moments eventually means that we lose connection with our children and miss the important bonding times that come from those serendipitous moments that are often unplanned but magical.

After traveling around the world and living for part of a year in South Africa, one of my favorite sayings is a simple South African Zulu greeting, "Sabona!" It is a greeting which is the equivalent of saying hello, but translated means "I see you." I love it because in our busy American lifestyles we often say hello without ever looking up and we don't stop to take the time to really *see* people. When my son was around four years old, I took him to the park, but mentally I was focused on all the things that I needed to do. At one point he called out to me to get my attention and I said "I hear you" without ever turning around. To this he said, "Then listen to me with your eyes!" With that comment he gained my complete attention. Since that day, I have never forgotten his words of wisdom and the important lesson that he taught me. Now when my children talk to me, I make a conscious effort to stop what I am doing and look and listen to them with my eyes, ears, and heart—at least on most days.

The Essentials of Prioritizing

When looking at the principles of prioritizing, it is important to start with the basics. Prioritizing involves several key steps: start with the end in mind,[8] create a task list, rank tasks, complete tasks in order of priority, and repeat this process each day.[9]

Starting with the end in mind essentially means that you need to work backwards. What is it that you want to accomplish and by when? This can be at the end of the day, end of the month or year, or end of life. Effective leaders must have time to form their vision of the future and to see where they ultimately want to go. Mothers must regularly access what is most critical at any given time, but also see beyond the immediate urgencies and ask long-term questions, such as, "What kind of children do I want to raise? What kind of relationship do I want with my spouse? How best can I accomplish this?" Beginning with the end in mind requires prioritizing the most important things first, even if they are not always the most urgent. Life regularly sends distractions that can take our focus away from the truly important things in life. Good leaders and good mothers must weed through the clamoring demands and focus on their top priorities.

The second step, creating a task list, is easier to do in the workplace than at home, yet it is critical in both places. Daily, weekly, monthly, annual, and multi-year task sheets are helpful in laying out a plan or strategy for accomplishing certain things and, later, for assessing how successful you were in accomplishing or completing those plans. Zig Zigler, businessman and motivational speaker, once said, "If you aim at nothing, you will hit it every time."

Part of the work in creating the list is to decide which things should be on the list and which should not. Today, as a mother of three young children and a wife of less than ten years, I have to regularly decide which things will remain off of my list, at least for a season, in order for me to really focus my window of time on those things that are most important to me. In order to do this more efficiently, I have started to apply what I now call the "Get-to-do/Got-to-do Rule."[10] Essentially there are two categories on a person's to-do list: things that you "get to do" and things that you've "got to do." Things on the get-to-do list are things that you want to do, things that excite and replenish you. Things on the got-to-do list are things that are important or urgent that have to get done, regardless of whether you desire to do them. During this busy season of my life, if a task doesn't fall into either my get-to-do or got-to-do lists, I politely say no, omit it, or simply don't do it. In saying no to some things, it enables me to say yes to those critical areas of my life.

The third step, ranking tasks, is traditionally what we think of when we conceptualize prioritizing. In various planning systems, tasks that are most crucial—having immediate deadlines or major consequences and importance—are ranked with an A. Those with importance but less of an immediate time frame are B-level tasks. C-level tasks usually have no penalty if they are not completed the same day, and D-level tasks are basically things that can be delegated.[11] As a mother and a leader, part of deciding which important things are addressed first begins with ranking them. The first ranking is to decide which level of importance activities possess, and the second is to rank them according to importance within each level. So, for example, activities that are ranked A-level items would then be given numbers such as A-1, A-2, and so on to display their importance at that level. What is interesting about this is that most women naturally do this when they are cooking. We estimate which item will take the longest to cook and start preparing that item, then gradually prepare other things, so that the longest and the shortest cooking-time items will be done around the same time. In a similar fashion, it is not enough for a mother to say that spending time with her children is a priority; she must be specific and outline which tasks and when she will engage with them to bring this priority into fruition.

In order to execute the fourth step—complete tasks in order of priority—respect must be given to time limits or deadlines, along with consideration for the consequences if ignored.[12] Two of the quickest ways to determine a priority are to ask when the deadline is and what will occur if I don't complete it. While these two questions may help mothers prioritize projects in the workplace, I realize that it is not always that simple in the home environment. This is because some of the most important matters at home, though they are important and there are real consequences, don't have designated deadlines, albeit sometimes for several years out.

Finally, the option to prioritize once, and only once, will not work for leaders or mothers. Prioritizing is a repeated process that must be done on a regular basis. Not only must we do this daily, monthly, and annually, but we often have to reprioritize several times a day. Good leaders and mothers must adapt to changing circumstances and reprioritize based on the more urgent and important issues that arise. Despite a mother's best intentions or perfectly planned day, everything can be overhauled in an instant with a sick child. Not long ago I was faced with the tough decision to attend an important board meeting at work or to care for my oldest daughter who was running a fever and miss the critical meeting altogether. Fortunately I was able to treat her fever and see it drop in time to make most of the meeting, but it was challenging to rid myself of this double guilt: leaving my sick daughter with my husband, on one hand, and being late for an important meeting on the other. At times it can feel like mothers can't win; regardless of the decision that they make, they wonder if it's the right one.

Even with their dedication to reprioritize their lives in favor of their family, working mothers are often stigmatized as being less committed to traditional family values because they are disengaged or away from their children for a period of hours each week. The following section looks at historical and contemporary criticisms related to mothers in the workplace.

The Great Debate

For decades, women and members of society have debated who is the better mother—the mother who stays at home with her children or the mother in the workplace? While this debate provides some scintillating content for women's magazines, it presents a false dichotomy that is overly simplistic at best and hugely divisive at worst. Having had an excellent mother as a role model, who was also a successful employee outside of the home, I don't believe it has to be either/or; it can be both/and. The criteria for what makes a *good mom* is not based on whether or not a woman has a profession, but on the woman. I believe that it is great if a woman is afforded the *choice* to stay at home, she wants to stay at home, and she does so. I also believe that if a woman *has* to work or *chooses* to work while caring for her family, that is also good and is often necessary—although likely more hectic. Regardless of the path a mother is on, we have to stop demonizing women for making choices that are different from our own.

Historically and traditionally, men have been associated with making contributions in the workplace and women in the home. When women decide to not only work outside of the home but take on a leadership role, they are often penalized by both men and women for exercising leadership, hence power, in a public domain.[13] In the home environment, a woman's *domestic* leadership may not be considered a threat, but a woman's leadership in the workplace causes some men to question their own identities as providers and some women to question their own life purposes in addition to being mothers. In response to these potential insecurities, men at times minimize women's workplace successes or compete with them for achievement and recognition on the job. Women, on the other hand, sometimes devalue women leaders so as to lessen power differentials and the sting of being compared to them.[14]

Women leaders who are also mothers face a double jeopardy. First, as parents, working mothers tend to be viewed negatively.[15] They are seen as less dedicated to their children and more ambitious or self-oriented. Many women are told after they have children that they should "cease being the picture and need to become the frame."[16] This could imply that a woman's children should be the center of her existence and the loss of self should be the new norm, even though this *child-centered* approach is unhealthy for the child, the mother, a marriage, and ultimately society.[17] Second, as workers, mothers are often associated with liabilities.[18] Employers may be concerned that a woman may choose to have a child and go out on maternity leave for an extended time, or expect that she will have high absenteeism due to caring for sick children. I have been privileged to work for an employer that values women and families. I was fortunate enough to be able to take seven months of maternity leave with my youngest child and not feel pressure to return prematurely. Research suggests that mothers are less likely to experience post-partum depression when they are not rushed to return to work right away.[19]

Conducting some independent research, I both read literature and interviewed women who identified a variety of challenges that working mothers face, including that of inter-role conflicts. Those inter-role conflicts encompassed scheduling clashes between work and home. When they were at work, they felt negligent of their families, and when they were at home, they felt guilt over not doing work.[20] Nevertheless, they viewed having a successful career *and* a thriving family as essential components of a fulfilling and complete life, and were committed to both. One study found that working mothers were able to resolve or lessen inter-role conflict by simply reframing their idea of what they believed constituted a good mother.[21]

Another challenge that this population faces is work inflexibility. In their edited book *Mama, PhD*, Elrena Evans and Caroline Grant highlight the many challenges that academic mothers face in an outwardly flexible work environment. Some of the things that they note include the tenure clock continuing during pregnancy and postnatal care, pregnant faculty perceived as failed scholars and pressured out of the tenure track, lower numbers of women faculty who obtain tenure status after having children, and pregnant faculty perceived as wanting special privileges and harassed by chairs and deans because of it. It has been said that the academy is only an "illusion of flexibility," and that, in many instances, it lags behind the corporate world in support of procreation and work-family balance.[22]

An additional challenge is condemnation and comparison. Working mothers often feel judged or condemned by others for leading in two fields—work and home.[23] They sometimes feel when they are not being judged they are being compared to other women who stay at home with their children. People assume that all working mothers have a choice to work or not, but for the vast majority this is false. Working is a necessity either because they are single parents trying to provide for their families or because they are in a dual career household where their salaries are just as essential as that of their spouses.[24]

Many women also discuss role overload. This is a feeling of being overloaded both at home and work and this overload impacts many areas of their lives, thus creating disequilibrium in their sense of work-life balance.[25] Sociologists refer to duties at home as the "second shift." The second shift is the idea that in addition to the hours worked outside of the home, women work the equivalent of another full-time job inside of the home when factoring in housework and child care.[26] On top of this, many working mothers struggle with the balance of caring for themselves in proportion to caring for others, such as their families and organizations.

A final challenge relates to battling the Superwoman Syndrome. This is where internal and external pressures force women to think that they have to do it all or that the weight of the world is on their shoulders. Kesho Yvonne Scott calls this superwoman mentality "warrior mode."[27] Scott points out that this syndrome can be the source of depression, suicide, or other damaging behaviors that affect women, especially women of color who often shoulder additional social and familial pressures. This warrior mode may affect working mothers both inside and outside of major leadership positions.

Having It All?

In one year, I presented at three conferences, took two domestic flights for business trips, traveled to five different countries, and attended countless evening and weekend work events. At one point my son asked the question, "How come we never see you anymore?" Hearing his question stunned me, hurt me, and gripped my heart! Although my two children at the time were with me for at least two of the domestic and one of the international trips, my son's question encapsulated my unresolved suspicion—the time that I spent with my children *was not enough*. I was gone too much and I needed to be more present during this season of my children's lives. Posed differently, his question struck at the heart of the long-debated question, "Can women really have it all?" In this section, we will look at classical and contemporary views on women balancing work and family.

In her seminal, albeit controversial, 1963 book, *The Feminine Mystique*, Betty Friedan discusses what she identified as the myth of the happy homemaker. In her work, Friedan challenged the post-World War II social structure that said a woman's place was in the home and her only true identity was as a married woman. She believed that women were socialized to see marriage as their pinnacle goal and to pity, as well as scrutinize, women who did not marry. A contemporary example of Friedan's point is a 2013 news article about single women in their late 20s in China negatively being called "leftover women."[28] Friedan also criticized popular women's magazines and literature of her day that taught women such things as how to catch a man and keep him or how to prepare homemade baby food, but did little in terms of teaching women self-actualization. Marriage, she charged, was a hegemonic institution that had enslaved women to unfulfilled futures at home while freeing men to be all that they could be.[29]

Although Friedan's views were considered radical during her day, such views are more common among professional and college-educated women today.[30] Although it was much more common for women to stay at home with their children when Friedan's book was published, today, over two-thirds of all American women with children work outside of the home.

In *Woman First Family Always*, Kathryn Sansone says, "If a woman gives up one aspect of herself—the woman in her, the mother, or the wife—the other two facets suffer."[31] She also mentions the importance of women listening to their own voices and being realistic. Thanks to the feminist movement, women today have more choices and are more empowered to listen to their own voices as they do what is best for themselves and their families, whether they stay at home or are in the workplace.

In her 2013 bestselling book *Lean In*, Sheryl Sandberg, the chief operating officer of Facebook, challenges women to lean into leadership opportunities that come their way as opposed to opting out or using their families, or future families, as an excuse for not being more professionally ambitious. She notes that, despite the feminist movement and the advocacy work that women have done, women still make less than men—about 25 percent less—women are still in the minority when it comes to leading countries and holding leadership roles in companies and parliament, and the numbers are even lower when it comes to women of color.[32]

Sandberg suggests two factors that hinder women from upward mobility: internal and external barriers. External barriers, structural and systemic hegemonic practices that hold women back, continue to need addressing and changing according to Sandberg, but she focuses her message on what she identifies as internal barriers that women *can* control. Internal barriers, according to Sandberg, are ways in which women hold themselves back due to a lack of self-confidence and internalized negative messages they have heard throughout their lives.[33] She goes on to say, "We hold ourselves back in ways both big and small, by lacking self-confidence, by not raising our hands, and by pulling back when we should be leaning in."[34] But she also talks about the challenges of many working moms who married later and found themselves in positions where their jobs were demanding a lot of time and attention at the same time that their biology demanded that they have children.[35]

Once again, can women have it all? More specifically, can working mothers have it all? While some would disagree with me, I believe that women with children, especially those in high leadership positions, have to choose some things while letting go of others, at least for a season. One working mother said it this way, "Not every woman has a choice about whether to work or not, but every woman has some choices, so do what is best for you and your family." For some this might mean stepping down from a senior level position, as in my case. For others, it could mean reducing the number of working hours or social networks and gatherings, and for others still, it could mean being more intentional about which professional activities they will or will not participate in.[36] As one of my mentors said, "You can have it all, but not all at the same time."

Leaning Back for a Season

Prior to getting married, one particular Sunday, I was bemoaning the fact that I was still single and in my thirties during an adult Sunday school class. The teacher of the class and mother of the church, in her wisdom, responded to my frustration by saying, "Right now you are traveling the world, so enjoy it! 'Cause once those children come, the only traveling that you'll be doing is from one bedroom to the next [caring for those kids]!" When I think back to that day, I often laugh, because she was right! Although I have not been quite as restricted as she originally suggested, things *do* change after you have children. I have had to alter my traveling itinerary, despite my love of traveling, in order to prioritize my family. The truth be told, while traveling the world is a lot more exciting than changing diapers, I wouldn't trade having children— and all that goes with it—for all of the traveling in the world. Although there are no accolades and news presses for the things that I do at home, and much of childrearing is delayed gratification, I and every mother must realize that for a short season I get to "change the world one diaper at a time."[37]

Aspects of a mother's leadership role are only for a season, so we need to maximize that time. In *Courage and Calling*, Gordon T. Smith talks about the seasons of leadership. He suggests that good leaders are able to discern when a season of leadership is over in a particular area and when to move on. They don't allow their egos, pride, or perceived power to prevent them from doing what is right for the organizations and people they are serving. In this way, good leadership is fluid rather than static and can allow one to move from one area to another at any given moment. The key to being current, viable, and valuable in one's leadership, according to Smith, is to transition to the right role at the right time, or to *prioritize* the role that is most needed at a particular time. This requires being tuned in to a sense of purpose and calling and regularly prioritizing what is needful.

A working mother's decision to pull back from a fast-paced career may be based on a season in her family life and the prioritization of what is most important for her and her family. Pulling back may also allow her space to create a margin for her own mental, spiritual, and physical well-being. Often this margin is critical for creativity and balance to flourish in one's life. In the absence of this margin, a crisis of focus can occur:

> There is a third crisis. . . . It is the crisis of hectic, unfocused activity. People have a remarkable capacity to live overworked and confused lives, caught up in hectic activity that in itself seems to have little meaning or purpose, but that is made up of so many things that have to be done.[38]

Pastor Rick Warren, author of the top-selling nonfiction book *The Purpose Driven Life*, speaks about three levels of existence: survival, success, significance.[39] He describes survival as barely making it in life or just going through the motions. He defines success as being comfortable in life—looking good, feeling good, and having the goods. Finally, he identifies significance as knowing that your life matters and knowing your purpose. This last category transitions leaders from solely indulging in the fruits of their own successes, and instead beckons them to move from "private success to public good."[40] In other words, our lives are not just for our own selfish gain, but for service to God and others. Warren goes on to say, "You can waste your life, spend it, or invest it in something that will outlast it. . . . We were made for more than the good life. We were made for the better life."[41]

While mothers in leadership positions often feel like they are in survival mode, trying to balance family and work, it is important for them to strive for significance as Warren has described it. Knowing her true purpose will help a mother to prioritize what is most important—*people* not positions. While it is true that women must occupy certain positions to help people, the ability to discern one's rightful purpose at the right time will accomplish just that. Looking back over my career I can think of pivotal moments when I vacated a position at the right time, benefitting me positively as well as my successors and those they served.

In his thought-provoking book *In the Name of Jesus*, Henri Nouwen, an Ivy League professor who left Harvard to work with the mentally challenged in L'Arche, said, "Everyone was saying that I was doing really well, but something inside was telling me that my success was putting my own soul in danger."[42] By Nouwen's account, although society lauded him as successful, he experienced inner conflict that led him to leave the prestigious halls of Harvard for a more humble, yet life-changing role. Nouwen went on to identify three temptations that he believed leaders experienced: the temptation to be relevant, spectacular, and powerful.

The first temptation, relevance, has to do with our own relevance or worth, which is tied to titles, accolades, and abilities. Nouwen noted that Christian leaders were called to offer their vulnerable selves—the *naked self*[43]—the true unpretentious identity that is dependent on God, not on one's own strengths or abilities. Mothers who step away from prestigious roles, away from the limelight, in exchange for "the mundane good"[44]—cooking dinner for the family or being home when their children get out of school—must overcome this temptation to be publically relevant.

The second temptation is to be spectacular. This temptation, according to Nouwen, centers around "stardom and individual heroism."[45] These are largely birthed out of an individualistic American culture that prides itself on doing things on your own, or being the lone ranger or a self-made success. This temptation does not acknowledge that it takes a village or team to accomplish things in the workplace and at home. Those who fall into this temptation are likely to lean toward two extremes: perpetrating either a messiah or a martyr complex. The beauty of collective collaboration is truncated by the individual's need to shine. This is competition at its weakest. Professionally successful mothers who pretend to do it all on their own without acknowledging their faith, supportive spouses, flex-work environments, paid help, and other "supporting cast members" are often snared by this temptation. I have said it numerous times, if it wasn't for the amazing support and role of my husband, help from a lady who periodically cleans my house, and the good Lord who keeps me sane, I could not participate in leadership opportunities in the workplace.

The third temptation is to be powerful. This temptation takes the focus off of the people we are serving, and instead places the attention back on the leader. Nouwen describes this as the antithesis of leadership. He says leadership means to be led.[46] For Christian leaders, being led starts with being led by God first and foremost, and by those we are leading, second. It is about emptying ourselves, putting ourselves on the level of the people that we are serving, and ultimately becoming servant leaders—*downward mobility*, as Nouwen calls it. He sees "power as an easy substitute for the hard task of love."[47] He explains that it is easier to control people than to love people. For the leader and the mother, *loving* people is in fact what makes us more powerful. For me, the choice to lay down my professional power to be led by God and to serve my family and others has empowered me to fulfill my truest purpose and calling, and for that I will always be thankful.

One Size Does Not Fit All

In conclusion, I believe there are seasons during which mothers in leadership need to lean back from prolific careers or executive positions in order to prioritize their families. For some this will be a short season and for others permanent; for some mothers this will occur at the beginning of their careers and for others in the middle or toward the end. Regardless of when, why, or for how long it happens, the decision to do so will likely be unpopular, uncomfortable, and anything but simple. Such a decision will likely cost money, as in the loss of wages or bonuses, as well as status and privilege. This decision must not be taken lightly. Ultimately, the choice to lean back lies with each mother and her discernment to do what is best for her and her family. To facilitate this process, it would be nice if mothers in leadership could apply a simple formula or had professional consultants who could help them prioritize both the well-being of their families and their careers. But we don't. Life is not simple and one size does not fit all. This process of prioritizing family occurs at different times and in distinct ways for each of us. Mothers and leaders must ultimately live their lives by the guidance and approval of One. For the Christian leader and mother, that One is God. In seeking to serve him, we are ultimately choosing the best for ourselves and others. In so doing, we will never go wrong.

❖ Discussion Questions ❖

1. What factors might influence your decision to step down from a major leadership role as a parent?
2. Do men with children have to consider their families as much as women with children when deciding whether to take a senior position? Why or why not?
3. What are the ramifications of mothers *leaning in* and *leaning back* when it comes to their careers?
4. What familial, social, or policy related supports are needed for women with children to be able to stay and progress within the workplace? Do you have these supports? If not, how can you create them?

5. When a woman steps down from a senior position, what are the social, psychological, and financial challenges that she might face? Which would be the most difficult for you?

Notes

[1] Robin Wilson, "Is Having More than 2 Children an Unspoken Taboo?" *The Chronicle of Higher Education* (July 10, 2009): B-16–19.

[2] Rick Warren, "What Drives You?" *Oprah's Lifeclass* on the OWN Network, February 24, 2013, accessed May 19, 2014, www.oprah.com/oprahs-lifeclass/Pastor-Rick-Warren.

[3] Nicholas Kristof and Sheryl WuDunn, *Half the Sky* (New York: Vintage Books, 2009).

[4] Bryan Strong and Theodore F. Cohen, *The Marriage and the Family Experience: Intimate Relationships in a Changing Society* (Belmont, California: Cengage Learning, 2014), 86–87.

[5] "Women in the Labor Force: A Data Book," U.S. Department of Labor: Bureau of Labor Statistics, report 1011, December 2008, accessed May 20, 2014, http://www.bls.gov/cps/wlf-table7-2008.pdf; National Women's Law Center, "The Reality of the Workforce: Mothers Are Working Outside the Home," February 2008, accessed May 20, 2014, http://www.nwlc.org.

[6] Neil Kokemuller, "The Importance of Timing in Leadership," Small Business Chron.com, accessed October 5, 2013, http://smallbusiness.chron.com.

[7] Stephen Covey, *First Things First: To Live, to Love, to Leave a Legacy* (New York: Simon & Schuster, 1994).

[8] Stephen Covey, *The 7 Habits of Highly Effective People* (New York: Free Press, 1989).

[9] James Manktelow and Amy Carlson, "To Do Lists: The Key to Efficiency," *MindTools*, accessed August 6, 2013, http://www.mindtools.com; John Wiley & Sons, "How to Manage Time by Prioritizing Daily Tasks" (2013), accessed August 6, 2013, http://www.dummies.com/how-to/content/how-to-manage-time-by.

[10] Dr. Steve Wilkins, Azusa Pacific University professor, introduced me to the idea of a "get-to-do, got-to-do" to-do list. After applying it to my life and seeing that it worked, I then made it into a rule.

[11] Erik Wolf, "10 Tips for Time Management," *FranklinCoveyReview.com*, accessed August 7, 2013, http://franklincoveyreview.com/featured/10-tips-for-time-management; John Wiley & Sons, "How to Manage Time by Prioritizing Daily Tasks."

[12] "7 Tips for Prioritizing Tasks Effectively," Vandelay Design, accessed August 6, 2013, http://vandelaydesign.com/blog/business/how-to-prioritize-tasks/.

[13] Elizabeth Parks-Stamm, "Motivated to Penalize: Women's Strategic Rejection of Successful Women," *Personality and Social Psychology Bulletin* 34 (2008): 237–47; Madeline Heilman, "Motherhood: A Potential Source of Bias in Employment," *Journal of Applied Psychology* 93 (2008): 189–198; Kimberly Battle-Walters Denu, "Sheroes: Mothers Make Great Leaders Naturally," *Women in Higher Education* 18 (2009): 23–24.

[14] Heilman, "Motherhood;" Battle-Walters Denu, "Sheroes."

[15] Ibid.

[16] Ibid.

[17] Ibid.

[18] Ibid.

[19] Rada K. Dagher, "A Longitudinal Analysis of Postpartum Depression among Employed Women" (doctoral dissertation, University of Minnesota, 2007).

[20] S. Womack, "Careers 'Put Family Life under Huge Strain,'" *The Telegraph*, July 17, 2007, accessed April 2008, http://www.telegraph.co.uk/news; Elrena Evans and Caroline Grant, *Mama PhD: Women Write about Motherhood and Academic Life* (Piscataway, New Jersey: Rutgers University Press, 2008); Battle-Walters Denu, "Sheroes."

[21] Diane Halpern and Fanny Cheung, *Women at the Top: Powerful Leaders Tell Us How to Combine Work and Family* (Malden, Massachusetts: Wiley-Blackwell, 2008), 68, 110.

[22] Sarah Gibbard Cook, "Mama, PhD: A Companion for Mothers and Scholars," *Women in Higher Education* 17 (August 2008): 21; Battle-Walters Denu, "Sheroes."

[23] Elizabeth Park-Stamm, "Motivated to Penalize"; Battle-Walters Denu, "Sheroes."

[24] U.S. Bureau of Labor Statistics, "2008 Annual Averages—Household Data—Tables from Employment and Earnings," accessed May 27, 2014, http://www.bls.gov/cps_aa2008.htm; Battle-Walters Denu, "Sheroes."

[25] Evans and Grant, *Mama PhD*; Battle-Walters Denu, "Sheroes."

[26] Strong and Cohen, *The Marriage and the Family Experience,* 114.

[27] Kesho Yvonne Scott, *The Habit of Surviving: Black Women's Strategies for Life* (Brunswick, New Jersey: Rutgers University Press, 1991); Battle-Walters Denu, "Sheroes."

[28] Kristie Lu Stout, "Chinese Women Fight to Shake Off 'Leftover' Label," August 21, 2013, accessed May 27, 2014, www.cnn.com/2013/08/21/world/asoa/cjoma-women-lu-stout/.

[29] Kimberly Battle-Walters Denu, "For Better or Worse . . . Is Marriage a Good Thing? Christian Women Give Advice to Singles Before They Say 'I Do,'" Carole J. Lambert, ed. *Doing Good, Departing from Evil: Research Findings for the 21st Century* (New York: Peter Lang, 2009), 73; Betty Friedan, *The Feminine Mystique* (New York: W.W. Norton & Co., 1963).

[30] Ibid.

[31] Kathryn Sansone, *Woman First Family Always* (Des Moines, Iowa: Meredith Books, 2006), 8.

[32] Sheryl Sandberg, *Lean In: Women, Work, and the Will to Lead* (New York: Alfred A. Knopf, 2013), 5–6.

[33] Ibid., 8.

[34] Ibid.

[35] Ibid., 15.

[36] Robin Wilson, "Gettysburg College Takes Work-Life Balance Seriously," *The Chronicle of Higher Education* (July 10, 2009): B-8; Robin Wilson, "Is Having More than 2 Children an Unspoken Taboo?," B-16–19; Battle-Walters Denu, "Sheroes," 23–24.

[37] Andrea Palpant, "Suburbia Needs Jesus, Too," *Christianity Today* (May 21, 2013): 3, accessed October 25, 2013, www.christianitytoday.com/women/2013/may/suburbia-needs-jesus-too.html.

[38] Gordon Smith, *Courage and Calling* (Downers Grove, Illinois: InterVarsity Press, 1999), 19.

[39] Rick Warren, "What Drives You?"

[40] Ernest Boyer, "Creating the New American College," *The Chronicle of Higher Education* (March 9, 1994), accessed May 27, 2014, chronicle.com/article/Creating-the%20New-American/93483/.

[41] Rick Warren, "What Drives You?"

[42] Henri Nouwen, *In the Name of Jesus* (New York: Crossroad, 1989), 10.

[43] Ibid., 16.

[44] Palpant, "Suburbia Needs Jesus, Too," 2.

[45] Nouwen, 39.

[46] Ibid., 57.

[47] Ibid., 59.

4

PASTOR ON CALL
Essentials of Flexibility in Leadership and Mothering

KELLY DICKSON, MDIV

> *"Besides being complicated, reality, in my experience, is usually odd.*
> *It is not neat, not obvious, not what you expect."*
>
> —C.S. Lewis, *Mere Christianity*

The sound of my cell phone pulsating against its temporary home in the cup holder of my husband's car brought me back from my relaxed state. My mind was still in Santa Barbara even though the car was nearing our return destination at our home in Orange County. My husband and I had taken a little more than a twenty-four hour retreat to the place where we first met and fell in love. Those twenty-four hours had been set aside for the two of us to celebrate our birthdays and to have a bit of uninterrupted time to reconnect in the midst of what I have been told is the most tiring season of child-rearing.

We both work full-time, he in business and I as a minister at a local church. We have a four-year-old and a sixteen-month-old. Life feels full, loud, and busy most of the time. Sleep, we have discovered, is a gift, not a right. Silence is rare and interruptions are an assumed element of every interaction.

It is amazing how long and glorious a twenty-four-hour getaway can feel once children have entered the scene. What once felt like a tease of a vacation now feels like a luxurious treat. There were meals (more than one!) where both of us ate at the same time, neither one having to settle for lukewarm or cold food. One full eight-hour night of sleep, devoid of cries triggered by the pain of teething. A visit to the beach without sand toys, Spiderman towels, gallons of SPF 50 sunscreen, swim diapers, every variety of flotation device, and countless Trader Joe's snack foods. Conversations had a start, middle, and end. Those twenty-four hours felt like an eternity.

Those twenty-four hours also felt long for an entirely different reason—two very significant people in our lives were not with us. While the two of us knew that our time should be spent catching up on the state of our marriage and filling the gaps that had formed through months of busy schedules and loud children, we spent much of the time talking about those two small people who weren't there—the things we love about them, their silly sayings, their cute mannerisms. . . . We missed them.

A text message flashed up on the screen of my phone. I picked it up from its place in the cup holder to read: "Where are you? I have your car keys in my pocket by accident." Immediately, I felt the relaxation melt away and a small rush of panic replace it. My mom, who had been watching our kids while we were away, needed to leave our house before we were able to get back to town, so we asked our regular babysitter to fill in until we returned. My mom had driven halfway up the state before she discovered that she had accidentally left my car keys in her pocket. I couldn't be mad because I had done this exact thing numerous times, leaving my husband stranded at home without a car while I assisted in the worship services on Sunday morning. Unfortunately, our spare key had been missing for months (and it was not unlikely that my four-year-old had mistaken it as "treasure" and hidden it while pretending to be Jake or one of the other Neverland pirates). How would I get to work the next morning? If I didn't have car keys and could not transport my kids to childcare, would we be stuck at home all day? How would I meet the deadlines at work that were pressing in on me if we all had to stay home carless together? This was a big week with some serious deadlines. I had already been suppressing the rising feelings of pressure from work over the past twenty-four glorious hours and this unexpected hiccup did not help.

What followed was about two hours of texting back and forth with my mom and our beloved babysitter making arrangements to ensure that life would continue on without any major setbacks the next morning. Fortunately, our babysitter was on summer break from college and did not have anything else going on in the morning, so she agreed to pick the kids up and drive them to the childcare program at the church where I work and where they spend three mornings a week. I made arrangements to work from home and woke early the next morning to drive my husband's car to my office to get everything I would need for a few days of working remotely. And my mom drove first thing in the morning to the post office near where she was staying to overnight the keys to me.

Introducing the Working Mother-Minister

Thus is the life of a working mom: changing plans, deadlines pressing, asking for help, finding gracious babysitters who constantly adapt to shifting schedules, working from home, resting *away* from home, missing the kids, being flexible, lost keys, chaos. "Motherhood and working are journeys of trial and error, and even after years of experimentation and analysis and data points, you sometimes feel like you know less than you did when you started."[1] There is no way around it . . . life is filled with unexpected surprises—some pleasant and some not so pleasant. For the working mother, some of these unexpected surprises have a far greater impact than they do for the stay-at-home parent. This is not to say that one is easier than the other. The difference is that while missing keys would, of course, be an inconvenience to any parent, to a working mother, last minute arrangements must be made, help must be enlisted, and flexibility must be practiced.

Working mothers of an entirely different breed are those who serve in leadership positions in the church. Similar to that of a mother, the pastor's role is not a nine-to-five job, nor is it a job that one can do mindlessly. Pastoring requires presence—both physically and emotionally. "Soul care is one way of describing the pastor's entire task, including the ministries of preaching and sacrament, teaching and administrative leadership. . . . Care of souls therefore means the care of the inner life of persons, the mending and nurturing of this personal center of affect and willing."[2] Soul care—a high and humbling calling considering that that same pastor is simultaneously trying to remember whether her kids brushed their teeth that morning, lunches were packed for the day, shoes and socks were put on, car seats were buckled, and sunscreen applied so as to not magnify the new stitches and scars on her four-year-old's face.

Additionally, her concern for the care of souls is not limited to the members within the congregation where she serves. There is an ache and a longing that runs deep for the tiny souls of these little people who wake her each morning before the sun rises and have depended on her from the very first moment they began to grow in her womb. This longing is that her children would come to know the heart of their God—the God who knit them together in their mother's womb. As she prays for the people she encountered throughout the day, she also prays for the two small people sleeping soundly in her home—that even now they would begin to discern God's presence in their daily lives. The stillness and intentionality required to juggle both roles feels daunting at times.

For the minister, each day presents different challenges and is met with numerous interactions with unique personalities. There are evening meetings, after-hour phone calls, hospital visits, and emergencies that require attention, sensitivity, and care. Pastors regularly receive visitors looking for pastoral counseling. Often pastors are sought out because they are viewed as "safe" and affordable. "In contrast to the confusing maze of professional helpers, the pastor is a known quantity, a familiar and reassuring face in a world crowded with strangers. There is already a kind of relationship with the pastor, making it easier and safer to take the risk of asking for help."[3] Each of these responsibilities is quite familiar to mothers—we frequent evening meetings, are hounded by after-hour callers, and are well acquainted with our local hospital staff. For the mother, "evening meetings" take place in the bathroom where baths are given or new potty training techniques are implemented. Mothers are called "after hours" to the bedroom to refill a water cup, administer Tylenol, or comfort the fears brought on by a bad dream. Hospitals become familiar places to all mothers beginning the moment she discovers that she is pregnant—visits only increase when her children become active, curious, or maybe a bit clumsy. Similar to pastors, the mother is sought out first and foremost because she is "a familiar and reassuring face in a world crowded with strangers." In many ways, these two roles mirror one another.

It is in the merging of these two roles that life must be navigated with great care and intentionality. There are a few things that can help make the grand task of juggling these two overtime, unpredictable jobs manageable. When either role can command the attention of the mother at any time, day or night, it is critical that flexibility be extended to and practiced by the mother-minister. Flexibility is both given and practiced when the mother leader has established and communicated clear expectations and boundaries in her personal and work life. She must know what she needs and be willing to release what is not needed in order to survive the chaos of these two permanently on-call roles. In this chapter, I will explore how mothers working in a ministry context must both receive and give flexibility within her work and home in order to carry out both roles successfully.

Called to Minister and Mother

I remember the first day I dropped my son (firstborn) off at the childcare program at the church where I was and still am employed. I was heartbroken. Despite the twenty-nine hours of labor he put me through and the endless colicky nights that followed my eventual C-section, that child had burrowed his way deep into my heart and I hated the idea of handing him over to the care of anyone other than myself, regardless of how competent they were. I am certain that I didn't get anything done at work that day and I am also certain that I cried more that week than I had the entire year previous (which is saying a lot considering the emotions of pregnant women). Thankfully, my boss extended a great amount of compassion to me and I was sent home early every day that first week. There were those working alongside me who had been where I was and knew what I was going through. I was thankful that, even from the start, I was shown grace and extended flexibility. What began that day, and has continued every day since, was a deep, internal wrestling over how to live out the call to be both minister and mother well and at the same time.

My job has never been just a means to collect a paycheck—it has always been a calling. I believe that I was designed by my Creator with the desire and specific gifting to pastor. In his book, *Pastoral Theology: Essentials of Ministry*, Thomas Oden speaks of the minister's process of being "called" into ministry. He points out that there should be both an "inward" and an "outward" call for those pursing a life in ministry. An inward call requires a private, inward, intuitive feeling that one is called by God into ministry. This calling comes through slow and patient internal self-examination in which one is asking questions of herself like, "How deep is my empathic capacity?" or "How much am I willing to give up in order to serve the poor, the alienated, the sick?" or "Can I learn to communicate the Christian message with persuasiveness and integrity?"[4] Once there has been confirmation of an inward call, Oden writes that one who is called into ministry must also experience an outward call—the affirmation of the visible believing community.[5] "The purpose of the outward or external call to ministry is to examine and confirm the preliminary intuition of an inward call by deliberately testing and assessing the candidate's potential for service to the body of Christ."[6] Essentially, do others see in me what I see in myself? Are there people in my life who can confirm that I have the ability to minister well?

When I was a junior in college, I experienced the first stirrings of an internal call. As a resident assistant in a freshman dorm at Westmont, I discovered for myself what Frederick Buechner meant when he said, "The place God calls you to is the place where your deep gladness and the world's deep hunger meet."[7] I came alive while ministering to the women in my dorm. I prayed for each woman by name every day that year. I listened as they processed what they were learning about God, themselves, and the world around them. I tried to encourage the strengths that I saw in them and provide a quiet refuge in my room when they needed a break from the noise and chaos of college life. When they missed home, encountered loss, or struggled with life decisions, I was there. We cried, laughed, grieved, and celebrated life together. Somehow, in the midst of that year, I believe that Jesus introduced me to a side of himself and myself that I had not known.

After graduation and a couple of years trying to do anything but go back to school, I found myself in seminary working on my Master of Divinity degree. If, in fact, I was being called into ministry, I felt ill-equipped and in need of training, so I forced myself back into the classroom—actually I believe it was God who forced me back into the classroom, but I listened nonetheless. It was there that I received what Oden referred to as an outward call. Though my time in seminary continually affirmed my desire to be in full-time ministry, on one very distinct occasion, a professor of mine sat me down and told me that he believed that most people should, at all cost, avoid ministry. It is not for everyone. In fact, it is not for most. However, he saw specific gifts and abilities in me he believed that if not used, would simply be disobedient. His words stuck with me and rattled around inside for a while. I began to pay more attention when others spoke of strengths they saw in me. Did they also see what that professor claimed he saw in me . . . the very thing I sensed in myself my junior year of college? Yes. This is an outward call.

For more than twelve years, God has been calling and preparing me for ministry. For more than four years, I have been made aware of just as strong of a call on my life to mother—both callings I am sure were there from the time *I* was knit together in my mother's womb. Is it possible for the two callings to be carried out well at the same time? What does *well* mean? What, aside from my definition of *well*, needed to change in order for this mother to simultaneously minister?

In her study on how motherhood changes ministry, Pamela Cooper-White writes, "At the core of the study's findings is the recognition that becoming a clergy mother, like all major life passages, is not an event but a process, impacting both the clergywoman and those she serves." [8] Both motherhood and ministry are communal callings that cannot be done without the help, support, and grace extended from others. Just as ministry is carried out in the context of community, parenting is a calling that requires community. When a new life enters the world everything changes. When a new life is welcomed into a church family, the whole family must flex to make room for this life. Flexibility is required. Just as the biological family must make room in the home for a new baby, so too does the church family need to make room. That is the key to the success of the mother-minister—flexibility. "Congregations or constituencies that were receptive to the announcement of the minister's pregnancy tended to be supportive of the clergywoman in preparing a space for the newborn arriving in their midst. Congregations that were less receptive were generally not described as hostile but as 'clueless' or in denial." [9] We must remember that mothering and ministering together is a process. It takes time, determination, perseverance, and patience on both the part of the mother as well as her community.

Where to Draw the Line: Which Calling Comes First?

The danger of ministry is that it is a role that, more often than not, extends beyond the confines of a forty-hour workweek. The challenge for the minister-mother is how *not* to steal the family time in an effort to make up the difference of what remains yet to be done at church. Often, pastors who are mindful that there will always be more people to care for, more calls and emails to return, and more contact to be made with members who have recently gone "missing" from the church, forsake time with their families to meet the ever-pressing needs of the congregants. On the other hand, the pull that a mother feels to be with her children and the guilt that so often crowds in when her work is begging for her attention can be suffocating at times and can lead her to neglect her call as minister if she is not careful. This is an ongoing daily battle. Figuring out how to be 100 percent present for the needs of family while simultaneously fulfilling the urgent needs that pop up at inopportune times from members of the congregation requires understanding and constant communication with employers and family members. It will also mean that some things need to be dropped. Not everything can be done perfectly from here on out. Something has to give.

In her essay, "Ministry and Motherhood: A Collision of Callings," Kristin M. Foster wrestles with this issue stating, "The easy harmony of balancing my own self-chosen commitments was shattered when I faced situations in which I was torn between two compelling calls, face to face with the terrible question, *Which comes first*? Is there room in one person's life for two primary callings, such as that of pastor and mother? Can I be faithful to one without betraying the other?"[10] Foster concludes her study by arguing that callings are *not* manageable—they compel us, we do not compel them. "I was now discovering that a calling by its very nature is not based on personal choice or subject to reasonable limits. A true calling defies our best attempts to reduce it to one among a set of factors in making decisions."[11] True. There are times when the bedtime duties need to be passed on to the spouse so that the minister can go sit with a member of the congregation who is convinced her marriage is over and just needs a listening ear and prayer. There are times when the mother needs to pass her worship service responsibilities on to another pastor so she can attend to her child in the emergency room. There are times when the minister will stay up well past her bedtime to respond to a call with someone in crisis and will be woken up only a few short hours later by her kids' needs for diaper changes and breakfast. These two callings are not manageable. They both require attention to what is needed in each moment and the willingness to let go of previously mapped out schedules and plans.

A few weeks ago I found myself in a situation where I was forced to practice this discipline of letting go. It was a Monday—enough said, right? I had just returned from a family vacation the night before, and aside from having my first of many appointments of the day scheduled at the same time that I was supposed to drop my kids off and a calendar that indicated that my day would end at 10:00 P.M., our childcare ministry had decided to move their morning program to a nearby park. The park added twenty-five minutes onto my morning commute, and they asked us to drop our kids off ready for a day in the sun and heat. Diaper bag packed, sunscreen applied, and lunches made, I pulled up to the park a few minutes before my scheduled drop-off time so that I wouldn't be late for a pastoral counseling appointment that was likely already waiting for me at the church. Conscious of the fact that I always want to be present with my kids, even when I am feeling rushed, I chose to release the growing sense of anxiety about being late—let it go. I trudged up the hill toward the playground in my heels with my daughter on my hip, sweat starting to form on my brow, signed the kids in, gave kisses and hugs, handed over the bags, and marched back down the hill to my car.

When I finally got to the church, the woman coming to meet with "a pastor" took one look at me and inquired about my age and credentials. My answer satisfied her enough to spend an hour and a half talking with me through some very personal issues in which she was seeking direction and insight. I consider it a great honor and quite humbling to be trusted with some of the painful or confusing aspects of the people's lives who sit across from me in my office. It is in these moments that I am reminded why I am doing what I am doing. I decided it was more important to meet with her than make it on time to my next meeting, so I ignored the clock and encouraged her to keep talking. The only thing that brought an end to our time together was a knock on my door from a co-worker letting me know I was already thirty minutes late for my next meeting.

Sometime between my morning meetings and picking up my kids at the park just after lunch, I ran to Costco to purchase the ingredients for a dinner party of ladies from the church I would be hosting at my house that night. Driving away from the park, I informed my four-year-old that we were on our way to the doctor to get the stitches removed in his lip that he had gotten days before from an attempt to impersonate Superman. Traumatized by the experience of getting the stitches, he cried the entire way to the doctor's office—an office I had never been to before and apparently neither had Siri, my imaginary iPhone friend who sent me thirty minutes in the wrong direction. An hour late to our appointment on a summer day in a car, with a broken air conditioner, and with one terrified boy and one sleeping girl—whom I knew would never take her afternoon nap at home because of this momentary car snooze—I had to let go of the work expectations I had for myself for the rest of the day, my master plan to be ready to host a group of women for a nice sit down meal at my home, and my anxiety over my son's growing up. I had to just be present.

Needless to say, holding a screaming child down long enough to get stitches removed while simultaneously keeping my sixteen-month-old from unloading the cabinet of medical supplies was not my idea of a restful lunch hour. Both kids fell asleep in the car on the way home and thus refused to take their afternoon naps . . . the time I depended on to finish my work for the day. While they played in their rooms, I prepared the house for a dinner meeting and sent off a few urgent emails. At five o'clock, a friend arrived to help me cook but had to lie down numerous times throughout the preparation process because the smells from our cooking made her pregnant body feel nauseous. The guests arrived at 6:30 P.M. for a dinner that was not yet ready and again I felt the anxiety rise within me. Let it go. Be present.

At 8:00 P.M., another wave of women arrived for a weekly gathering that I had stupidly booked back to back with the first group. Both groups stayed. Not a seat was unused in my house—poor scheduling on my part. There I was in that place once again of needing to let go. My home was filled with a mix of women I loved and new faces with stories yet to be learned. No one seemed to mind the chaos—not even me. By the time the last guest left, I fell into bed exhausted, and yet so fulfilled. Mother. Minister. Tired. Grateful.

This is what I love: people, their stories, the journey, hospitality, being present for my kids, new friendships, good conversations, days that are full, and letting go. It will not be neat and tidy. Chaos abounds and flexibility is required. In order to get what she needs to succeed as a pastor and mother on call, the leader must be able to articulate and ask for what she needs.

Work toward Flexibility in the Workplace

In her book *Equal to the Task*, Ruth Haley Barton encourages families to consider their needs and to not allow fear to determine the circumstances of the family. "In order to keep working toward a lifestyle that is satisfying and supportive to men, women and children, we must confront belief patterns that do not serve us well . . . the Christian, however, must reject the scarcity mentality in favor that in God there will always be enough of whatever we need to live as whole persons and do His will."[12] For a mother who desires or needs to work, she must be willing to step out in courage and ask for what she needs, not fearing rejection. Even if the answer is no, she must remember that in God there will always be enough.

At the time I returned from maternity leave after having my first child, our church staff had only one other baby "on staff"—the daughter of a husband and wife team who both served full-time in the youth department. When their daughter was born, it had been decades since any staff member had been pregnant. I am eternally grateful to my friend and co-worker who spoke up, articulated her needs (and the needs of all the future mothers on staff), and joined forces with the human resource department to put together a staff maternity leave plan prior to her child's arrival. She was not as fortunate as I was. She had to pioneer her way into the fully-employed mothering world with a fairly seasoned church staff whose experience with babies and new mothers had long since expired. I have greatly benefited from her courage and experience.

We had a nursery on campus for mothers who needed childcare for an hour or two while they attended Bible study, but the idea of childcare throughout the workday, and especially during the summer when most Bible studies were taking a break, was not an option. Two weeks before I needed to return to work, I still did not have childcare coverage for all of the days that

I would need to be back in the office. I had arranged for my mom to watch my son every Thursday and my aunt would watch him Tuesday afternoons, but had no plan for the rest of the week. I asked a family friend if she might be willing and available to watch my son one afternoon each week, but she declined saying that she did not agree with mothers who chose to work rather than raise their babies. I was hurt, offended, and confused. I was *called* to this job . . . wasn't I?

I contacted the childcare coordinator at the church and asked if she would consider having my son in the nursery two and a half days each week. After twelve uninterrupted weeks of being with my son, it was painful to think of handing him over to someone else for the day—he was so tiny, so helpless, so new. The childcare coordinator—a woman known for her deep love for young families and her heart for ministry—desperately wanted to help, but there were a million hurdles to clear before this would be a possibility. She told me that she would look into some things and call me back. Two weeks later, I checked my son into the nursery where he would be cared for two and a half days each week.

That was almost four years ago. Today, there are thirteen staff kids (and four more on the way) who are daily loved and cared for by the employees of the church nursery five days a week from 8:30 A.M. to 5:00 P.M. Half of those kids also attend the wonderful preschool on campus, which has been there for decades, and when school is over, their teachers walk our kids over to the nursery where they will have lunch, take a nap, and play. They are taken on excursions to local parks, read stories, and are celebrated on their birthdays. What once did not exist has now become a family.

There was a change taking place within the culture of our church staff and rather than run from it, our church leadership embraced it. All it took was a little courage and prompting from a few pregnant staff members, along with the combined efforts of our human resources department and church administration team, and a way was made for employees to continue working while our kids were safely and affordably cared for right there on campus. What a gift! What a necessity!

A study that explored the impact of flexibility offered to employees within the workplace found that when there was a perceived sense of flexibility, there existed consistently less family-to-work conflict and less stress and burnout.[13] Flexibility was defined in this study as "the ability of workers to make choices influencing when, where, and for how long they engage in work related tasks."[14] Employees were evaluated on the following five workplace flexibility options:

- Flextime: a work schedule that enabled employees to have flexibility in determining, within limits, when their regular workday would begin and end so long as each week totals forty hours worked.
- Compressed work week: a work schedule where the typical eight-hour workday, five days a week might be compressed into fewer, longer days
- Telecommuting: the employee works in a location other than the designated worksite or office
- Part-time employment: the employee works less than a forty-hour work week
- Job sharing: two employees share the responsibilities of one full-time job

Though workplace flexibility was originally created with mothers in mind, studies now reveal that men and women of various ages and life stages have become more effective at work and experience less stress at home as a result of the flexibility extended to them from employers:

The suite of work-life policies now considered core to workplace flexibility (e.g., flextime, compressed work week, telecommuting, part-time employment, job sharing) was originally targeted at mothers with small children. Thus, flexible work arrangements were generally called *work-family* programs. Coupled with strategies for childcare, they were designed to ameliorate mothers' stress and burnout in order to retain women in the workforce and reduce women's family-to-work conflict to enable them to be more effective on the job. Research generally supports that such arrangements facilitate these goals.[15]

The study found that different forms of workplace flexibility appealed to different people depending on their age, stage, or gender. Employers who were willing to be flexible with their employees, depending on their needs and life stage, had employees who were more satisfied in their working environment. Interestingly however, though women tended to differ from men in the type of flexibility they used and preferred, the study also revealed that at every stage, women valued almost every flexible work option more than men valued them. The study concluded that the more employers sought ways to understand their employees and provide options of workplace flexibility, the more these efforts "would facilitate the development of effective programs, policies, and work-life strategies to meet employee and organizational needs."[16] A leader must know her needs and be able to articulate them so that when the time comes, she is able to maintain her responsibilities at both work and home, not only for her own benefit but also for the benefit of her employer and family.

Historically, flexibility in the workplace has been seen as a threat, and as a result of that perspective, many women were quietly forced out of the workforce or found it very difficult to progress professionally once they began having children. "Corporate America harbors a dirty little secret. People in human resources know it. So do a lot of CEOs, although they don't dare discuss it. Families are no longer a big plus for a corporation; they are a big problem.... It's fine to have the kids' pictures on the desk—just don't let them cut into your billable hours."[17]

Fortunately, the tides are shifting and employers have discovered that in order to keep the right people, the good people, they have to be willing to flex and to provide options, not only for the growing workforce of women, but the needs of both men and women of all ages who have endured long commutes and have juggled families and caretaking responsibilities under very stringent expectations. These opportunities will not likely develop on their own. Mothers need to be confident in what they need and feel the freedom to articulate what will help them to work most effectively and efficiently given their present circumstances. They also, however, must expect to work hard, to be more accessible by phone, email, and, text, and to "manage up" by keeping open and frequent communication with their bosses and co-workers.

Articulating What You Need

Because I work at a church, one of my work days is Sunday. If I am helping to lead in the worship services, I typically arrive at 7:30 A.M. and leave around 1:00 P.M. Though it is only a partial day, I am still away from my family for a good chunk of the day, and because my kids are young, I return home just in time for them to go down for naps. Additionally, I have a weekly evening work requirement that ends just in time for me to help my husband tuck our kids into bed. Between those ongoing commitments and a number of other irregularly scheduled evening events and meetings, most weeks have the potential to demand far more than forty hours, and I often won't know what the week will hold until it is well underway.

Ministry is irregular, unpredictable, and often, last minute. That is why I love my job. On the Myers-Briggs, I am labeled "P" for perceiving, as opposed to a "J" for Judging. This simply means that as I go about my day-to-day tasks, I prefer a more flexible and adaptable lifestyle rather than being more structured and decided. I was made for the ministry lifestyle. I enjoy each day looking different from the previous and never knowing when someone will pop into my office to talk, cry, or share a little glimpse into what they are going through. That being said, I was also made to be a mom. I have a responsibility to my children. I desire to pour into their lives and to be present as they grow—not just physically, but emotionally, too. I want to allow time in each week to play with them, to listen to their stories, and to interact in their imaginary worlds. I want to take them on adventures, read to them, and spend whole days in our pajamas. If I want both, I need to create time and space in my week for both. This *is* possible. This *is* attainable.

In their article, "Work-Life-Balancing: Challenges and Strategies," Eva Chittenden and Christine Ritchie explore the challenges faced by full-time employees who do not set boundaries within their work and home lives. "Balancing our work and personal lives is difficult but incredibly important. It is critical to avoid a pattern of delaying what we value most and prioritizing those things that are ultimately of less value to us. Examining and living by our values, while hard, is a vital step to achieving balance and happiness in our lives."[18] Mothers in any kind of leadership position must revisit the ways they spend their time (both at work and at home) on a regular basis to ensure that they are achieving the balance they desire in both spheres.

In an attempt to seek balance between work and home, I asked my supervisors if they would allow me to take Fridays off. They requested that I map out my weekly hours and show how I planned to spend my time. When they saw that I had a plan to fulfill my work requirements and was willing to be accessible to them if they needed to reach me when I was not in the office, they gladly gave me the opportunity to implement a compressed work week and take Fridays off. Their willingness to extend this flexibility to me has helped keep our childcare expenses down and has allowed me one, and often two, full days to be with my kids. "Flexibility in the timing and location of work, whether full-time or part-time, had been shown to promote work-life balance."[19] Our staff leadership agreed that church-work rarely stays inside the lines of a nine-to-five day. So long as I was able to continue working in effective partnership with our ministry team and maintain presence and connection with our congregants, they agreed that taking Fridays off was the best option for the health of my family, and ultimately, the health of our team.

Additionally, I realized that my longest workday would also mean a long day in the nursery for my kids. We were scheduled to arrive at nine in the morning and would not leave the church campus until eight at night. I did not want my kids to be in childcare for that long of a period of time, so again, I asked my supervisors if they would let me take my kids home once a week on that particular long day after lunch and work from home while they napped. They graciously agreed to my request. This allowed me to put my kids down for naps on a day when I would not otherwise see them until bedtime, and it also gave my kids time to rest in their own beds rather than nap at the church where they often slept half the amount of time they would if they were home.

I am deeply grateful for those afternoons for two reasons: First, I tend to be much more efficient and focused in my work during those hours. My kids take good naps—typically around three hours each day. I can work uninterrupted for a much longer period of time than I would if I were in the office, and I am much more accessible to my co-workers than I am when I am on campus. Second, it shows that I have managed to gain a level of trust with my supervisors that I have worked hard to achieve. This did not happen overnight, nor did it happen without great effort.

I acknowledge that this level of flexibility is rare and I don't take lightly that it has been extended to me. Not every mother has this ideal of a work situation. One of the greatest concerns of employers is that, without the accountability of the office, her work will not get done. To alleviate these concerns, she will need to show that she can get work done while staying at home with her children. If the work cannot be done during the hours that she would typically be in the office (let's be honest; kids don't always nap for as long as we plan or expect), the work will need to be done after her children have gone to bed or her kids will need to be distracted long enough for mother to tie up any loose ends before calling it a day. I am not proud to admit that I have been known to stack mountains of snack food in front of my kids or turn on a DVD (typically we don't allow any TV time during the week) to buy myself twenty or thirty minutes of additional work time. It's a challenge and will always feel like a juggling act. At the end of the day, some employers are simply not ready or comfortable extending this kind of flexibility to their employees. These are merely external factors that impact the mother-leader—factors that may not be controllable.

Learning to Be Flexible

Having children has completely uprooted my sense of order and control. I used to think I had some sort of control over my day. Even in ministry, there are few true emergencies. Calls can be returned later, other pastors can fill in for me in a pinch, I can schedule my own appointments, and for the most part, the day tends to run as my calendar predicts it will. Kids have a way of changing all of that. Nothing is predictable. Tantrums happen—all the time—delaying work time arrival by a minimum of fifteen minutes. Diaper blowouts seem to come right as the last buckle is fastened in the car seat and every bag has been packed in the car for the day. Sippy cups spill all over clean work clothes just as keys are locking the front door, or random birds fly into the house after the kids are already in the car and you find yourself chasing it throughout the house with a broom in your high heels. (Yes, that happened to me twice in a period of three months.) Mornings are insane. I mean, literally, insane. Any time I manage to arrive on time to work (rare), I feel like there should be a crowd of people cheering me into the parking lot like they would at the finish line of a big race. It is a *huge* accomplishment. Most days I feel like I want to collapse into my own little puddle of Ann Taylor LOFT work clothes on the floor of my office before the day has even begun because I am already so tired from getting my two little ones up and out of the house, clean and alive.

I am learning that flexibility is not just something that needs to be offered to me in order for me to do my job well—I need to extend flexibility to myself as well. I need to be comfortable with the chaos and the mess. I need to be okay leaving for the day with a bit of clutter scattered around the house. I need to give myself a few minutes after arriving in the morning to gather my thoughts and catch my breath. I need to ask my kids for forgiveness for my short temper and constant pushing to move faster because "we're late." I need to build extra time into the mornings and lean into the chaos. Control is merely an illusion. I never had it, and kids have reminded me that I *will* never have it. Being flexible is the only way I will make it from my door step to my office each and every day.

The Internal Life of a Healthy Mother-Leader

It seems as though there is endless information available for working parents on how to maintain health and order in the midst of a chaotic existence—suggestions that guarantee to reform the personal and working life. If the parent can only master these "six things," her life will be better. Keep a calendar, plan ahead, eat well, exercise regularly, go on weekly date nights with your spouse to keep the marriage alive, and engage in some sort of hobby that is "just for me." True. These are all methods that lead to healthy *external* habits that most likely will have a positive impact on work and personal life. But what happens when I run out of time to exercise? What if I just don't have enough energy to prepare a healthy meal for my family after a long day at work and need to pick up some take-out on my way home? What if the "babysitter fund" has run out and my husband and I are stuck at home watching episode after episode of West Wing together? Will our marriage fall apart? The guilt is unbearable.

These are all habits that promise to alter my external circumstances, but what about the *internal* habits that shape who I am becoming—who my kids are becoming?

In her book *Daring Greatly*, Brené Brown describes people as "wholehearted" who believe that they are worthy and display courage in a "never enough" culture through their willingness to be vulnerable. She says that courage and vulnerability are traits that, if modeled by parents, will equip children with confidence. In her chapter on parenting, she says, "Who we are and how we engage with the world are much stronger predictors of how our children will do than what we know about parenting."[20] While healthy external habits are good, Brown suggests that the transformative behavior is passed on through our own embodiment and practice of vulnerability. She charges parents to:

- Acknowledge that we can't give our children what we don't have and so we must let them share in our journey to grow, change, and learn.
- Recognize our own armor and model for our children how to take it off, be vulnerable, show up, and let ourselves be seen and known.
- Honor our children by continuing on our own journeys toward wholeheartedness.
- Parent from a place of "enough" rather than scarcity.
- Mind the gap and practice the values we want to teach.
- Dare greatly, possibly more than we've ever dared before.[21]

I have a friend who is a mother of two, a pediatrician, and one of the smartest women I know—seriously. When I was getting ready to return to work after having my daughter, she placed her hand on my shoulder, looked me in the eyes, and said to me, "I am going to give you the talk that I give all the mothers of my patients just before they go back to work from maternity leave." It was as if she was able to peer into my soul, and as she spoke, she affirmed my ambition and character. She reminded me that the very fact that I was returning to work was teaching my daughter that women are strong and that they can pursue their dreams. She reminded me that as I juggle the chaos that comes from being a wife, mother, and minister, I am modeling for my children how to manage stress, how to organize time, and how to pour myself wholeheart-edly into two things that I believe in: mothering and ministering. In the days and years ahead I will have to ask my kids for forgiveness—giving and receiving grace is a profound lesson for them to learn, especially from their mother. I will be tired—this will teach them perseverance. I will have to make sacrifices, and how I decide what to sacrifice will teach them discernment. More than anything, she reminded me that I have been called to these roles—to be both a mother *and* a minister. And by pursing these callings, I am teaching my son and daughter to be obedient first and foremost to Jesus:

> The root issue is not some historically fixed way of structuring family, economic, domestic, and childrearing tasks. The root question is one of priorities. How can a given Christian family, with its particular constellation of talents, limitations, and needs so structure itself that it contributes to the advancement of God's kingdom here on earth? Perhaps the best environment for children is not the one in which mother stays home, but one in which the whole family, as part of the larger family of God, reaches out to meet the needs of others.[22]

Pastor and Mother on Call

My kids may not have all the same opportunities that other kids have. They may wish they could spend more time at home playing with their toys and they may have days where they didn't get enough sleep because they had to nap in the church nursery, surrounded by their friends rather than at home in peace. They might not get to spend all morning long in their pajamas every day of the summer because I need to get them to childcare by nine. They might only be able to have friends over in the evenings or on the weekends. They might not get to go on as many adventures or have as much time with me as they would if I was at home full-time. Some days that makes me sad. But God has written a different story for my life and, if I am obedient, it is a story that ends in deep, meaningful, and lasting life.

I believe that God has composed a unique story for each person and that we navigate our way into and through that story when we listen to the longings that emerge when all is still and silence has time to settle in. Mine is a calling to my family and to God's church. If he moves us, we will go; but for now, we are here and I am thankful. I want my kids to know that I fear God more than I fear the opinions of others who think that I might not be a good mom because I don't stay home full-time.

I want my children to know that their lives are not their own and that they were made to be bearers of God's image wherever he may lead them. I want them to know God is in the process of shaping them and preparing them for their own unique calling—that in serving others they will experience far deeper joy and greater satisfaction than they would if they lived each day for themselves. I want them to know life is meant to be lived in community and that asking for help is not a sign of weakness but an opportunity for deeper friendship. I want them to know their mother loved them from the moment she found out they were growing inside her and that love has grown stronger and fiercer with each passing day. I will fail. I will ask for forgiveness. I will cry . . . a lot, I am sure. But I will never regret teaching my children the value of obeying God's call. And so I am both mother *and* pastor on call.

Discussion Questions

1. What has been your experience with flexibility in the workplace?
2. How has that experience (either positive or negative) impacted your ability to mother? To lead?
3. When have you had to extend flexibility to yourself as a result of your work? How did that impact your family? Your work?
4. What boundaries have you set in place to strengthen and develop your internal life? Do you see yourself on the path toward wholeness or breakdown?
5. Brené Brown, in her book *Daring Greatly*, charges parents to practice vulnerability with their children in order to strengthen and develop their confidence. How does this strike you? What are some ways you have modeled vulnerability to your children? How did they respond?

6. In her book *Equal to the Task*, Ruth Haley Barton challenges a traditional view when she says, "Perhaps the best environment for children is not the one in which mother stays home, but one in which the whole family, as part of the larger family of God, reaches out to meet the needs of others." What systems need to be in place in your own family and work life so that this might be accomplished?

7. What challenges do you face as a woman who is called both to lead and to mother? What are some specific joys you have experienced in each of these callings?

Notes

[1] Kristin Van Ogtrop, *Just Let Me Lie Down: Necessary Terms for the Half-Insane Working Mom* (New York: Little, Brown and Company, 2010), 8.

[2] Thomas Oden, *Pastoral Theology: Essentials of Ministry* (San Francisco: Harper & Row, 1983), 186–187.

[3] William R. Miller and Kathleen A. Jackson, *Practical Psychology for Pastors* (New Jersey: Prentice Hall, 1995), 2.

[4] Ibid., 19.

[5] Ibid., 20.

[6] Ibid.

[7] Frederick Buechner, *Wishful Thinking: A Theological ABC* (New York: Harper&Row, 1973).

[8] Pamela Cooper-White, "Becoming a Clergy Mother: A Study of How Motherhood Changes Ministry," *Congregations* 3 (2004): 15.

[9] Ibid.

[10] Kristin M. Foster, "Ministry and Motherhood: A Collision of Callings?" *Theology and Mission* 16 (1989): 99.

[11] Ibid.

[12] Ruth Haley Barton, *Equal to the Task: Men and Women in Partnership* (Downers Grove: Intervarsity Press, 1998), 182.

[13] E. Jeffery Hill, et al., "Exploring the Relationship of Workplace Flexibility, Gender, and Life Stage to Family-to-Work Conflict, and Stress and Burnout," *Community, Work & Family* 11 (2008): 166.

[14] Ibid.

[15] Ibid.

[16] Ibid.

[17] Betsy Morris, "Is your Family Wrecking Your Career?" *Fortune* (1997): 71–72, cited in Ruth Haley Barton, *Equal to the Task: Men and Women in Partnership* (Downers Grove, Illinois: Intervarsity Press, 1998), 175.

[18] Eva H. Chittenden, MD, and Christine S. Ritchie, MD, "Work-Life Balancing: Challenges and Strategies," *Journal of Palliative Medicine* 14 (2011): 873.

[19] Chittenden and Ritchie, "Work-Life Balancing: Challenges and Strategies," 871.

[20] Brené Brown, *Daring Greatly: How the Courage to Be Vulnerable Transforms the Way We Live, Love, Parent and Lead* (New York: Gotham Books, 2012), 243.

[21] Brown, *Daring Greatly*, 219.

[22] Barton, *Equal to the Task*, 175–76.

5

DEFINING REALITY
Raising a Very Special Child

CARLA D. SANDERSON, PhD

> *"Reason itself is a matter of faith. It is an act of faith to assert*
> *that our thoughts have any relation to reality at all."*
> —G. K. Chesterton, *Orthodoxy*

Leaders give definition. They define vision, values, mission, and strategy, and in so doing, they define the future of the institutions or organizations they lead. Before leaders know what the future will be, they must first fully understand the present. The leader's role begins with defining reality—acknowledging and owning the set of circumstances, challenges, and risks inherent in the work that lies ahead. Knowing and embracing the reality of where you are is essential to leading forward.

The same principle can be applied to parenting. From the moment we learn we are parents-to-be, we begin to envision the life we want to give our children. We begin to think about the values we want to instill, the purposes we want our family to live out, and the social environment we want our children exposed to. We dream of the future we hope they will have. And we embark on the highly intuitive and amazingly instinctive task of parenting. By our very nature, we examine our circumstances and ponder the opportunities before us in raising our children. We define the reality of our homes and lives to see what we must do to achieve the environment necessary to reach our set dreams and ideals.

Some parents raise children whose daily well-being and future may be compromised and threatened by unavoidable circumstances such as disease, disability, impairment, poverty, or family dysfunction. For these parents, acknowledging and owning the reality of the circumstances, challenges, and risks inherent in raising their children may not feel as natural and instinctual, and in fact can be quite overwhelming. This chapter is intended to encourage and equip parents who are raising special needs children by bringing the leadership principle "defining reality" to bear on shaping the brightest possible future for them.

A Methodology for Defining Reality

Parenting is one long and steep learning curve that requires decision making all along the way. How do we learn to parent? How will we decide what is best for our children, especially when their circumstances are complex and their opportunities uncertain and limited? What can we learn about parenting from our work as leaders, and vice versa? How can we achieve a healthy balance between our roles as parents and leaders?

Leaders have widely used a number of problem-solving methodologies in providing a framework for complex decision making. Each methodology identifies several steps that take the leader through a system in order to arrive at a needed solution. The steps include action-oriented verbs such as name, define, identify, assess, measure, analyze, plan, implement, improve, enhance, control, and evaluate.

Since 2011, leaders in a wide variety of fields have adopted a methodology that has meaningful application. Originated by Eric Ries, the Lean Startup is a method of continuous innovation and improvement where "validated learning" results in radically improved outcomes.[1] Lean starts where many other methodologies start, with recognition and acceptance of reality. With Lean, the critical first step in the process is to clearly identify and communicate the circumstances, challenges, and risks until everyone involved in the situation recognizes and accepts reality. A key feature of this methodology is to recognize the "true north," the destination that you have in mind—the vision and strategy needed to achieve the desired outcome.[2]

Letting go is a strategy necessary to achieve a healthy and balanced lifestyle for mothers who are leaders. Leaders who become mothers may go through a process of letting go of former work habits and patterns when the reality of caring for a child becomes top priority. Parents who become leaders may go through a process of letting go of peripheral things (such as a spotless home or warm cookies awaiting children after school) when assuming the responsibility of leadership.

Parents raising special needs children must further let go of their dreams, visions, and ideals for parenting when the circumstances of a child's life are radically different than the norm. Many of us dreamed of having children since we ourselves were children; we enacted being perfect made-up parents to our perfect made-up children. But an important first step in becoming effective parents is to accept the real circumstances of our lives and the real circumstances of the life of each child. Some children do not fit the norm; some children are very special children with very special needs.

The Very Special

At-risk. Atypical. Unique. Extraordinary. Special. Special needs. The language we use to describe the children and adults we parent is critical. While "special needs" is the common phrase used by practitioners and the general public when referring to children and adults living with a disability, I have found "the very special" to resonate well with many parents. However we refer to these individuals, there is a staggering number of very special people being served today—early detection and advances in special education strategies have resulted in increased diagnoses and treatment plans. For all of them, a strong family support structure is essential.

The Very Special: One in fifty children today has an autism spectrum disorder (ASD) and 41 percent of those have an intellectual disability as well (the encouraging news is that 37.5 percent of individuals who receive an ASD diagnosis will go on to lose that diagnosis).[3] The incidence of ASD remains staggering.

Seven percent of children ages three to seventeen have a diagnosis of attention deficit hyperactivity disorder (ADHD). Broken down, that statistic is 11 percent of boys and 4 percent of girls. An overlapping statistic suggests that 8 percent of children in that age group have a learning disability.[4] These disabilities include a range of disorders of sensing, interpreting, and responding to information, such as an auditory processing disorder, and when psychological testing identifies these as "severe," they are referred to as intellectual disabilities.

The data are inconclusive and inconsistent regarding the family dynamics in which these children are being raised. Some studies suggest that the frequency of divorce in families raising children with ASD and ADHD is twice that of families in the general population. In a study by Hartley et al., the divorce rate among families of children with ASD was 10 percent higher than families who had no children with ASD (23.5 percent versus 13.8 percent), and remained higher into early adulthood.[5] Predictors for divorce in families with a child with ASD included younger maternal age and the child being born as a younger sibling in a family. The divorce rate in the comparison group decreased after about eight years of age. In contrast, a large study by Freedman and Kalb indicates that there is no evidence to suggest that children with ASD are more likely to be raised by parents who are divorced.[6]

The presence or absence of support structures in which children and adults with disability live is also a reality to address. For families of faith and for those seeking faith, God designed the church to provide the ultimate supportive environment. The church is the body of Christ and each member—made in the image of God—is indispensable. It is God who arranged those members. The very parts of the body that may seem weaker are in fact indispensable, and the parts that may seem less honorable are to receive the greatest honor. Scripture says that every child and adult, even if living with any kind of disability, impairment, or dysfunction, is indispensable.[7]

There is a widespread perception that a large number of families with special needs children and adults are un-churched. Vanderbilt special education professor Dr. Erik Carter's research shows a growing and encouraging trend toward churches offering disability awareness programs and support groups for families with special needs children. Acceptance of church members with disabilities has never been higher, yet Carter's research shows that two-thirds of special needs youth are not involved in what he calls an "inclusive youth ministry."[8]

Thus, we recognize that a growing number of children and adults experience life as difficult, challenging, and risky. We recognize the likelihood that an above average number of them are raised by parents who are divorced and that the church itself is not the supportive environment that it is commanded to be. These realities help shape the macro perspective from which we accept the circumstances and challenges facing this segment of our nation's children and adults, and from which we proceed to innovate, improve, and control the outcomes we desire for their lives.

Our Story

Twenty-five years ago, a homeless man sitting on a sidewalk in Philadelphia fixed his gaze upon mine as I passed by. In that instance, I accepted the reality that my then-four-year-old son was at risk for the same circumstances that I saw before me. As a nurse, I was not unfamiliar with homelessness and the life of social isolation and poverty that frequently go with it. Establishing eye contact with this man did not make me uncomfortable—quite the opposite. I was not confused about how to help him. What I experienced was immediate connection with this man I had never seen before, connection that came through a very familiar blank stare of one who also had special needs. I felt as though I was looking into the face of my own son. What followed was the overwhelming realization that perhaps I knew a bit about the childhood circumstances that led this man to the realities of his adult life.

At home I was looking into a blank little face every day and was coming to see the risks that my son, by age four, faced through his inability to learn, adjust, and relate. The man who looked back at me was at one time some mother's four-year-old son, someone's next-door neighbor, someone's preschool student, perhaps someone's Sunday school student. And thinking about my older son back at home, I knew that perhaps this man was also once a special somebody's brother.

Three times my husband and I were able to say, "It's a boy!" Three times! Our oldest two sons were six and five when I transitioned to a deanship position at the university where I serve. By the time I moved to an executive level administrative position our sons were thirteen, twelve, and five. Leadership became a way of life for me.

The decision to accept the leadership position had been a family decision. After my husband and I worked through the changes that we would have to make if I assumed the role, we took our oldest son to dinner to discuss the decision with him. We defined the reality of the administrative life for him— evenings when I would return to the college after dinner for events, weekends when I would pursue work-related projects, travel that would take me away from home at times. The decision to move forward was a shared family decision between my husband, our oldest son, and me, and was based on assessing the situation together, recognizing the lifestyle changes that were ahead, and accepting the sacrifice of family time that the opportunity would require.

From there, we began to weave our home life together with the amazing opportunities university life affords, all for the good of our family and to the maximum extent possible. Our children's exposure to the arts has meant involvement in college theatre and music department concerts at the university where I lead. Our spectator sport has been college basketball. Our international travel has been through mission trips and establishing faculty/student exchange programs. Etiquette lessons have taken place around scholarship banquet tables, and history lessons at the annual history lectureship. We have sacrificed precious family time to be in community with the university and have received many benefits from university life for the good of our family.

The reality of being in a leadership role during the critical parenting years must be confronted head on. The realities of home come first. A sense of feeling prepared, productive, and in touch at home helped give focus to the reality of many conflicting demands on my time as an administrator. We navigated the long list of childrearing activities related to church commitments, athletics, music lessons, scouting, and time together as a family and with friends. A reality for my husband and me was the value we placed on friendships for our sons. Because friendships did not come easily for our son with special needs, we fostered friendships as a childrearing strategy. For example, in order to be prepared at all times, we consistently kept the ingredients for a "company meal" on hand—Santa Fe soup and chocolate oatmeal cookies—a meal that could feed an army of friends on very short notice. I never once remember saying no to the boys' request to bring a friend home for dinner, or even a crew over to spend the night.

Most of all we valued our relationship with each son, the "being in touch" reality. I loved my work and was easily drawn to new opportunities and new commitments. Yet my goal for raising godly sons who were well adjusted and at peace with themselves was always at the forefront of my thinking.

Leaders know not to ignore risk. Sometimes I had to forego work opportunities in order to be in-touch with the situations my sons were experiencing. There was a time, during his adolescence years, when our son with special needs came face-to-face with the reality of suicide—a child at church camp went into the woods and took his own life. I was scheduled to go on an international trip for a very good cause, but after seeing the real sense of confusion and despair on his face, I cancelled the trip. We were not perfect parents, but having the goal to be prepared, to be productive, and to be in-touch helped us pay attention to the realities we faced.

It was seeing risk factors for developmental abnormalities that first made me recognize that something was different with our second son. Over the changing table when he was ten days old, I articulated aloud what I had been sensing for a few days: "This baby is not establishing eye contact in an age-appropriate way." And it went on from there, "This baby's infantile reflexes are persisting beyond what is normal," "this baby's head control is weak," "this baby should be rolling over . . . sitting up . . . crawling . . . walking . . . talking," "this child has no math skills," "this child cannot read." The diagnosis of pervasive developmental delays (PDD) was made at age two, and a mild to moderate intellectual disability was confirmed by psychological testing during his school years.

It was clear to us from the beginning that we were facing the reality of our son's disability earlier and more easily than other parents who were facing similar circumstances. In an article entitled "Building New Dreams," researchers suggest that parental adaptation is key to the necessary emotional attachment, growth, and development of children with special needs.[9] Instead of acceptance and resolution, these researchers use the term adaptation when referring to the essential process parents go through. Adaptation is defined as "an ongoing process whereby parents are able to sensitively read and respond to their child's signals in a manner conducive to healthy development."[10] On the basis of our review of the research, we contended that parental perceptions, thoughts, and emotional reactions to their child's condition are effective avenues for promoting adaptation.

As parents of a very special child, we reacted quickly and embraced the risks of learning deficits and the isolation that comes with being behind. We wanted to be prepared, and we wanted to prepare our son. Speech therapy started very early, followed by occupational therapy. "Inclusion" or in-classroom learning as opposed to separate special education started in first grade. Vision therapy came later during his elementary years. When concerned about unusual childhood behavior, my husband and I sought advice from a counselor.

Our main focus was on reading. We wanted to be productive in our goal for our son to learn to read. We did a homeschool reading program, an assistive technology reading program, and reading tutoring programs one right after the other—before school, during school, after school—with college students, with college professors, and with special education specialists. Our son had significant visual processing difficulties. We participated weekly in an intensive vision therapy, with lots and lots of homework, requiring travel to a city seventy-five miles away. Our goal was for our son to be productive in developing the skills necessary to read.

All along the way, we implemented our own parenting strategies to develop the interpersonal skills necessary for our son to be in touch with the people all around him. We went to great lengths to expose our son to normal childhood activities, even as we knew we had to provide extra support for him to be successful with those activities. "Play dates" are quite common today. Twenty years ago, children played outside with others in neighborhoods and parks. Nothing had to be arranged, except in special circumstances like ours. Because of the delayed developmental timeline of our son's growing-up years, he was at risk for being left out. For instance, toddlers are known to participate in parallel play. They like to be with children but they really don't interact with them in play until they are preschool age. By the time our son started school, his peers were interacting together, but it was much more comfortable for our son to watch from afar, preferring to play by himself. In order to challenge him to develop interpersonal skills, we arranged play dates, often with children who were younger or who had their own set of challenges.

Our son was on ball teams, went away to church, Young Life, and Scout camps, participated in water sports and boating, and did most everything his older and younger brothers were doing. But it was not without careful assessment of every situation and intense strategic planning to give him the support he needed to be successful. For instance, in order to participate in camp experiences, my husband went along as a camp counselor. In order to be on the team, my husband signed on as a coach. In order to experience scouting, my husband became the scoutmaster. In order to be included, we hosted the after-church sleepover and the weekly Young Life club nights. Our goal was a socially well-adjusted son who would overcome the risk of isolation and despair, and instead come to learn the love of God and of his people, and to give love in return.

After high school, our son attended a very fine school for individuals with disabilities. A good number of the student body had survived storms such as automobile accidents and sports-related head injuries only to face a life filled with risks of a different kind. I marveled at the decision many parents made to send their children away to learn to live with the physical impairments they faced. It would have been "safer" for all of us to keep our children at home, away from the responsibility of navigating a big city without help and away from the homesickness and frustrations they faced learning independence. Yet we embraced and managed the risk because we thought it was the right thing to do for our children; and despite significant hardships at school, it was. I don't like to think about what my son's life would look like today if we had done otherwise.

Children with very special needs grow up to be adults. Many of them grow out of their limitations while some have afflictions that worsen as they age. In our case, our son continues to mature in his late twenties. Our non-reader with a visual processing impairment has a driver's license—oh the risk assessment, preparation, and intervention that were put in place in making *that* decision! His vocabulary continues to grow—he recently surprised us by using the word audacity! He understands the importance of his job at a riding stable and appreciates the value of a dollar.

Above all, thanks be to our faithful God, our son is in touch. He knows the value of friendship, he has good friends, and he is a good friend. He knows the beauty of the woods and the rivers, and the good it does to visit the sick and to attend funerals. He knows better than anyone just when I need a hug. He knows how to pray and ask God to bless those he loves. And he knows God loves him. He is not anxious about anything, but in everything our son has joy.

Realities to Live By: Parenting Very Special Children and Adults

Reality One
The Facts Are Brutal

Jim Collins, in his book *Good to Great*, describes three tiers in the process of achieving successful outcomes—"disciplined people, disciplined thought, disciplined action."[11] We must develop the "disciplined thought" required for special needs parenting in order to achieve the outcomes we desire for our children. Collins says we must first "confront the brutal facts."[12]

I once had to confront the fact that I could not give the time and attention parenting and leadership required while still being involved with other aspects of life I had previously enjoyed such as watching television, being in book clubs, and taking shopping trips with other women. My husband and I have maintained our family holiday traditions, monthly "Supper Club" night with friends, and biannual visits with my college roommates. We also exposed our sons to our hobby of spending time on the water early on in their lives. While it was essential to face the fact that a lifestyle of parenting and leadership meant sacrifices, it was equally essential to plan for the activities that mattered most.

In learning to parent my very special son, I had to start by confronting facts about myself. What were the true emotions that led to the flood of tears? Was it more than a sense of loss? Was it embarrassment? Frustration over lack of control? Fear of rejection?

Special education services require regular and frequent Individualized Education Program (IEP) meetings in the child's school where the teachers and parents review progress. Every IEP meeting, from when my son was age four and we started interventional therapy within the school system to the last ones when he was in high school, provoked the same response. The lack-of-progress report brought a knot in my stomach and a chill around my heart. I would listen, sputter out my questions, and try to rush the document signing that signaled the end of the meeting. I would walk-run the long school hallways, eyes brimming with tears, a smile pasted on my face, greeting children and teachers along my exit route. Taking deep breaths, I would hurry to my car and drive away to some isolated place where I could pull over and weep my heart out.

The brutal facts of parenting very special people will break your heart, but only for a moment. Yes, we all must face the fact that our children are not the made-up perfect children we dreamed they would be. We have to confront the dream we had and let it go. With time, the idea of the made-up perfect child becomes more and more remote. Time heals and our hearts mend. We become more prepared, more determined to accept the reality and make good of it.

One afternoon our son announced that a neighbor had called him "dumb." My spirit sank. I knew this day was coming. But I rebounded quicker than I had in similar situations before. I said, "You know, you do learn differently from him. Your brother has a foot that curves in, so he runs differently than everyone else. Your friend at school has to take shots because she is missing some important chemicals in her body. I knew a child once whose ears didn't work so he couldn't hear, and another one who was born without one of her hands." That afternoon I confronted the brutal fact that my son had been and would continue to be made fun of. I decided to turn it around to make something good of it.

Collins' work has shown that when we deal with the facts, the decisions we make are more grounded in reality and more likely to provide a frame of reference. For Collins it is establishing a culture of disciplined thought.[13] The frame of reference for parenting our son was this: to nurture the development of a godly man who exceeds his predicted potential and becomes all God designed him to be. I have found Collins to be right—when you "start with an honest and diligent effort to determine the truth of the situation, then the right decisions often become self-evident. You cannot make a series of good decisions without first confronting the brutal facts."[14]

In that same book, Collins suggest that we "build 'red-flag' mechanisms" as an early warning system that forces us to adjust quickly when we see realities that cannot be ignored.[15] In raising our son we experienced almost daily disappointments of one kind or another. There is temptation to put up a wall of self-protection, to develop thick skin, or to simply brush the emotion aside. I fought that temptation and developed a system of limits. I learned to live with daily setbacks but I learned to see certain things as huge red flags. I previously mentioned the red flag look on my son's face as he faced suicide for the first time. From adolescence on, a Friday night with nothing to do was a red flag night. A flurry of activity involving something good happening for both brothers was a red flag time. I remember one New Year's Eve when several families had assembled for dinner and football. Slowly, one by one, all the other teenagers were leaving the family party to head to other activities, leaving our son sad and my heart broken—the pain of his red flag expression has never gone completely away.

If I could see red flag circumstances developing, I intervened. I made many a Friday night happen for our son by inviting friends over or planning pizza and a movie. I avoided invitations where things might not work out well for us. We didn't retreat or capitulate; we regrouped and persisted, determined to prevail.

Jim Collins has built his understanding of what it takes to be successful in leadership on his research of what happens when leaders experience serious adversity. "People fall generally into three categories: Those who are permanently dispirited, those who got their life back to normal, and those who use the experience as a defining event that made them stronger." He calls this the "hardiness factor."[16] Nothing has shaped a spirit of hardiness in me more than parenting a special needs child.

When our son was in first grade, I was sitting in a chapel program one morning, feeling quite dispirited after a particularly difficult parent-teacher conference, when I heard a quote credited to Kenneth Caraway that worked to make me stronger: "There is no box made by God nor man but that the sides can be flattened out and the top blown off to make a dance floor on which to celebrate life."

I recognized each side of my box, and the top, by giving them all names: the sides—impatience, frustration, guilt, and pain; the top—fear. This simple "acknowledging and owning" activity propelled me to a new place. A celebration of my son's life became my focus. These five emotions would be with me, but from that point on I put them in their place . . . under my feet. My son's future took on a whole new appearance from that day forward.

Reality Two
There Are No Right or Wrong Answers, and No Assembly Instructions

Special needs parenting requires thousands of little and big decisions. We long for advice, examples, success stories, object lessons, and carefully mapped out plans of action, and there simply are none. Each child and each situation is unique. The variables to consider are many: the parents' unity of thought, the presence or absence of support structures, such as grandparents and other family and friends, travel distance to services, the impact of decisions on other children in the home, when to stop a therapy that is not working, when to medicate, and on, and on. Specific to our situation, do we move to a metropolitan area where there are more resources? Do we medicate for ADHD symptoms when the underlying problem is pervasive developmental delays? Knowing special education services are only available in public schools, do we send our other sons to private school as most families in our neighborhood and church are doing, or choose public school for all three? Do we retreat and stay at home where our son is happiest, or do we embrace extracurricular opportunities and social settings that will stretch us all?

Leaders know that effectiveness in decision making is both instinctive and learned. I have profited much from the book entitled *Decisive*. Its authors, brothers Chip and Dan Heath, offer new and fresh perspectives on decision making. Their WRAP method can guide our process of choosing when the options facing us are not clear. Think WRAP: "When faced with a choice, Widen your options. When you analyze your options, Reality-test your assumptions. Before making a choice, Attain distance before decision. Live with the decision, but Prepare to be wrong."[17]

Heath and Heath warn against confirmation bias, which suggests that when we want something to be true, we gather information that supports our desire and confirms our assumptions.[18] I contend that this is especially true for special needs parents. By our nature as mothers and fathers, our wants for our children are embedded into our very being. It takes a deliberate act of will to confront the biases of our own beliefs about what is best for our child. But in reality, we may need to widen our options, test our mother-nature assumptions, give distance to our gut-level thinking, and be prepared to see our situations in a more objective light.

When faced with the decision about whether or not to give our son medication to address his ADHD symptoms, our immediate reaction was no. Leaning solely on my understanding and assumptions about early childhood neurological development, for two years I declined the medical advice recommending ADHD medication. Seeing the dysfunction in our family and the intense restlessness brought on by constant hyperactivity in our son, I continually questioned my own decision. What if I was wrong? Heath and Heath suggest this question, "What if our least favorite option were actually the best one? What data might convince us of that?"[19] I began to widen my options by reading articles, talking to other parents, listening to special education teachers, and seeking the counsel of a wise prayer partner. I finally relented to a twelve-week trial of Ritalin therapy.

My assumptions were reality-tested when we were visiting a museum just before our son's sixth birthday. For forty minutes, during the medication's therapeutic window of optimum effectiveness, our son stood still before an incubator and learned how baby chicks hatch. Before the medication was started, we were accustomed to actually holding his face in place to get his attention when trying to explain or show him something. If he was going to have the focus and attention needed to learn, medication was going to be necessary. I was prepared to be wrong and I was—our son was on Ritalin therapy until age fourteen, and then again during his post-secondary program of study.

From experience raising our child, I strongly endorse Heath and Heath's decision-making approach, which they refer to as "zoom out, zoom in," saying,

"Zooming out and zooming in gives us a more realistic perspective on our choices. We downplay the overly optimistic pictures we tend to paint inside our minds and instead redirect our attention to the outside world, viewing it in wide-angle and then in close-up."[20]

As parents, we tend to overly trust the internal impressions we have painted in our minds. Those internal, close-up impressions are valid and worthy, but may be insufficient. There are other sources of close-up information. Instead of just mental impressions, we can seek to form other legitimate impressions. Heath and Heath say go "see for yourself." If we are trying to choose the right learning environment, we can go see the options for ourselves. If we are determining the impact of a particular therapy, we can go observe. Close ups create the texture and color you need to see the picture more clearly, say the Heaths.[21]

Over an eighteen-month period, we made three trips to the post-secondary school our son attended as a young adult. Before choosing that particular setting, we sat in on classes and we visited the various places at the residential complex where he would be living. We walked the route from the school to the apartment and back. We ate in the diner where he would eat and visited the church most accessible to him. Our visits provided rich texture to the decision to enroll him later on.

Taking an external, wide-angle view on a parenting decision might mean inviting the impression of someone with more experience than we have, such as a grandparent, a trusted friend, or an expert. The external view allows us to learn from the experience of others, informing us about how things generally unfold in situations similar to ours. The Internet offers an amazing wealth of wide-angle information on raising special needs children, from blog sites to scientific research articles. Zooming out broadens our thinking and develops our reasoning when we are faced with the need to make decisions and find answers.

No child ever came with the assembly instructions provided. Parenting requires a lot of what the Heaths call "ooching." Ooching is a diagnostic, a way to reality-test your assumptions. Ooch before you leap, they say.[22] It is the same prototyping that we know as putting a toe in the water before we jump in.

Special needs parenting is a lesson in experimentation where we explore options through small tests of change. The goal is to discover reality rather than predicting it. "To ooch is to ask, Why predict something we can test? Why guess when we can know?"[23] We were ooching as parents when we tried a short play date before allowing our son to stay overnight at a friend's, when we tested impulsivity with money by placing a five-dollar bill in our son's pocket instead of twenty dollars, when we experimented with home-based vision therapy before we committed to 150 miles of travel two days a week for therapy with a specialist, and when we rode with him on every route he would take as a driver, sometimes several times over, before he drove those routes alone.

In learning to find the best options and directions for our very special child, the ultimate lesson we learned was to keep our eye on the goal. Effective strategy is key for leaders, and it always starts with naming the goal, followed by executing the plan. In the book *Execution*, Bossidy and Charan discuss meshing strategy with reality, aligning people with goals, and achieving the results promised.[24] Having a clear understanding of the goal is the place to begin.

As parents, our "zoom in, zoom out" approach leads to strategy that we trust to be the very best we can offer our children. When our strategy isn't working or when new circumstances, challenges, or risks come our way, we ask the "critical issues" questions all over again. We try to see things as they are, not the way we hope them to be. We confront the fact that we will never be totally objective when it comes to the way we see our son—the reality is, at times, too painful. Yet we combine our huge vision and great ambition for our son with a mindset of innovation applied to our parenting.[25] We strive to be disciplined people, pursuing disciplined thought, and taking disciplined action.[26]

Reality Three
Answers to the "Why" Questions Will Come

Some of us are more bent on asking "why" than others. I sometimes admire those people who accept life's circumstances and move on, but I am not one of them. As a leader, I approach every question searching for context, causes, and conditions. I do the same thing in my parenting, coming alongside my children in an attempt to help them understand "cause and effect" and "if this, then that" in their thinking and decision making. The big questions of life intrigue me; in fact, if I had to name the single most significant, common thread running between my role as a mother and as a leader, I would say through both roles I have found the joy of probing life's most important questions. I would also name the question, "Why was my son born with an intellectual disability?" to be the most helpful question I have pursued as his mother.

While in high school, our son took on the responsibility of being the water boy on the boys' football and basketball teams. One February night in a basketball gym, his younger brother answered the "why" question for our special needs family.

The score was Hardin County High School (HCHS) 60, Jackson-Madison County High School (JMCHS) 79 with a minute thirty to go in the final game of the men's varsity basketball season. There's a new player on one of the benches, though not a new face to the team.

For the entire season, the JCMHS players had pestered their coach about letting the team water boy dress out. "But he's maybe 5'6" and maybe 105 pounds; he could get hurt," the coach probably thought, listening to the deep-voiced pleas of his anxious players as they towered over his own tall frame. Game after game they pressed for their teammate to play.

The word finally came: our son would dress in the #5 green and gold uniform for the last away game in Savannah. He badly wanted his hair braided in cornrows to match the team's, but no one could seem to make his thin, fine blond hair cooperate.

JCMHS maintained a healthy lead throughout a fast and furious game of basketball. With less than two minutes left in the game, the coach motioned for our son to move from the end of the bench next to him. The players and fans alike erupted in long chants calling his name. Then he was at the scorer's table. The ecstatic and anxious team was on its feet cheering for a break in the action when the referees could introduce a new player into the game.

The clock kept ticking. Finally the coach grew anxious himself and called a time out, a minute thirty to go.

The senior water boy was in. The bench coach took over coaching the game, shouting out the set-up they had practiced a thousand times over. Our son darted around his guards from one wing to the other and back again. His teammates were passing carefully, strategically, all eight eyes on their target. The ball went out of bounds. The referee motioned that the ball still belonged to JCMHS. The entire gym of spectators, who now seemed to have caught on to what was happening, breathed a sigh of relief!

There were 5.5 seconds left on the clock. The point guard headed in toward the goal. Our son made another skipping dart around his opponent and headed for the right wing inside the three-point circle. The pass was made. He connected. He turned, dribbled outside the paint, turned back in . . . and eyed the goal!

A lifetime of growing-up challenges flashed in an instant. Countless "you can do its" rang out across the years. Loud noises once caused our son great panic. I could see his little hands folding his little ear lobes into a tight clutch at the sound of fireworks, or circus clown horns . . . or gymnasium buzzers.

But the gymnasium buzzer that night blared out just milliseconds after those once little hands, now raised high in the air, released and took the shot of his lifetime.

The basketball? It went in for three points as a Savannah gym exploded. Why? So a gymnasium full of people could experience the joy that goes beyond race and runs deeper than socioeconomic barriers as a team of rough-and-tumble ball players worked good in the life of a less fortunate white kid they had come to care about.

Special needs children belong to special needs families. Our youngest son turned immediately to us as the ball went in and said, "*THAT* was God, doing some of his finest work ever."

Ultimately for our family, the "why" questions of life are answered in the supernatural, and best explained in the context of a coherent Christian world and life view where we see life as God's plan and purpose for this world. A Christian world and life view is "an energizing motivation for godly and faithful thinking and living in the here-and-now. It also gives us confidence and hope for the future. In the midst of life's challenges and struggles, a Christian worldview helps to stabilize life, serving as an anchor to link us to God's faithfulness and steadfastness."[27]

My favorite definition of a leadership goes like this: a leader is a dealer of hope. That is a pretty good definition of godly parenting, too. Applied to the question of children and adults with special needs, the ultimate answer to the "why" questions is an answer that gives great hope. God is the Creator of all things—he made heaven and earth and all that is therein. We are told in Scripture "God created us in His image and likeness" and each one of us for a purpose.[28] We see this when Jesus' disciples asked why a man they were passing by was born blind. Jesus answered, "That the works of God might be displayed in him."[29] Oh, the times we have seen the work of God displayed in the life of our special needs son, like experiencing a basketball team working good.

The imperfections of this world are universal. Some children are born with physical and intellectual limitations—a child's pancreas doesn't function properly and she has juvenile diabetes, another's foot is malformed, another's skin has no pigment, another's immune system cannot break down the oil in peanuts, another's brain doesn't effectively process visual or auditory stimuli. The reality is all of us come short of the glory of God.[30] Our special needs children, and you and me.

There is good news—we are all indispensable and God loves us all. We know he cares and works in the details of our lives according to his good purposes. We can take hope in one day being made perfect, when this life is over and we can spend eternity in a perfect relationship with God our Father. Therein lies the ultimate reality for every "why" question that will ever come our way.

My very special son has taught me more about the faithfulness of God in my home and work than I ever would have learned without him. The more I zoomed in on the questions I had about how to raise my sons, the more I found God in the answers. When I zoom out now to take a look at the men my sons have become, it is evident to me that God's purposes prevail even when I cannot see what he is doing. I may not be able to answer the question about what will happen to my very special son when I am no longer able to parent him, but because of the lessons I have learned from watching God work in his life thus far, I am content in knowing that God is in control and nothing can ever separate my son from the love of God that is within him. That is a reality I cherish like none other.

Discussion Questions

1. Discuss the unexpected and unique realities you faced both as a new leader and as a new parent. Give one positive outcome of having defined the reality and a subsequent decision to address it, and one negative outcome of having ignored the reality and the consequences that resulted.

2. Name a time as a parent when it became necessary for you to let go of a long-held dream, vision, or fondness in order for a true recognition of reality to be established and a new vision to begin to develop. Discuss how letting go allowed you to define and accept a reality.

3. Identify a choice facing you as a parent and leader. Apply Heath and Heath's WRAP methodology as a guide to making the choice. Give particular attention to the first step and widen the number of options you can choose from. Stretch your thinking. Identify at least five options. Discuss how "widening your options" can impact decision making.

4. Name a goal that you wish to achieve as a leader or a parent. Using Bossidy and Charan's critical issues assessment, map out your plan for assessing the issues that are inherent in reaching your goal.

5. A part of defining and accepting reality is finding resolve with the "why" questions that come up in life and work. Give an example of how resolving the "why" question of a particular situation allowed you to move forward.

Notes

[1] Eric Ries, *The Lean Startup: How Today's Entrepreneurs Use Continuous Innovation to Create Radically Successful Businesses* (New York: Crown Business, 2011), 18, 38.

[2] Ibid., 22.

[3] "Autism Spectrum Disorders (ASDs): Data & Statistics," Center for Disease Control and Prevention, accessed September 2013, http://www.cdc.gov/ncbddd/autism/data.html.

[4] Barbara Bloom and Robin A. Cohen, "Summary Health Statistics for U.S. Children: National Health Interview Survey, 2006," Center for Disease Control and Prevention, accessed September 2013, http://www.cdc.gov/nchs/data/series/sr_10/sr10_234.pdf.

[5] Sigan L. Hartley, et al., "The Relative Risk and Timing of Divorce in Families of Children with an Autism Spectrum Disorder," *Journal of Family Psychology* 24.4 (Aug 2010): 449–57, accessed September 2013, doi: 10.1037/a0019847.

[6] Brian H. Freedman, et al., "Relationship Status among Parents of Children with Autism Spectrum Disorders: A Population-Based Study," *Journal of Autism and Developmental Disorder* 42.2 (2012): 539–48, accessed September 2013, doi: 10.1007/s10803-011-1269-y.

[7] I Corinthians 12:4–26 NIV.

[8] Erik Carter, "What Matters Most," presented at The Summer Institute on Theology and Disability, 2012.

[9] Douglas Barnett, Melissa Clements, Melissa Kaplan-Estrin, Janice Fialka, "Building New Dreams: Supporting Parents' Adaptation to Their Child With Special Needs," *Infants and Young Children* 16.3 (2003): 184-200.

[10] Ibid.

[11] Jim Collins, *Good to Great: Why Some Companies Make the Leap . . . And Others Don't* (New York: HarperBusiness, 2001), 12.

[12] Ibid., 88.

[13] Ibid., 88.

[14] Ibid., 82.

[15] Ibid., 78.

[16] Ibid., 82.

[17] Chip Heath and Dan Heath, *Decisive: How to Make Better Choices in Life and Work* (New York: Crown Business, 2013), 23.

[18] Ibid., 11.

[19] Ibid., 100.

[20] Ibid., 133.

[21] Ibid., 129.

[22] Ibid., 138.

[23] Ibid., 151.

[24] Larry Bossidy and Ram Charan, *Execution—The Discipline of Getting Things Done* (New York: Crown Business, 2002), 20–21.

[25] Reis, *The Lean Startup*, 20.

[26] Collins, *Good to Great*, 126.

[27] David S. Dockery, *Renewing Minds* (Nashville: B&H Publishing Group, 2008), 38–44.

[28] Genesis 1:27 NIV.

[29] John 9:1–3 NIV.

[30] Romans 3:23 NIV.

6

MY STRAND OF PEARLS

IRENE NELLER, MA

"Each pearl on your strand represents someone who has been a Pearl to you in some way along your journey."

—Christina DiMari, *Cultivating Pearls*[1]

Raising my two sons and leading a team of professionals proved to have more in common than I ever imagined. I'm not saying that my staff acted like children or that I treated my children like my staff; rather, what I discovered in motherhood can be applied in the office and vice versa. When I found myself pregnant with my first child, I was poised to take my job to a more serious level and to pursue a master's degree. But I believed mothering and leading in the workplace were mutually exclusive, and thus my career aspirations would never play out. One role would force me to compromise the other. I found myself at a serious crossroad.

I had been raised with the impression that mothers who worked professionally could not take on more responsibility in the workplace because the family would suffer. Yet I wanted to weigh my options. With the support of a very encouraging husband who knew that this little Latina girl from east San Jose wanted to overcome stereotypes, labels, and confidence deficits, I began graduate studies. Along the way, women of leadership came into my life at just the right time to encourage me—women I now refer to as *my pearls*.

What I discovered in my personal journey, as I reflect upon it now two decades later, is that these two worlds blend in so many ways. What's more, living fully in both—as a mother and a leader—is an extremely rewarding experience unmatched by anything else. The two roles share so much in common. Each role truly enhances and benefits the relationships we build with our families, our children, and our work teams.

I was fortunate to have women interested in my personal development surround me during the formative years of my life. They were the ones with wisdom and insight who told me repeatedly that I was wired for leadership. I didn't want to accept this defining label. I was thirteen and I wanted nothing to do with being a leader. That role was clearly for my sister, the firstborn, and she mastered it so well that there wasn't much left for me to do to impress my parents, or so I thought.

It's not typically expected of the youngest child either, according to psychological profiles of children's birth orders. Psychiatrist Alfred Adler (1870–1937), proposed the first theory on the effect of birth order on personality. And since Adler, human behavior experts have studied the birth order as a factor in shaping an individual's personality traits as an adult. The oldest tends to be the leader, the middle child the mediator, and the youngest, the entertainer, overcompensating to gain attention.[2] As the youngest one in my family, I didn't believe I could be a leader. I liked hiding behind others and truly enjoyed being the loyal and trusted follower more than the aspiring, motivational leader. I wasn't the team captain, but I definitely would cheer everyone to the finish line. So when it came time to discover what to do with my life after high school, I ventured off to college, following of course in my sister's footsteps, to discover this "leadership trait" and put my so-called inherent leadership abilities on some career path. But I wasn't that girl who wanted to be the president of clubs or associated student organizations like my sister—the firstborn in my family. I lacked confidence. What I did have was a surplus of effort and a will to succeed coupled with a strong work ethic that I credit to my father. Confidence would come much later in life after a series of discoveries, failures, successes, and experiences as a mother who just happened to find herself in leadership.

My mother dreamed of my becoming a teacher, but I chose instead to pursue the general field of communications. I didn't like having all eyes on me, so teaching was out of the question. I liked discovering and telling a story and sharing it in such a way that persuaded people to take action. I learned the power of the written word and the art of the sales pitch. After several jobs in retail, I landed my first professional job as an international admissions counselor for a private Christian university—what a profound training ground that job became! I met people from all walks of life, from all continents, eager to pursue a college dream. Each time, as I walked them through the complicated application and immigration process for enrollment, I was able to pull from some experience in my life and from my rich and diverse heritage to encourage these students to move forward. I felt empowered in this role and I liked it.

That was the beginning of using my influence. Someone defined leadership as having influence over another person. I poured myself into becoming a college admissions counselor and I was able to do so freely without distractions. I was young, energetic, driven, ambitious, and married to a husband busy in graduate studies, so I had lots of time to focus on my job. And I did. I worked long hours and traveled to various countries to recruit students. Eventually, I was noticed by my superiors and asked to take on more responsibility. With more responsibility came the demand to exercise the traits expected of leaders. But what exactly were those traits? Does someone pull you aside and train you or do you just learn on the job? I was about to discover that leaders—and mothers—are best trained by firsthand experiences. No one gives you a playbook that diagrams how to best respond to *all* situations.

I accepted my first promotion and decided to venture into being a leader. However, I suddenly found myself pregnant. My surprise pregnancy at the onset of this promotion began the best training needed to bring my life into balance. Otherwise, I was headed down a path of becoming a very self-absorbed and overly zealous professional who would have bulldozed over others who didn't see the world like I did. I quickly learned as a young mother that I would no longer be in full control of anything or anyone. I was exhausted, sleep-deprived, and hanging on by a thread mentally and physically after the birth of my first son. I had to find more meaningful purpose to the demanding schedule I had stepped into as I began my journey, discovering how to use my talents and what I believed was my calling to lead others effectively and with purpose.

Being a working mom has never been easy; I've shed many tears over the internal struggle of feeling I am disappointing my family or my boss or my staff or all of them at the same time. This is when I have to accept I cannot be everywhere at once or perform perfectly at all times for everyone around me. I am grateful for a husband who supported my ambitions with all the demands placed on me. I can't give women the formula to a happy, balanced, and successful career or family, but I can say without reservation that the following three personal discoveries and recommendations are vital to maintaining balance and perspective as a mother and as a leader:

1. Find a job you are passionate about and a work environment that is family friendly and allows you to blend your worlds, because they will blur together.
2. Don't make excuses for being a mother at the workplace and don't make excuses for enjoying your job when you're at home. Not everyone is gifted to serve in these two leading roles, so embrace what you have and let others around you witness you in action.
3. Don't seek to please everyone because you never will! As women, we often live under the guise that we have to be perfect, performing at maximum capacity on all cylinders at all times. Find what makes you happy and then do it with all your heart and soul.

Justice Sonia Sotomayor, the first Latina and third female justice in the Supreme Court of the United States was being interviewed on all the morning television news shows following the release of her book *My Beloved World*. An anchorwoman on the morning show asked her, "Can women have it all?" Justice Sotomayor vehemently answered:

No. It's a ridiculous question. It suggests that at every moment of every day, you can be completely happy and have everything you want. What a ridiculous notion. I don't know of any working mothers or stay at home moms who aren't in perpetual conflict about the choices they're making. If it's working moms and they're on the job, they're thinking of what event they're missing of their child's day. Or, if they're at home with children and going to soccer games, they're thinking in the back of their head about what they have left behind at home, wondering, "How am I going to catch up and get everything done?" What we need to be discussing is how we build relationships not just with spouses and extended family but with others to manage our very complicated lives.[3]

In this often-complicated life I had embraced, I could not forget those relationships. I found myself going to those who had helped me get to where I was in order to seek wisdom, consultation, and a shot of confidence to carry me into whatever I faced next. I chose to surround myself with positive forces and influences. These were women who appeared to manage their full plates well. Not perfectly. But well. The more authentic they were about sharing their flaws and struggles with me, the more confidence I gained that I too could follow in their steps. I learned valuable lessons from these women and knew it was my turn to pay it forward. No one achieves success on his/her own. A trail of supporters and mentors line the way. Ignoring those persons and not serving others likewise is selfish and irresponsible.

Many years later during National Women's History Month (NWHM), I met a woman who would become a strong spiritual influence in my life and confirm what I believed to be the purpose for my life as a mother and a leader in higher education. Our worlds seemed to intersect by divine encounter. As one of the leading women on my campus, I initiated our celebration of NWHM and our team invited a speaker who, we discovered, was also the mother of one of our students. At our "Pearls in Process" event, Christina DiMari shared with us how difficult it had been growing up without a mother—how alone you feel, not sure who you are or what your potential is. She said that after she surrendered this "missing piece" in her life through deep personal and spiritual reflection, she began to experience everything she was missing in a "strand of pearls." She read from one of her books:

Each pearl on your strand represents someone who has been a Pearl to you in some way along your journey. Because she crossed your path you have been encouraged to fly, pursue your dreams, and reach your highest potential. She spoke words that brightened your path, or she walked with you awhile or cheered from afar. Authors motivated you; music moved you; and unexpected strangers inspired you. Think about the people who have added value to your life. These are your Pearls. When you put them on, you will carry the blessing they passed on to you. Focus on taking the irritations out of your life to be molded into a beautiful pearl. It is time now for you to take what you have learned and pass it on to girls coming up the road behind you.[4]

Her story moved me on many levels. Tears rolled down my cheeks as I listened to her experiences and those of girls at my university who confided in her about their painful and often very lonely journeys. I agreed with everything she shared—that even if we are blessed with mothers, we still need other women who are willing to take time to invest in us and believe in us. And we can be those pearls for our families, and for those at work and in our communities. She left us to ponder two questions: Who are your pearls—who has invested in you and how— and whom can you invest in and what can you do?

Who Are My Pearls?

The following day I sat in my office looking at my bookcase filled with biographies and memoirs of iconic women of generations past and present. Women who have modeled grace, poise, wisdom, and leadership—often under much public scrutiny—and who have risen to roles of prominence because of the obstacles, challenges, and clichés they overcame. I also reflected on the pearls in my own life and made a list of them and how they had poured into me. One thing stood out: the simple investment of their time and heart as they believed in me, encouraged me, even prayed over me, and nurtured me by sharing with me their own life stories. They weren't women of significant wealth or prominence and they didn't hold impressive pedigrees or higher education degrees; they were simple women. I was not alone when I became a mother or when I joined the workforce. They journeyed with me. Their selfless acts of friendship, care, and compassion are reflected in who I am today. They are my strand of pearls.

I was convicted to take much more seriously and purposefully my experiences and the influence I have been given over others. This epiphany about mentoring needed to be carried out intentionally toward my two sons. I was reminded that the simplicity of loving and serving those nearest to us is the highest calling. Being a mother shifted my focus to look more inward than outward. It was as if someone put a mirror in front of me and asked, "What do you see behind this face?" That reflective perspective drove me to ask myself, "How am I being perceived? And what kind of influence am I having over my family, my staff, and my circle of influence?" Self-reflection is a scary process; the right advisors and counselors are critical.

Realizing the Need for Pearls: My Background

I was raised in a very traditional Hispanic family where girls didn't leave home until they were married and definitely didn't leave home to go to study. But my parents desired more for my two siblings and me and broke the stereotypical Latino traditions by sending us off to college. I chose a small school close to home but lived in the dorm. College was excellent for me, allowing me to experience independence away from a very controlled environment.

It also introduced to me a series of identity challenges I was not prepared to handle: Who am I? How can I fit in as one of only a handful of Latino students? What is my purpose on this earth? It would have been a perfect time to have a role model, to journey with a female leader whose ethnicity could identify with my culture. I soon discovered there were too few women leaders around me in my formative professional development years.

Years later in my young professional career, I discovered the value of a professional role model—a woman who came to speak in a college course I was taking as a prerequisite for graduate studies. She was an executive in an advertising firm and I could only hope to become like her. I sought her out and we developed a relationship that would last for decades. She became a significant pearl in my strand.

Women in Higher Education

I've served in higher education most of my life, and the number of females in executive leadership positions at colleges and universities are few. College, for the traditional student age seventeen to twenty-three, is the foundational time and the formative years for discovering and homing in on skill sets, personal callings, and professional ambitions. The national trends of women in leadership are still disconcerting in the twenty-first century: according to a *Washington Post* article, women lead 26 percent of universities in the United States and 4 percent of the Fortune 500 companies.[5]

What I have found ironic in higher education is that females outdo males in enrollment numbers across our college campuses in the United States. Yet the majority of support programs, leadership roles, and professorship are acquired by men and are oriented toward men. There is a real female leadership gap that the Council of Christian Colleges and Universities (CCCU) is attempting to address by requesting schools to develop leadership programs aimed at cultivating the next generation of female leaders. In addition, college and university accrediting agencies, such as the Western Association of Schools and Colleges (WASC), are placing higher expectations and demands upon schools to develop programs and leadership opportunities for females, but few schools and colleges have the resources and support to respond to this request.

Female enrollment growth trends at colleges and universities show no signs of slowing down, either. In a 2011 study commissioned by the White House Council on Women and Girls, entitled "Women in America: Indicators of Social and Economic Well-Being," women are projected to account for nearly 60 percent of total undergraduate enrollment by 2019 and have surpassed males in graduate schools since 1984.[6] Women also have higher graduation rates at all academic levels and account for the majority of undergraduate enrollment across all racial/ethnic groups. So who will educate the next generation of female leaders if they are the predominant demographic in colleges and universities?

Amy Gutmann, the president of the University of Pennsylvania, says in an article in the *Washington Post*, "Time for More Women to Lead Our Schools,"

> It will only be with more sponsors, a sharper focus on developing women in the career pipeline, and more public accountability of our results that we can bring the numbers in line with the student populations we lead. If leadership matters—and in today's world it matters more than ever—then there must be a consistent message from the

top that recruiting and promoting talented women isn't just the right thing to do, it's the smart thing to do.[7]

She goes on to say,

Almost anyone in a position of leadership can point to a highly placed individual who took an interest in fostering, and took pains to help develop, the trajectory of her career. They are not mere mentors but "sponsors," or senior people who advocate on others' behalf. Research shows that such powerful individuals are far more effective than mentors who simply offer feedback. Therefore, we as higher education leaders must do more to retain and recruit role models and provide such sponsors for emerging women in our field.[8]

I knew that the best way I could help other women and girls was to pass on the lessons I had learned on my journey. I decided long ago to fully embrace my gender first and not compromise it any way while aspiring to achieve and lead.

Embrace Your Femininity and Your Motherly Traits

My office is purposely decorated with feminine pieces. I want girls coming to visit me to know they are encountering a woman who has embraced her identity as a female and who hasn't compromised it in any way to become a leader. Sometimes we try hard to appear different than we are or mask our true identities, says Jonalyn Fincher in her book *Ruby Slippers: How the Soul of a Woman Brings Her Home*. Perhaps we do so because we are insecure about who we are or unaware of how to use our God-given abilities as women. She goes on to say that how we use and discover our natural femininity will depend on our family of origin, birth order, personality, resources, and our soul's growth; each woman works out her characteristics depending on how she chooses to use them. She asks, "Which characteristics form your natural, God-given womanhood and which are you using?"[9]

I have learned to use the characteristics of my womanhood in working with students, parenting two boys, being in university leadership, and mentoring girls. As an admissions counselor, I learned firsthand that girls, like boys, choose to go to college because of a personal dream they hope to accomplish.

They want to matter in life and matter in someone else's life. I used this experience and insight to educate myself as a mother. Was I taking every opportunity to talk with my sons about their dreams and aspirations? I was having these conversations with students each day, but was I having those same interactions with my sons? Every day I had great moments to interact with my sons as we traveled to school or to one of their sporting events. I began treating those times together as if they were conversations with a student in my office or a staff member having one-on-one time with me to go through their projects and ideas. I found annual reviews with my employees an ideal time to be purposeful in my reflections of their skills and personal development. Being with my sons in the car was like a daily scheduled appointment, and I needed to take advantage of this time.

On the other hand, could I do the same with my employees in each of our scheduled appointments? Or was that time sanctioned to just get through the agenda items? I needed to shift my professional and personal perspectives on how I used these moments and this scheduled time to interact with others with purpose. I shifted my motherly focus on providing for my son's basic needs (running them here and there for sports commitments) to include those psychological needs that would help lead them to self-actualization. As mothers, we need to know when to push the pause button on our busyness and shift with laser-like focus to character development. This same mindset should occur with the teams we lead as well. I had to shift my priority on task orientation with my team to also focus on professional/personal development.

I remember one particular female student who gently tapped me on the shoulder while I was standing in line at the campus coffee café: "You don't know me," she said, "but I've watched you around here and admire how you carry out your job. Do you think we could grab coffee together sometime to talk? I want to be a leader like you someday and would love to know how you do it all." That tap on the shoulder would be repeated many times over, and it increased significantly when I was asked to serve as a vice president.

Female students usually seek me out for this one reason: they want to know how I handle leadership as a woman and how I balance family, career, and life. They are eager for someone to hand them a playbook on how women can balance achievement and ambitious pursuits while maintaining personal and family relationships. I tell them that they don't have to compromise their femininity or man-up their personalities. Too often, women feel the pressure to put their femininity in the backseat as they pursue a fulfilling career. What they need to be told is that the characteristics of a female will serve them exceptionally well in the workplace! Furthermore, if they are fortunate to become mothers along the course of their professional careers, their skill set has just doubled in value.

Understanding how to show and practice empathy, care, compassion, flexibility, and patience are traits mothers will come to learn if they truly want to be effective and influential. These same traits will also serve them very well in the workplace. I mention these specific traits because they don't come naturally or easily for me (according to the StrengthsQuest and Myers Briggs tests), yet they are the ones that have been pointed out to be highly effective and useful in leadership. I knew I needed to be intentional about focusing on these in particular. Had I not stepped into the role of a leader, I wouldn't have had the opportunity to take these self-evaluative tests so seriously. Remember that mirror in front of you? I needed to do some serious personal reflection to work on those areas necessary to be an effective leader.

Once I discovered my strengths, weaknesses, and challenges, it took a lot of work and much purposeful effort—at home and in the office—to address and correct them. I shared this discovery with my sons, then in their teens, and they looked at me like I was sharing with them the day of the week it was! How did they know these were my weaknesses before I did? That was an eye-opening experience. I bared my soul, became very vulnerable, and shared these discoveries with my direct reports and I asked them to also hold me accountable to the practice of showing empathy and compassion, grace and patience. Being vulnerable with my sons and my staff made a profound difference in the way I approached a situation. While I've been naturally inclined to produce an end result without paying much attention or care to the process required to get there, I became more thoughtful than reactive. I still work on this daily. After all, I am a pearl in process, being shaped and molded, my rough edges continually being smoothed out. As mothers and as supervisors we must address our rough edges in order to achieve the outcomes we desire in others. Our children can help us become more intentional too, and they are much more outspoken on progress you're making, whether or not you ask for their feedback!

Being a Plate-Spinner

Most women are naturally wired to multitask and can do it very well. We are the plate-spinners in our families and we certainly can be plate-spinners in the workplace. Maggie Wilderotter of Frontier Communications believes women are better at multitasking than men: "We do it naturally. I see it in our organization. Men seem to be more asynchronous." According to John Bussey, *asynchronous* is "a tech term that means, among other things, starting a new operation only after finishing the last one. That asynchronous linear drive can be good for meeting a specific objective. But it may not leave much room for nuance that might shape that objective—or win over an audience."[10]

I met Moe Girkins, the first female CEO of Zondervan Publishing and one of the top female executives of corporate giants such as AT&T, Motorola, and Dell, when she spoke at a university event. I knew I had met another pearl to add to my strand. In my inquisition of her during our time together, she said I was asking questions about leadership that she, too, had spent much time contemplating as she rose through the ranks in leadership. She states in her book *Mother Leads Best*, "It is simply that mothers have certain advantages because of nature and nurture that men lack. Hormonally, they are predisposed towards compassion and caring."[11] Her book recounts what she discovered after studying and interviewing fifty women in leadership—vice presidents and CEOs of Fortune 500 companies.

Girkins identifies five nurturing traits top women leaders possess that make them more effective—empathy, sensitivity, caring, warmth, and patience—qualities, she says, that were brought out when they became mothers. These leaders also discovered that as mothers, they became selfless and the maternal instincts unleashed through motherhood strengthened their character and broadened their perspective on life. They learned to let go of the need to control, and in turn lead with both mind and heart. So if we are wired to be more nurturing, how do we display that tendency outside of our families and in the workplace?

"The biggest myth that I'd like to set to rest is that women can't have a family and a successful career," says Ilene Gordon, CEO of Corn Products International, Inc. "The skills that make a good business leader—organization, drive, trust, delegation, and compassion—also go a long way to balance the responsibilities of work and family life." Gracia Martore of the Gannett Company says, "in order to lead an organization, you have to be incredibly comfortable in your own skin, . . . to be confident in who you are."[12]

That confidence rarely comes naturally. It is an acquired trait. And a mentor can help a young person attain confidence and believe in herself. Nothing is more powerful than another person speaking words of encouragement, affirmation, and confidence into another. Are we actively and intentionally speaking these words to our children? To our staff and direct reports in the workplace? In the process of mentoring, I've discovered that taking an active role to believe in another significantly bolsters confidence levels in that individual, and positive productivity follows.

Female leaders in corporate settings also recognize the high value of believing in other women coming up the ranks. *Advertising Age* magazine featured over one hundred of the most influential women in advertising in a special September 2012 issue. Among those featured was Joyce King Thomas, CEO of Longreads and creator of MasterCard's famous Priceless advertising campaign. She exhorts women to mentor women:

> I have a suggestion for every woman. Starting today, let's all pick three women to mentor. I'm not just talking to those at the top, but to those in the middle and those scrambling up by their fingernails. There's always someone lower down the rung than you are. Reach out and give them a yank up. Get a woman an internship. (Paid, please.) Give a woman some killer advice. And if you have even a smidgen of power, get a woman promoted. Right now.[13]

Who I Am as a Mother Who Leads

After the first National Women's History Month event I sponsored on my university's campus, I couldn't walk through campus without looking into the eyes of every young woman I passed, and I wondered whether I could be effective with these females just because I was a female. Mentoring others was not something I thought I could do easily. I didn't even have daughters, so how could I relate to these young women? They are so different from boys and I was out of my experienced comfort zone.

I reminded myself that mentoring is investing in others. It is a simple act of loving and caring for another person. Simplicity. Being a pearl is tapping into everything I am as a woman and mother. I reflect on mothers as possessing traits to be compassionate, insightful, forthcoming with wisdom, but caring along the way—even when the truth hurts. A mother is expected to believe in the best of her children always. To fully see each child's worth and potential. She has to find a way to be direct and supportive, authoritative but caring, so not to crush the spirit of the child. Do these sound like traits that can work effectively in professional settings? She is not to be a "friend," but someone who combines accountability with love because she knows what the child can accomplish. That does not mean there are not intense challenges at times. My personal challenging experiences would require hundreds of pages. And learning to relinquish control and exercise trust and compassion is not easy in the process of nurturing a child. But it is not difficult to extend love and care for our own children. It should come naturally. But not everyone experiences the love and care from a mother, as they should.

I began to look at investing in girls in a whole different way. What they needed from me was not hard to give. The girls on my campus were looking for women who could be pearls in the strand they were putting together. They were looking for accountability, caring, and understanding from someone who would speak truth to them, believe in them, and care even in their toughest and most unlovable moments. I kept feeling God prompting me, "It is time now for you to take what you have learned and pass it on to girls coming up on the road behind you."

I started by meeting with three young women—all juniors in college—who were exhausted with life but searching for more, something deeper to give to. We met at my house and I pulled out some simple decorations and refreshments; they found that time together in a home setting away from their dorm rooms valuable and enriching. It was a simple beginning as I opened my home for us to get to know one another and exchange life stories. As we came to know each better, they were encouraged to learn that a woman who appeared to have everything figured out in life in fact felt very much like they did in one way or another. My self-confessed insufficiencies somehow strengthened theirs and gave them hope of striving for personal achievement and development. I gave them confidence by sharing my weaknesses.

I learned that women learned best when I was honest with them about my own journey, struggles, and successes. Authenticity and transparency were what they craved from me. I learned that my regrets about the past could cripple my ability to live for the future. And fear of the future doesn't let me thrive in the present. So I needed to face my fears and live with more openness about the personal hurts and disappointments I was dealing with as well.

As my sons progressed in their teens, life became very difficult and complicated for us. Loving and caring for their internal needs and personal development would be among the most challenging life experiences. My character was being challenged, broken, and stretched, and I needed to gain courage and strength from these moments of uncertainty, emotional exhaustion, and weakness. Eleanor Roosevelt said,

> You gain strength, courage, and confidence by every experience in which you really stop to look fear in the face. You are able to say to yourself, I lived through this horror, and I can take the next thing that comes along. You must do the thing you think you cannot do. No one can make you feel inferior without your consent.[14]

Divine Encounters

What I call my divine encounters, because I believe a higher power brought them about, have been some of my most fulfilling life experiences. On vacation one summer, I randomly opened the local newspaper to review what artisan fairs were occurring and came upon a front-page story about a local girl graduating from high school. She was the homecoming queen and a star student who was dedicated to serving special needs kids. She wanted to prepare her life for this cause. And then the words in the news article jumped out at me—she was heading to my university!

I knew it wasn't coincidence that I had read this story and that I was at the same location as she at the time. I contacted her via Facebook (one of the great perks of social media and instant connectivity) and asked if we could meet. I've learned that my VP title opens many doors and allows immediate connections to take place. This divine appointment led me to ask her to join the mentoring group I was forming for the upcoming school year. Tears filled her eyes as she looked at her mother and said, "This is what we've been hoping for. I wanted to journey with someone who could help me figure out my calling and my life as I go to college." This simple engagement led to scholarships for her and now she is a thriving leader on the university campus with confidence and purpose for her future endeavors and aspirations. She will go on to have a major impact on those persons who are challenged with special needs. I too, as her mentor, will have a direct influence on a group of individuals I never could have if it were not for my personal investment in her. She will go on to touch the lives of others beyond my reach, and that reality is the greatest gift I can see in mentoring others.

The same is true for our children. If we support their personal development and prepare them well for life's challenges and opportunities, their reach and influence can change the lives of hundreds. It just takes one life to make a difference in our world and in our communities.

When I met another pearl, she had come to college after having lost her mother to AIDS. She was serving as the care provider for her younger siblings. Her father had also been killed in this war-torn African country where she would have lived a life consumed with immense struggle and little hope of a future. But a family serving this country on a humanitarian trip discovered her and, after years of a relationship with her, provided what she needed to attend my university. The family was seeking a female influence that could care for her as she transitioned to this new life/world in the United States and at a university. They knew her life would be radically exposed to change she was not going to easily navigate through, so they pursued a mentor. We found each other and not by coincidence. Her story is one of amazing personal transformation, and I got to be a part of it and witness it firsthand!

She became a part of my group and I witnessed all her firsts—such as ordering from the drive-through at fast food restaurants and feeling overwhelmed at the sight of the abundance of food available so easily in the cafeteria—but I also got to witness the transforming work taking place in her heart and character. She went from being a timid, fearful girl with a very limited worldview to one who, today, is leading others, speaking at events, and planning to return to her country to work in healthcare facilities and hospitals that can help rebuild desperate and broken lives torn apart by war, AIDS, and destruction.

You cannot script these moments in life. You cannot plan whom you might come across and influence. But in each instance, you must be ready to be used with purpose.

Dream Big!

Every great dream begins with a dreamer.
Always remember, you have within you the strength, the patience,
and the passion to reach for the stars to change the world.

—Harriet Tubman, Humanitarian

My greatest fulfillment comes from knowing that because of my simple investment in the lives of these young women each year, they will go on to reach hundreds more—people and communities I could never reach or have an impact upon. But they can do so and go places I could never even dream of going. I know one life can change a world. History shows us this. My time with these students, during which I encourage them to dream big, is one of the greatest rewards of my life. When I hear of them going on humanitarian mission trips to third-world countries and places I will never visit or have an opportunity to reach, I am blessed to know that they will, and that I was used for this purpose at this time through my leadership. These girls are stepping into classrooms, courtrooms, and boardrooms, and my reason for existence has just been validated.

My advice and messages are simple to my (staff) marketing team, my sons, my students, and women in my circle of influence (pearls): Dream big! And remain faithful to your calling, to what you are passionate about. Live with intentionality and purpose. Give 100 percent and then watch what you do when you advance to a level beyond what you could have imagined!

At the end of the academic year, when I release these female students into the next leg of their journeys more confident in who they are, courageous in their pursuits, and encouraged to go for their dreams, I ask them to write down what they want me to continue praying for to support them, and I keep these notes in my journal to remind me of the continuous work in progress in their lives. Here are some of these cherished requests:

- "I want people to see hope for a future when they see me caring for their needs."
- "I want to grow to be a woman of peace and I don't want my failures to pull me down."
- "I want to change education in America! I want to empower the students that I'll have in my classroom to believe in themselves so they can influence others positively."
- "I want to go to other countries and work with girls who have been rescued from human trafficking."

These young lives have years ahead to give to others and to impact our world. If I can be a small part of the reach they will have, I will have served my purpose for being on this earth. The reason for being and serving others is to show them what purpose they can achieve with their lives so that they too can eventually serve others, and so the effort continues to move forward! When the girls walk across that graduation stage, I am the one cheering from my seat: "The door is wide open for you to realize your dream, girl! Walk confidently into your future and never look back regretfully, for every season has lessons to learn. Go out into the world and shine!"

Joyce Meyer, an influential international advocate of teaching women to live with confidence, says, "Each of us must decide how we will live and what we will live for."[15] As I reflect on words posted on the United States White House website for the Council for Women and Girls in recognition of National Women's History Month, I am inspired:

Let the Courageous vision championed by women of past generations inspire us to defend the dreams and opportunities of those to come. We must advance the status of all women and girls around the world, as this remains one of the greatest unmet challenges of our time. We must ensure that women and girls, including those marginalized, are able to participate fully in public life, are free from violence, and have equal access to education, economic opportunity and health care. We are grateful for the continued leadership and unwavering commitment of champions and advocates who are advancing a future in which the dreams of our daughters [and sons] are equally within reach.[16]

I look at the framed black-and-white photos of women of the past in the university hallways, and I think, *What might they have had to overcome in their personal lives to pursue their dreams and callings?* May I never forget those who invested in me and championed leadership for me. Reaching out to others honors their legacies and leadership.

Be a Giver

I always say there are two types of people in the world: givers (generously, outwardly focused) and takers (selfishly ambitious). In her book *From the Heart: Seven Rules to Live By*, Robin Roberts says, "If you scratch the surface of a successful person, you will see the generosity and sacrifice of others that went into making it happen. It is important to acknowledge those who help you. Equally important is reaching a hand back to lift up and support those who are following behind. You can make the legacy of generosity more generosity."[17]

The girls I have met have shared with me how hard it is to find support. They have learned the hard way that not everyone is a giver. I encourage them to look for the signs of healthy people and put up boundaries with unhealthy people. Christina DiMari spells out some of this:

Signs of Healthy People
They show up to give you brief support.
They respect you for who you are and don't try to change you.
They give you space and honor you as a person.

Signs of Unhealthy People
They show up to take all they can from you.
They are clingy because they are not comfortable with themselves.
They are manipulative and will use all types of tricks to get what they want.[18]

She goes on to point out, "For the most part, you get to choose whom you travel with," and urges us to be honest with ourselves about what kind of persons we have around us and what kind of person we are. "If you are around people who struggle with jealousy, manipulation, anger, resentment, bitterness, lying, and activities you don't want to be a part of, realize that in most situations you can change this. . . . Look for friends who rejoice with you when you succeed, ones who reflect qualities like joy, peace, patience, and courage."[19]

Personal investment and mentorship are powerful and so critical to practice. They initiate a spiritual internal reaction and true heart transformation. We can create a ripple effect by purposely investing in our children and in the women and girls in our communities. As we become maturing adults, mothers naturally shift from teaching and instructing their children to mentoring them in their choices as adolescents and adults. This same process takes place in the workplace with our employees, and certainly can take place when serving as a mentor. We can build one another up, encouraging dreams to become realities. I have a sign that hangs prominently in my home that reads, "Don't just chase your dreams, live your dreams." I encourage my sons to read it each day.

A Pearl for Every Girl
After a Pearls in Process event, Christina and I sat by a beautiful fountain, a preferred sacred space for personal reflection and solace many use on my university's campus, and we started dreaming together of the possibilities of connecting each female student with a pearl (a caring mentor).

We dreamed that every girl from every nation, community, and college campus would have a pearl that was willing to shine light into her life and she would be a pearl for other girls. We thought it would be beautiful to host an event around the fountain each year and then model that event on other college campuses. We began to imagine what we wanted it to be like. We imagined pearls coming together to be encouraged, equipped, and inspired to go back and shine on their campuses or communities. And as they came to these events, heard stories shared by others who overcame challenges, and pursued their dreams, their hearts would be inspired and eventually transformed, and they would be refreshed by being in the company of other females who cared about similar things.

We walked around the fountain and read a large plaque that explained the vision of the lady who donated the fountain for the campus. Her name was Marjorie. And I remember her insisting upon having this fountain built in the center of our campus. There were so many other resources we needed on our campus, but we could not steer her away from this fountain idea. It was a way for her to remember her late husband. So she gifted the campus with the fountain so that students could have somewhere to go to be reflective in a peaceful setting. I now know her desire took on a higher symbolic purpose, and it's being lived out each fall when we gather around it with a young group of women seeking to be refreshed and renewed in their hearts and minds.

We did our first pearl gathering event the following year. Pearls flew in from all over the world! It was everything we both had imagined and more. The highlight of the whole event, for me, was Friday night at the candlelight service around the Fluor Fountain of Faith on Biola University's campus. Each female student received one singular fresh-water pearl and a verbal blessing from mentors who came to be connected with students interested in journeying together. During this beautiful moment, Jessica McLean, a singer and songwriter, performed a song she wrote specifically for this aspect of our vision, called "The Fountain."

Several girls wanted to speak to me afterward, so I had them form a line and I sat at the fountain's edge. I wanted to hear a bit from each one. Standing in front of me was a beautiful young Latina. I asked for her name. She replied, "Marjorie." In the back of my mind, I was thinking, *Oh! That's interesting. Her name is Marjorie, like the lady who had the vision to build this fountain.* Before I could ask her another question, streams of tears began flowing from her eyes. She told me how much the night meant to her and how significant all of the lessons about the meaning of the pearl are—because her name, *Marjorie,* means *pearl!*

The Meaning of a Pearl

Christina defines being a pearl this way:

> When a single grain of sand enters the living membrane of an oyster, it causes the oyster conflict and irritation. The oyster's reaction is to continually coat it with a substance called nacre, eventually transforming the grain of sand into a beautiful pearl. The Latin word for pearl literally means unique, attesting to the fact that no two pearls are identical. You and I are like that grain of sand. Through that refinement process, something of beauty is created in us that, each in our own unique and creative way.[20]

For me, true balance comes when I allow God to be the center of my life, to transform my imperfections by his grace, and to reveal the value and beauty in my world so I can invest of myself in others. People need a kind word, a strong example, or a listening ear. Why not send a note or give a call to someone who has been a pearl in your life? Don't underestimate the long-term value of relationships from long-past contexts. Princess Grace Kelly of Monaco—whose personal journey from an American Oscar-winning actress to an international princess is shared in *What Would Grace Do?*[21]—understood the value of investing in others' lives. She was a prolific letter writer who understood the power of sharing words of affirmation. Her encouragement through those written words have been collected by biographers eager to gain her insights and wisdom. I was reminded, as I read her story, how important it is as leaders and mothers to take the time to write notes of encouragement to others. It's a gesture Princess Kelly modeled, and her words have inspired hundreds of others. I hope you have both pearls that bless your life with their wisdom and experience and girls and women to whom you are a pearl. As you keep the plates spinning at home and at the office, may you lead as a woman who encourages and gives a hand up to others: *shine on!*

Discussion Questions

1. Who has invested in you? Name some of the women who have come alongside and encouraged you, who's written or spoken words have inspired you?

2. Who are some women or girls coming along the road behind you that you have invested in? Who are the people you seek to encourage?

3. Are you a giver or a taker at home? At work? In your community?

4. What words come to mind when you think of what kind of mother you want to be?

5. What words come to mind when you think of mentor? As you reflect on who you are, do you see these characteristics within you? What do you feel you need to continue to work on?

6. If you could do one thing to impact another person, what would it be? How can you accomplish this goal?

Notes

[1] Christina DiMari, *Cultivating Pearls* (Fort Collins, Colorado: Mountain Fountain Creations, 2013), 224.

[2] Diana Walcutt, "Birth Order and Personality," American Psychological Association's Psych Central, accessed May 26, 2014, http://psychcentral.com/blog/archives/2009/07/22/birth-order-and-personality/.

[3] "Sonia Sotomayor: From Bronx Housing Projects to the U.S. Supreme Court," interview by Katie Couric, *The Katie Show*, February 8, 2013, http://katiecouric.com/videos/sonia-sotomayor-from-bronx-housing-projects-to-the-u-s-supreme-court/.

[4] Christina DiMari, *You're Designed to Shine Study Guide* (Loveland, Colorado: Group Publishing, 2011), 48.

[5] Georgia Nugent, "Can We Stop Talking about the Glass Ceiling?" *Washington Post*, February 22, 2013, http://articles.washingtonpost.com/2013-02-22/national/37232957_1_female-leaders-first-female-president-higher-education.

[6] White House Council on Women and Girls, "Women in America: Indicators of Social and Economic Well Being," U.S. Department of Commerce Economics and Statistics Administration, accessed March 30, 2013, http://www.whitehouse.gov/administration/eop/cwg/data-on-women.

[7] Amy Gutmann, "Time for More Women to Lead Our Schools," *Washington Post*, February 22, 2013, http://articles.washingtonpost.com/2013-02-22/national/37232960_1_higher-education-women-universities.

[8] Ibid.

[9] Jonalyn Grace Fincher, *Ruby Slippers: How the Soul of a Woman Brings Her Home* (Grand Rapids: Zondervan, 2007), 139.

[10] John Bussey, "How Women Can Get Ahead: Advice from Female CEOs," *Wall Street Journal,* updated May 18, 2012, accessed March 30, 2013, http://online.wsj.com/article/SB1 0001424052702303879604577410520511235252.html.

[11] Maureen Grzelakowski, *Mother Leads Best: 50 Women Who Are Changing the Way Organizations Define Leadership* (Chicago: Dearborn Trade Publishing, 2005), 1–15.

[12] Quoted in Bussey, "How Women Can Get Ahead," 2.

[13] Joyce King Thomas, "Joyce King Thomas Offers Tips on Getting Ahead," *Advertising Age*, Special Report: 100 Most Influential Women in Advertising, September 24, 2012, accessed May 16, 2014, http://adage.com/special-reports/100mostinfluentialwomeninadvertising/191.

[14] Eleanor Roosevelt, BrainyQuote, http://www.brainyquote.com/quotes/authors/e/eleanor_roosevelt.

[15] Joyce Meyer, "How to Enjoy Life," *Charisma Magazine* (January 2011), accessed August 23, 2014, http://www.charismamag.com/spirit/devotionals/loving-god?view=article&id=8428:how-to-enjoy-life&catid=1527.

[16] Valerie Jarrett, "Women's History Month Proclamation," Council on Women and Girls, March 1, 2012, accessed May 14, 2014, http://www.whitehouse.gov/blog/2012/03/01/womens-history-month-proclamation.

[17] Robin Roberts, *From the Heart: Seven Rules to Live By* (New York: Hyperion, 2007), 59.

[18] Christina DiMari, *Ocean Star: You're Designed to Shine, A Memoir* (Carol Stream, Illinois: Tyndale House, 2006), 50.

[19] Ibid., 48.

[20] DiMari, *You're Designed to Shine Study Guide*, 49.

[21] Gina McKinnon, *What Would Grace Do? How to Live a Life like the Princess of Hollywood* (New York: Penguin Group, 2012), 82.

7

THE REAL ME
The Importance of Authenticity in Leadership

Melanie P. Wolf, MA

"I'm not a bit changed—not really. I'm only just pruned down and branched out. The real ME—back here—is just the same."

—L.M. Montgomery, *Anne of Green Gables*

Having four children is challenging for me on my very best day. Having four children on the first day of school requires stunt doubles and superhuman skills like traveling at the speed of light that I simply do not yet possess. Last September, our four children were attending three different schools, and for three of the four, those schools were brand new. My youngest son was beginning kindergarten and my youngest daughter moving on to second grade. My older daughter was beginning middle school and my older son moving up to the upper middle school. Not only was it the first day of school for my kids, it was the start of the second week of classes at the university where my husband and I both work.

We had just moved from Dallas, Texas, to San Diego, California, where we had both taken jobs at a private Christian university: my husband coaching soccer and I working in campus ministry. I was only four months into a brand new job in a brand new state, and only four months into being back at work full-time for the first time since having my first child twelve years prior.

A big day on all accounts. New shoes, outfits, lunches, environments, and nerves for all of us.

We took the classic first day of school photos, reviewed pick-up plans, and my husband left with our two older kids. Just as I was heading out the door to walk the younger two kids to their elementary school, I got a frantic phone call from my husband stating that I had failed to send a copy of our seventh grader's immunization card proving that we had, in fact, taken him to get the newly required immunization. I rushed around apologizing profusely and convinced the registrar to accept a photo of the vaccine record with the promise that we would bring the original to the office as soon as possible. I grabbed my camera, forgot my phone, and headed up to the elementary school a bit frazzled but thankful that I was able to fix my mistake without too much distress for my son on his first day of seventh grade.

I returned home to find multiple missed calls and a message stating I had taken a photo of the wrong side of the immunization card. The wrong side! I gasped, and with wide eyes I flung my hand over my mouth like a scene out of a cheesy movie. This day was certainly beginning to feel like a movie. After many failed attempts to get a hold of me, my husband had finally left the middle school and taken my son with him as he was not even allowed to enter the school without the correct proof of vaccination. My guilt-ridden tears did not do much to ease my son's disappointment and I left for work even more frazzled than I already was. Not only was I feeling like I had failed my son on his important first day of upper middle school, I was carrying the enormous weight of the week ahead on my already slumping shoulders. I was utterly overwhelmed. I would lead meetings with brand-new-to-me student leaders, preach in chapel for the first time in my new environment, and lead a three-day retreat for forty students at a location that I had never even seen a photo of. My I-totally-dropped-the-ball mommy morning was not the start to my stressful work week I had hoped for.

This tension of feeling pulled in two entirely different directions is something I have become quite familiar with. My roles as mother to four school-age children and member of the campus pastoral team at a Christian university often seem to require me not just to wear two different hats, but almost to be two entirely different women.

I don't think I'm alone in feeling this tension and this tension is not a new phenomenon. It is even found on the pages of the 1955 classic, *Gift from the Sea*, by Anne Morrow Lindbergh. An author, wife, and mother of five, she poetically describes the distracted, often fragmented life of a mother:

> The life I have chosen as wife and mother entrains a whole caravan of complications. It involves a house in the suburbs . . . food and shelter; meals, planning, marketing, bills, and making the ends meet in a thousand ways. . . . It involves health; doctors, dentists, appointments, medicine, cod-liver oil, vitamins, trips to the drugstore. It involves education, spiritual, intellectual, physical; schools, school conferences, car-pools, extra trips for basketball or orchestra practice; tutoring; camps, camp equipment and transportation. . . . It involves clothes, shopping, laundry, cleaning, mending, letting skirts down and sewing buttons on, or finding someone else to do it. It involves friends, my husband's, my children's, my own, and endless arrangements to get together. . . . What a circus act we women perform every day of our lives. It puts the trapeze artist to shame.[1]

This balancing act and the necessity to "remain whole in the midst of the distractions of life" seem like a common challenge for every working mother I know.[2] The feeling that one foot is firmly placed in the family, mothering, home-life world while the other is planted in the professional, work place, work-life world can leave a working mother feeling like she might be torn right down the middle. This issue highlights the importance of living and leading from the deepest, most honest places, the places that ground and anchor the mother. As I seek to do this—to live and lead from this deepest, most honest and grounded place—I am increasingly convinced that it is about knowing and being who I really am. It is about *authenticity*.

Identity and Authenticity

Identity and *authenticity*. These are big words. They are used in a variety of contexts and each holds quite a few definitions. Identity and authenticity are critical issues in the life of any leader. Though it doesn't seem completely obvious at the onset, these terms are intricately related. While issues of authenticity and transparency regarding goals, budgets, and policies are indeed important in the work of an effective leader, the authenticity I am talking about is the authenticity of self, about knowing and engaging one's true self.

I have been a leader for most of my life in one context or another. As a child, I loved to play teacher, mother, doctor, big sister, and virtually any other role that made me feel "in charge." I loved to babysit and help in the church nursery as I got a little older. I was the captain of sports teams, a student council member and officer, and could be counted on to take the lead in a small group or class. Many people referred to me as a natural leader and the role was one I was comfortable in and very often sought out. I worked as a camp counselor and was a youth group volunteer and small group leader as I entered late high school and college. While I wasn't entirely sure what type of job I would have when I graduated from college, I was certain that I would be some type of leader.

My operating definition of leader as I entered college could be summed up in just one word: perfect (or pretty close to perfect). I am not entirely sure where I got that definition, but it seemed to me that I had to have (or appear to have) everything completely figured out and squared away before I could lead anyone anywhere, and I was pretty sure I was supposed to be leading. I put a great deal of pressure on myself and others seemed to do the same.

Keeping up an image of perfection was a central goal of mine. I couldn't imagine what would happen if people found out the truth about my shortcomings. I was quite aware of some of my faults and limitations, but accepting those and letting others see them did not seem like a very good idea.

Following my sophomore year of college, I went to a camp in the Northwoods of Wisconsin to take part in a wilderness leadership practicum. (That is really a fancy title for an extended backpacking and canoeing trip through the Northwoods in May in the snow . . . yes, *SNOW*!) I had done quite a few backpacking trips both as a camper and as a camp counselor in the Blue Ridge Mountains of North and South Carolina over the previous five years. Frankly, I felt like a bit of an expert. This would be the longest I had ever backpacked and my canoeing skills were moderate at best, but I was sure that my previous experiences had somehow prepared me thoroughly for the trip.

On the second morning of our trip, we woke to find that our trip leaders would be placing one of us in the role of "leader" for the day. That person would be in charge of literally everything: choosing which snow-covered trail to hike or blaze that would ideally get us closer to our goal destination, as well as taking the lead in any and all meals, stops, and decisions regarding where and when to set up camp for the night. One of the men in our group was assigned leader for the first day. He led us fearlessly and flawlessly. He guided us by compass through miles of forest and miraculously found a dry, snow-free clearing with the perfect trees to tie up our tarps for camp that night. He knew everything about everything related to hiking, orienteering, and camping. He was *backpacking trip leader extraordinaire* (and is probably now working as a professional *backpacking trip leader extraordinaire* somewhere)! The day went off without a hitch. Our campfire conversation was centered around his excellent leadership skills, how we trusted him because he was confident and knowledgeable, and how our trust in him grew his confidence even further. It was a leadership success by any and all accounts.

To say that I was shocked the next morning to find that I had been assigned as the leader for the day is an absolute understatement. How could I follow *that*? The trip leaders pulled me aside, handed me the compass and map, and said, "Today, we will all follow you." The end. That was the extent of my instruction. Wide-eyed and suddenly very unsure of myself, I walked away to have a closer look at the map—honestly not too certain where we even were, much less where we were headed. My previous backpacking trips had been on well-marked, familiar trails. I had never had to use a compass to actually find my way through the wilderness. Orienteering was so far down on my skill list that it felt irresponsible for me to accept being in charge for the day.

I returned to my leaders and said I would like to wait until another day. *No luck*. I said I wasn't ready. They said they would follow me. I asked if I could switch with someone. They calmly grinned. I questioned whether I had to be the one to physically lead us or if I could ask someone more skilled at orienteering to do the job. They simply said I was the leader. "Yes, but can't a leader make someone else lead?" I frantically asked. They said again that they would follow me.

Standing in the middle of the wilderness in Wisconsin, I found myself in a bit of an identity and authenticity crisis. I was not very happy with who I was and wasn't at that moment. And I was certainly not very happy about the prospect of anyone else learning who I was and wasn't at that or *any* moment in the near future. Everything in me wanted to be someone else. I wanted to have better skills and more experience. I wanted to feel even the least bit comfortable and positive about hiking and orienteering in the snow. I wanted to be *backpacking trip leader extraordinaire 2.0*!

I was forced to see and admit who I really was that day. I had to look honestly at both my strengths and my limitations. The task to lead was mine and I needed help. I was a good hiker and had a reasonable amount of backpacking experience, but I did not have the skills necessary to guide us by compass through the snow. I called the group together and told them I had been assigned the official title of leader for the day. I told them the things I felt very good at and confident in: hiking, motivating, general camping skills, and making a killer meal over a campfire out of not much at all. I then told them the things I was not very good at or confident in: orienteering, being in snow in general let alone navigating trails that were covered in snow, and therefore all things related to the combination of orienteering and snow. "Remember, I'm from Georgia . . ." I said as I smiled. My fellow backpackers all looked at me. The truth was out. I had seen and admitted my limitations. I then asked them for help. I said that my first decision as the leader for the day was that I should not actually be the one leading through the wilderness. I said I needed someone else to be in charge of the map and compass. I was apparently also going to be learning how to delegate!

It was scary to look my peers in the eye and confess that I needed more help than I felt I could give. I considered pretending that I actually was *backpacking trip leader extraordinaire 2.0,* or faking an injury so someone else would have to take over. I decided instead to face the truth and tell my team the truth about who I really was. I took what felt like an absolute leap into authenticity. Being an inexperienced orienteer did not make me a bad leader. I was actually a really good one. It just made me aware of what I was and was not good at. All in all, the day was a fantastic success! I was proud of my decisions and felt respected for being honest and asking for the help I needed. I learned that leading from my true self means recognizing and admitting my strengths as well as my limitations.

In addition to my belief that I needed to be flawless in order to be a leader, I bought into the myth that there is no permission to be anything other than an effortlessly perfect mother. My first child actually helped me lean into the idea that I could be a perfect mother and have a perfect child. He was smart, adaptable, appropriately quiet, and stunningly charming all on cue. Mothering him felt like second nature to me, and juggling my new role as mom with the other responsibilities in my life seemed highly doable.

When my daughter was born just nineteen months later, the façade of perfection crumbled almost immediately. My easy-going toddler became active, messy, and incredibly loud. It took me longer to get back in physical shape and it seemed my house would never be the same again with two little ones in diapers and someone almost always awake. I didn't love people stopping by unannounced as I once had. A surprise guest who used to find me well-rested, put together, and happily reading either alone or to my son in the middle of a tidy family room would now find me eating peanut M&Ms for lunch, un-showered, and trying to breastfeed a squirmy baby with a toddler feeding himself animal crackers off of an un-mopped kitchen floor. My disguise of perfection went out the window. Quickly.

Accepting my imperfection and limitations as a mother was *not* my favorite thing. I very much wanted to be in shape, in style, well-rested, in a clean house, with happy children, with close friendships, deeply fulfilled by my meaningful job, and all with grace, ease, and a loving smile. I wanted people to think it was all really easy for me. And it wasn't. I would show up to the college writing course I was teaching quite unprepared, very tired, and regretting not waking up my baby to breastfeed before I left for class out of fear that I would soon be wearing a breast-milk stained blouse in front of my class whom I desperately wanted to convince that I could handle it all.

It was in this year of having a baby and a toddler while teaching and working in campus ministry at a Christian university that I had a glaringly imperfect and utterly embarrassing experience in a local spa. I was given a gift certificate for a massage by a dear friend who knew I could use a break. After the blissful hour-long massage that I drifted in and out of sleep during, the massage therapist came back into the room to discuss the *growth on the bottom of my foot* that she had "tried to be delicate around." She wanted to make sure she hadn't caused me any pain. I had absolutely no idea what she was talking about. She was shocked by my unawareness and suggested that I head to a doctor immediately. Embarrassed and a bit confused, I let her leave the room before I checked the bottom of my foot only to find a squished raisin on my arch. Now, this was not a freshly squished raisin, but a dried-out, dirty, *very* stuck-to-me raisin. I wanted to stay in that room for the next three weeks. Instead, I got up, looked at myself in the mirror, and went to find my masseuse so I could tell her not to worry about the *growth*. "It was a raisin. A squished raisin." I told her. "That is why I needed this massage today. So thank you." She nodded politely and gave me a demure smile under the, "*Oh, I cannot WAIT to tell this story . . .* " look. I laughed as I drove home, wondered if I would ever confess the story to anyone, and vowed not to darken the door of that particular spa again.

I have realized that whether I like it or not, I am deeply flawed. I am so far from perfect it is comical that I ever thought perfection was something I could attain. I have to operate within my life and limitations as they are. I need to maximize my strengths and learn to roll with my weaknesses and limitations. And I don't need to pretend that none of it took any effort. It takes a lot of effort. Every day. A huge part of that journey has come from a commitment to just be real. With myself and with others. Tired, un-showered, strong, ambitious, with raisins on my feet and all.

Self-Knowledge and Self-Acceptance

There is nothing more comforting and liberating than the permission to just "be yourself." We seek human relationships where we feel welcome to bring all of who we are. Most of us however, struggle to know and accept who we really are, therefore making it impossible to bring that genuine self. We spend a great deal of time and energy trying to be someone else.

When I was eight years old, I went to my first overnight camp at an all-girls camp in South Carolina. I took the opportunity that being away from my family for a full week afforded me and decided I would tell everyone at camp that my name was Paige. Paige is my middle name and there was an older girl on my swim team named Paige who I remember as funny and absolutely beautiful. It was the perfect time to pretend to be her. The plan worked out fairly well except that my counselors had to call my name three, four, or five times before I would ever respond. I was constantly confused and unsure if someone was talking to me because I was not used to responding to "Paige." When my parents came to pick me up, the counselor told them that despite my hearing challenges, I (Paige, of course) had a wonderful time at camp. I dodged the awkward interactions and was eager to be in the safety of our station wagon where I wouldn't have to stress over which name to respond to or wonder if my secret would be out. It takes a lot of effort to be someone other than yourself. That was only my first and most innocent attempt.

While the story of me pretending to have a different first name at camp is perhaps just childish and fairly harmless, many of us walk around not knowing or not wanting to be who we really are, even into adulthood. As I matured and moved into other leadership roles, I became more aware of the things that I was good at and the things that came naturally to me. Professors, supervisors, mentors, and friends called out areas of strength and giftedness in me and I continued to gain confidence in those things. But something very interesting was happening at the same time. I was still trying to hide my insecurities, anxieties, and failures for fear that they would negate the good, strong things I was learning about myself. I was still trying to keep up the illusion of virtual perfection. This was only intensified as I entered a career in vocational ministry and felt the pressure to be free from weakness, struggle, doubt, and even sin.

Ultimately, I felt the need to deny and ignore—or at the very least, disguise and hide—a lot of things that are true about me. This desire is rooted in shame and fear, and what psychologist Dr. David Benner calls "the soil of self-ignorance."[3] What is needed instead is self-acceptance and self-knowledge. At first, it seems backwards to think that we should accept things about ourselves that we might want to change, but even the things that we most want to change about ourselves must first be accepted. "Self-transformation is always preceded by self-acceptance. . . . Only after we genuinely know and accept everything we find within our self can we begin to develop the discernment to know what should be crucified and what should be embraced as an important part of self."[4]

Benner states that transformation affects our identity by changing the identifications and attachments in each of our lives.[5] "Our identity is grounded in our attachments. We are what we most identify with. If my body is what I most deeply identify with, then I am my body. If, however, my thoughts, history, religion, symptoms, accomplishments, reputation, competencies, or longings are what I most identify with, then this becomes my identity."[6] These attachments are not where identity should be based. There is a danger in letting circumstances define identity. Suddenly, a person who suffers from an illness can let that define her as sick or weak, not just someone with an illness. Benner suggests that there is a major difference between *having* thoughts, beliefs, or opinions and *being* those thoughts, beliefs, or opinions.[7] This happens with both strengths and weaknesses in the life of a leader. A leader can let her successes and failures define her, or she can see them as things she experiences while being grounded in the deeper reality of her unique identity.

Basing her worth or identity on the skills, behaviors, or personalities of her children can be a tremendous and dangerous temptation for a mother. It is easy to let my children's lives and identities define my own. When my kids have been recognized as compassionate, articulate, or intelligent, I feel successful and competent. When my kids throw temper tantrums, scream in defiance, or tell muscular men with tattoos covering a vast majority of their bodies that they look silly wearing earrings (yes, this really happened!), I feel lame and like a total failure. Of course, appropriate pride or even embarrassment can be a natural response for a mother, but there is great danger in letting the choices, ideas, and actions of *anyone* define her identity.

In Christian spirituality, it is recognized that the "true self-in-Christ is the only self that will support authenticity. It and it alone provides an identity that is eternal."[8] True identity and knowledge of self are most fully known in relation to God. No other created thing struggles with the issue of identity. A hydrangea bush just pushing up through the soil does not wonder what it will become or whether what it is becoming is what it was intended to be. We would laugh at the notion that a skunk wonders how it should be a skunk, and yet as humans, we struggle with authenticity, with becoming and being our true selves.

The acceptance and knowing of self is built upon God's full knowledge and unconditional acceptance of us, just as we are. Benner writes, "Real knowing of ourselves can only occur after we are convinced that we are deeply loved precisely as we are."[9] Henri Nouwen refers to this as recognizing and claiming our *belovedness*, stating that the greatest trap and greatest enemy to the spiritual life is self-rejection.[10] Believing that we are fully known and fully loved by God just as we are gives us freedom to be ourselves because we are no longer operating out of the fear that disclosure will result in abandonment and rejection.

This task seems particularly challenging for the working mother. She is pulled and twisted not only by a variety of tasks and responsibilities but also by the expectations of herself and what seems to be the rest of the known world. Everyone seems to have an opinion about whether a mother should work full-time or part-time or no-time at all. It is challenging to both respect the opinions of others and silence them when necessary in order to fully lean into what is right for the only person who can actually make that decision: the mother herself.

Once that decision is made, the questions and opinions only increase. The working mother must continue to map out what it looks like to fully be herself in the roles and responsibilities she finds herself in. If her identity is based on her job title or on her status as a wife and mother, there will be a continual search for how others are responding to her. If her identity is based upon the successes and failures in her job or in the lives of her children, she will either have an inflated view of self or a deflated view of self. Basing identity on anything other than God's full knowledge and acceptance will always leave the mother in an unstable and ultimately unfulfilling place.

As a young leader and mother, I fought the battle to know and be myself with a great deal of passion and confusion. I swayed between full confidence that I was gifted and called to ministry even while my children were young, and zero confidence that I should be working and ministering at all while I had children under my roof. Some of the battle was external; there were a number of voices weighing in. But much of the battle was internal; the voices inside my own head seemed loudest of all. It took me a long time to admit that I really *wanted* to work. When our first son was born, I took a part-time job to supplement our income and supplement my sanity. That is the truth. We did need the money in order to help pay our bills, but I needed to work for myself as well.

In all honesty, this was not something I found easy to accept about myself at first. It was tempting in those early years to say that I only worked because I *had to*. I did not have many models of young working mothers in my life. Somehow having to work for financial reasons was far more acceptable and respectable than working because I wanted to, even to me. I bought into the temptation to try to be who others, or I, thought I was *supposed* to be. I listened to the voices of what I have come to understand are the false selves that chatter away in my soul and muddle the voice of who I really am and want to be.

Mothering my four children has presented more than a few opportunities for those false selves to engage in what seems like a full-blown opera of songs, chatter, wailings, and whispers. While I haven't anticipated that my children would never be loud at unfortunate times or throw tantrums in public, I have constantly had to battle the voices in my head that say I am a horrible mother when they do those things.

A recent conversation—one that could also be described as a rather emotional argument in my driveway—with my next-door neighbor was fertile ground for the weeds of shame and self-doubt to grow. Angered that my children kept kicking the soccer ball into her yard, she told me that I needed to "step up to the plate and get my children under control." Now, this seemed extreme. Unreasonable. These are merely soccer balls that end up in her yard on occasion. They break nothing and harm no one. Everything in me knows that having a frustrated neighbor does not mean that I am a bad mother who has no control of her kids, but for the rest of the afternoon after the confrontation, I found myself convinced that I was an incapable mother. I suddenly felt exposed and insecure. All of the times when my children had not listened the very first time or talked back or been outright disobedient became evidence in this case against me as a total failure. It took many more tears, and hours, than I would like to admit to settle into the reality that I am raising four human beings who make mistakes. And disobey. And say mean and hateful things. And kick soccer balls over fences. Sometimes I do not have control of my children. And those things do not make me a bad and incompetent mother. My identity has to be based upon a much deeper reality.

The Journey toward the True Self

Sue Monk Kidd's journey toward the "True Self," as told in *When the Heart Waits,* is both personal and universal. Her desire to "whittle away the false selves" she recognized in her own life led her toward the work of C. G. Jung and what he called "the Self with a capital S." This Self refers to "the Center, the image of God within us." In order to connect with this true Self, one must confront the false selves that are vying for center stage in our lives. She writes, "As we attempt to adapt to and protect ourselves from the wounds and realities of life, we each create a unique variety of defense structures—patterns of thinking, behaving, and relating designed to protect the ego. *These egocentric patterns make up our false selves.*"[11] The work of recognizing these false selves is not easy. We are often blinded to the patterns of thinking and behaving in our own lives that are informing the ideas we have about ourselves and the roles we play.

It is easy to feel a bit lost amid the demands of balancing family and ministry. I forget what it feels like to be me apart from being someone's mother or wife or campus pastor or colleague. My well-rehearsed patterns of seeking the image of perfection and who I am *supposed* to be often sneak in and squelch the *real* me that is longing to be seen and known. There is a great temptation for me to want others to believe that juggling motherhood and ministry is smooth and picturesque, that I have made a fantastic decision and am handling it with grace and ease. I don't mind if people know it is challenging, but I would love for them to also believe that I never question if I can really pull it all off. In reality, the juggle is incredibly tiring and often confusing.

Without a sense of my belovedness, belonging, and acceptance, the voice of false, self-seeking perfection and who I am *supposed* to be reacts to my imperfections with shame and fear. One of my mentors shared with me the internal dialogue she has chosen to debunk the shame that sneaks in when she is faced with her mistakes, limitations, and inadequacies: "Good enough." I have chosen to adopt these words myself, believing that "good enough" is just that. When I am tempted to feel guilty for forgetting one of my kids needed to wear a special shirt for their field trip or for bringing store-bought cookies to the bake sale, "I am a good enough mom" is a message I repeat to myself. When I feel not fully equipped for a small group leader training meeting that I have to lead at work, "I am a good enough leader" helps me engage in my work, with all that I have, at the moment.

Dr. Brené Brown refers to this perspective as "wholehearted living." After over a decade of research and three books about self-acceptance, perfectionism, shame, and vulnerability, she writes in the introduction of her widely popular book *Daring Greatly*:

> Wholehearted living is about engaging in our lives from a place of worthiness. It means cultivating the courage, compassion, and connection to wake up in the morning and think, *No matter what gets done and how much is left undone, I am enough.* It's going to bed at night thinking, *Yes, I am imperfect and vulnerable and sometimes afraid, but that doesn't change the truth that I am also brave and worthy of love and belonging.*[12]

"Wholehearted living" frees us to live authentic lives. It frees us to face the truth about ourselves and not feel the need to hide. The confidence and empowerment birthed in the belief that we are enough is unmatched by any other gifting or talent. Leaders and mothers who know who they are focus on their strengths, admit their areas of limitation, and offer their very greatest asset: their authentic True Self.

The Necessity of Authentic Connection

"In the wilderness of the mind, the desert wastes in the heart through which one wanders lost and a stranger. When one is a stranger to oneself then one is estranged from others too. . . . Only when one is connected to one's own core is one connected to others."[13] A significant part of authentic wholehearted living is having people who can hear the truth and speak the truth into the life of a leader and mother. Motherhood and leadership are tasks that should not be done alone. Period.

Wholehearted living allows people to connect at a deep and meaningful level with those in their lives. At the very core of what it is to be human is the need for connection; we are hardwired for it.[14] In order to connect, we have to be vulnerable, and true vulnerability is rooted in the True Self. Being vulnerable feels exposed and raw because it is the commitment to let our true selves be seen. Much of life seems to be about hiding and covering up the parts of us we aren't very happy with or proud of. Being vulnerable is being willing to be honest, first with the self and then with others, telling the truth about what is really there, being willing to be who we really are.

This does not at all mean having to be flawless or perfect. It can, in fact, feel quite far from that because it is actually being honest and authentic about the fear, pain, joy, sorrow, and desire that exist in the soul. I thought I had to appear flawless or perfect in order to be a good mother or a leader of any kind. I expected perfection from myself and, without recognizing it, from my children as well. I have come a long way on this particular journey and can truthfully say that one of the places I have grown is in the space I seek to give myself and my children to be honest and present even when that isn't pretty— space for each of us to make mistakes, be scared, sad, lonely, even depressed.

Though now more willing to admit my limitations and lessons learned from mistakes I've made as a mother and as a leader, I have remained hesitant to be vulnerable and authentic about some of the deeper areas of struggle in my life. For a number of years, I have battled varying degrees of depression. At first my depression was fairly manageable. In the last few years, this "dance with depression," as I have often called it, has felt more like an all-out onslaught and has left me, at times, feeling completely unable to achieve my tasks and responsibilities as both mother and leader. I recently wrote to a friend that while this darkness had not always hovered oppressively over me, there had been a swooping in, a swaying, a shadowy presence that always felt close by. That swaying turned into a steady and heavy soaking.

In her important book, *Darkness is My Only Companion*, Episcopal priest Kathryn Greene-McCreight shares her journey of living with bipolar disorder. Her description of her own depression is a window into my own experience as well:

> The experience as a whole and the experience that constituted
> the eventual illness were at the least bewildering and at the most

terrifying. The blue sky, which normally fills my heart, stung my soul. Beautiful things like oriental rugs and good food like bean soup absolutely exhausted me. Noise was amplified in my ears, and I fled sound and conversation in search of silence. Small tasks became existential problems: how and why to fold laundry, empty the dishwasher, do the grocery shopping. My memory failed me. I was unable to read or write. And it went downhill from there. A back and forth in and out of darkness lasted for years.[15]

I have spent afternoons with my back against a wall and my knees pulled to my chest. I have spent hours in bed during the day and have lain awake at night consumed with what I have come to call my "darkness." I have felt the haunting of unexplained sadness and loneliness. I have been paralyzed by fear, sorrow, anxiety, and extreme apathy. All the while, as a leader and a mother.

Most of the time, I have been able to manage these seasons by adding some things into my days that help me. Even when I don't feel like it, I know that things like exercising, having meaningful conversations, reading, writing, taking a long bath, engaging in some type of craft or creative expression, eating healthy foods, spending time in nature watching birds and whales, and looking out onto the ocean asking the waves to take my heaviness back out to sea with them can help me find my way out of the darkness. This list of things that help me has been tested and added to over the years. I have shared with a few trusted people in my life about this struggle and my need for extra time and intention to take care of myself when the struggle is in full force.

My most recent and most severe bout of depression was triggered by a string of significant losses and heartbreaks. A pretty long and twisted string of them. It seemed to be strangling me. I came to the place where the well-tested weapons in my arsenal of defense were insufficient to pull me through the engulfing darkness. My known resources were totally used up. Self care became not just an important aspect of my life—it became almost all I could do. I returned to weekly and, at times, even semi-weekly therapy sessions with a licensed psychotherapist, continued monthly sessions with my spiritual director, engaged in any and all of the things that usually help me, and, with the counsel of some kind and honest friends, became open to taking an antidepressant.

Women are no strangers to depression. About one in five women develop depression at some point in their lifetime, and postpartum depression affects between 10 and 25 percent of women.[16] That is a lot of women. Certainly many of them are leaders and mothers like me.

Part of self-acceptance and self-knowledge for me is facing the reality that I battle depression. I have to be honest about that in order to take care of myself. It takes a great deal of effort and intentionality for me to care for myself amid a life of motherhood and ministry when I am struggling with depression. I have become deeply committed to the practices of self care that keep me healthy and whole, and I have worked hard to listen to my body and soul in order to know what I need. Sometimes I can't hear or know those things on my own. I need the people I have asked to speak into my life to do just that.

Those who have journeyed the dark days of depression with me have been few. Some of my closest companions have been authors who have battled depression themselves. Their words and stories have brought comfort and hope. They have given language and images to things that felt too big and too formless to speak or see on my own. Friends who have shared that they have at times found themselves in a similar swamp of sorrow have given me energy and courage on even my hardest days. We have sent photographs, poems, scriptures, songs, quotes, books, and movie suggestions to one another in an effort to speak into the darkest places of the soul that needed to be seen and heard and healed. We have taken walks, shared tears and conversation over coffee, and sat for literal hours in a car or at a kitchen table. The faithful companionship of these few has often felt like the very breath that I have so desperately needed.

As a mother, I have grieved the days when my children have seen me cry far more than I usually do or have looked concerned because I was quietly lying in bed in the middle of the day. I have told them what a dear friend remembers her mom saying when she was battling an intense and dark depression: "I am not okay right now, but I am going to be okay." I have leaned heavily on my support systems and hired babysitters even when money was tight so I could make taking care of myself a priority. Perhaps the best encouragement I have received is to let go of the shame and guilt that I am tempted to feel and instead believe that taking care of myself is the most loving thing I can do for myself and the people in my life, including my children.

I am aware that my children have seen me struggle. They have also seen me fight—for myself and for our family. My older children know that I have taken an antidepressant. They asked what my medication was and I told them it helped me see the things in my life with better perspective and less cloudiness. They know I am committed to my work in therapy and in spiritual direction. I have worked hard to not need them in ways that are unhealthy for them and for our relationship. That means I have to be fierce about getting the help and support I need from the places where it is appropriate and healthy. I am not interested in completely hiding the pain and struggle, but I am also not willing to have my children play a particular role because of it.

Pain and struggle are universal. They are part of the human experience and mothers and leaders are by no means excluded. As a mother, I have felt like I am not allowed to struggle because my children and family need me. Additionally, as someone in ministry, I have fought embarrassment and shame, not feeling that it was acceptable for me to be anything less than 100 percent okay. I have felt misunderstood and honestly wondered if I had anything to offer my children or my students in a time when I felt so empty myself. And while those feelings have been deep and very real, I have also found that somehow my own darkness and battle with depression has been perhaps my most treasured gift in ministry and motherhood. Henri Nouwen's insight into this concept has, for years, encouraged and challenged me. Nouwen referred to ministers as "wounded healers," writing that "those who proclaim liberation are called not only to care for their own wounds and the wounds of others, but also to make their wounds into a major source of healing power."[17] I am continually humbled that the wounds of my past and even the pain of my struggle with depression could be used to help me empathize with, serve, and lead my family and those I minister to.

Jean Vanier refers to this mystery in the life of a Christian when he writes, "And not only are we loved, but we too are called to heal and to liberate. This healing power in us will not come from our capacities and our riches, but in and through our poverty. We are called to discover that God can bring peace, compassion and love through *our* wounds."[18] In my specific roles, being willing to be vulnerable and authentic about my own pain has often helped me connect at a deeper level and has afforded me the sacred privilege of walking with others in their times of sorrow and struggle. Students who come to my office and apologize for their own tears hear me sincerely say, "I am familiar with tears . . . they are a gift . . . this office is a place where tears are welcomed." They know it is a place where it is okay to not be okay. Because I have had many days when it was far from true for me, I don't expect or demand that my kids "have it all together." I am fully aware that they, like me, have limitations and are beautifully imperfect. Hopefully, they experience a more honest, gracious, and loving mother because my capacity to understand and forgive has been grown in and through my own mistakes, wounds, and struggles.

A Symbol of Authentic Living

At a recent retreat for female seniors in college, I had the opportunity to present the closing session, which was on "faithful living." Knowing that every woman in attendance would find themselves in seasons of orientation, disorientation, and new orientation in their life and faith journeys, I chose to share about some of the seasons of disorientation I had experienced.[19] I wanted to speak authentically about the things that have helped me survive and so shared about a specific season in my faith journey that occurred roughly ten years ago. It was a time in which I found myself questioning a number of things about God and Christianity. Due to depression, I found myself completely overwhelmed by the doubt and questions that flooded my heart and mind, feeling entirely hopeless. It was a dark and confusing time, and it felt incredibly similar to the one I experienced as I prepared for and spoke at this retreat.

I shared about symbols: physical objects that can trigger the mind to remember a truth when remembering feels impossible. I shared about leaning into tradition and liturgy: letting the words of others become those words I could not create on my own. I shared about connecting with God in creation: seeing birds soar gracefully through the sky, waves rolling into the shore, or trees dancing in the wind as prayers to the God who created them. I shared about the importance of community: people who could and would make time and space for the pain and questions that come, people who were willing to accompany me on the journey even when the journey was dark.

I shared from an honest, authentic place, admitting my doubts. I held on my lap the blanket that I sleep with every night, a physical reminder of God's presence and comfort. It was incredibly liberating to not pretend that everything had always gone smoothly for me and that somehow I had to present myself as someone other than who I really am.

As I sought a symbol to give the women as a reminder of our weekend together, I wanted something that would embody the importance of being who we really are and sharing who we really are with those we share life and community with. I immediately thought of a clear glass coffee mug. When I think of a coffee mug, I picture conversation and relationship, taking time to talk and listen. The clear glass symbolized authenticity, being who we really are and seeing others for who they really are. We closed the retreat by sitting in a large circle all facing a table that was covered in clear glass coffee mugs.

One of the other presenters at the retreat explained the symbolism of the mug and the women were asked to choose a mug from the table in silence and present it to someone who had encouraged them on their journey over the weekend. My mug from the weekend sits on my desk at work. I keep it there as a visual reminder that I want to bring my True Self into the opportunities and relationships in my life. I want to live wholeheartedly. I firmly believe that doing so gives those I am in relationship with the encouragement to do the same.

Bringing my full, True Self into my roles as leader and mother is an all-day, everyday challenge. My students see me fail. My kids, of course, see me fail. They see me make mistakes and they are often the recipients and witnesses of those moments. When I can admit my weaknesses and apologize for my mistakes, I have an opportunity to practice authenticity. They hear me articulate my feelings and see me laugh, take some deep re-grouping breaths, and even cry.

Perhaps the greatest gift I can give my children is to love them as they are. All of who they are—strengths, limitations, pain, and all. In order to be free to do that, I have to love and be who I really am. All of who I am. When we are operating out of fear, insecurities, and false selves, we are not free to engage with others in ways that are truly meaningful. I don't want that to be the case in my life and certainly not with my children.

I want my kids to know that even though I struggle, I keep going. I am okay with the fact that they see me mess up, because they too are bound to mess up. When they do, I want them to know that they can survive in the midst. I want them to know that they can actually grow and change and become even better leaders, friends, students, family members, and professionals if they fight through the temptation to cover up every mistake, struggle, and limitation. I want them to remember that I took time to take care of myself, that I was intentional and fierce in making sure that I had the support I needed. I want them to remember that I didn't do it all perfectly. Not even close. But I did it, and I was committed to the pursuit of finding, being, and celebrating my True Self in the midst.

Here is what I know: authenticity is really hard. But it is absolutely worth fighting for. Embracing and revealing what is true about the self is an essential aspect of living and leading well. Being a leader and mother, and most importantly a healthy human being, I have learned that I have to know and take care of myself and be authentic in the process. If I am going to live, lead, and mother out of the most honest, deepest parts of me, I must continue through the process of knowing and accepting my True Self. In order to be a healthy and whole person, I need authentic connection, and in order to have that, I have to be willing to show people who I really am. I have to be the real me.

Discussion Questions

1. What are some of the cultural mores that have informed your understanding or assumptions about what motherhood is *supposed* to be or what a leader is *supposed* to be like?
2. What leader and mother whom you know or have observed seems to truly know and accept herself? How is this evidenced in her life and leadership?
3. What do you see as essential elements of living authentically for women who are navigating leadership and motherhood?
4. What step(s) could you take to live more authentically today?

Notes

[1] Anne Morrow Lindbergh, *Gift from the Sea* (New York: Pantheon, 1955), 19–20.

[2] Ibid., 22.

[3] David Benner, *The Gift of Being Yourself* (Downers Grove, Illinois: Intervarsity Press, 2004), 21.

[4] Ibid., 58.

[5] David Benner, *Spirituality and the Awakening Self* (Grand Rapids: Brazos Press, 2012), 60.

[6] Ibid., 61.

[7] Ibid.

[8] Benner, *The Gift of Being Yourself*, 15.

[9] Ibid., 65.

[10] Henri Nouwen, *Life of the Beloved* (New York: Crossroad Publishing House, 1992), 31, 33.

[11] Sue Monk Kidd, *When the Heart Waits* (New York: HarperCollins Publishers, 1990), 50–52.

[12] Brené Brown, *Daring Greatly* (New York: Gotham Books, 2012), 10.

[13] Lindgergh, *Gift from the Sea*, 38.

[14] Brown, *Daring Greatly,* 10–11.

[15] Kathryn Greene-McCreight, *Darkness Is My Only Companion* (Grand Rapids: Brazos Press, 2006), 20.

[16] "Depression in Women: Understanding the Gender Gap," Mayo Clinic, January 19, 2013, accessed August 24, 2014, http://www.mayoclinic.com/health/depression/MH00035.

[17] Henri Nouwen, *Wounded Healer* (New York: Crown Publishing Group, 1972), 88–89.

[18] Jean Vanier, *From Brokenness to Community* (Mahwah: Paulist Press, 1982), 21.

[19] Walter Brueggemann, *Spirituality of the Psalms* (Minneapolis: Fortress Press, 2002), 8.

8

SPIRITUAL MOTHERHOOD
Nurturing Souls at Home and Beyond

JAMIE NOLING-AUTH, DMIN

*"The secret to a strong, healthy, and fruitful ministerial life
lies in how we work with God."*

—Dallas Willard, *The Great Omission*

My eyes open at 5:45 A.M. to the sounds of my six-month-old son crying over the baby monitor on my nightstand. My husband lays the baby down beside me. I hold my son's tiny hand in mine. Today is Ash Wednesday, the day in the Christian year when the Church calls Christians to remember our human frailty, to confess our desire to be powerful, and to recall that our lives are short. On this day, we are reminded to rest in the knowledge that God is our Creator and Sustainer, our Real Strength, and our Redeemer. Today I will help lead our campus's Ash Wednesday worship services. "From dust you have come and to dust you will return." The words settled on my heart with a new poignancy brought on by motherhood.

After portioning out my baby's daily bread—in this case, three five-ounce bottles of milk, a small bowl of pureed avocado, and some sawdust-looking rice cereal—I pull my son out of his bouncer and give him abundant kisses. I hate saying goodbye to him. I have been back at work for three months, and still the morning goodbye is not easy. No amount of kisses will do. "I love you," I whisper in his ear and then I say it five more times rapidly. I place him in the arms of the woman who saw me in the same light thirty-five years ago.

The worship team approaches the stage as I step away from the pulpit and pick up my votive of ashes. The words of the liturgy were lovely and powerful: "We have sinned . . . by what we have done and by what we have left undone." I press my thumb into the black ash and then sweep the sign of the cross onto the forehead of a colleague. The students come forward. One after the next. Sweet children of God who want to take part in God's story. "From dust you have come and to dust you will return." Each of these is beloved by God. This year, the boys have a special place in my heart—the big ones who need to bend down so I can put ash on their foreheads, the ones who remove their hats as they reach the front of the line, the shaggy ones with mounds of hair that need to be held to the side for the mark of the cross, the contrite ones who look down as they receive the ashes, the delighted ones who happily look into my eyes to receive the words I whisper. "From dust you have come and to dust you will return." These students—all of them—are some mama's baby, and they are God's dear ones.

❖   ❖   ❖

When I was growing up, adults would tell me that time goes by faster and faster as one grows older. Now that I am an adult, I know this to be true. A school year used to be an eternity. Now, it is hardly enough time to get a lunch date on the calendar with one of my dearest friends. I can see that, in what will feel like five minutes, my infant son will transform into a toddler. Today we celebrate his two tiny little teeth and his new ability to crawl, and in no time at all, we will be celebrating that this teething phase is done and we'll be chasing a running little boy enlivened by freedom-bursts. Time will pass by quickly.

Many women come into leadership outside of the home after they have children. This was not my experience. I was in my ministry leadership position years before I became pregnant with my son, and so my work-life patterns were already well established. I have had to learn new patterns of living and working, create space for what is most important, and find hidden opportunities within both areas of responsibility that are advantageous to the other. I am a new mom in my first year of figuring out how to do this dance between motherhood and professional leadership. I am in the months when my recent maternity leave, feeding my baby, and setting good habits for the long term are at the forefront of my mind. From this vantage point as a new mother reentering her leadership role, I will tell my story. I will then make two observations about the integrated life of my callings as both campus minister and mother: first, the rarely addressed observation that these tasks of motherhood and pastoring are deeply similar; and second, the truth that the nurture of one's own soul is essential to both roles, even though in both contexts it can be a significant challenge to undertake.

Each mother has a unique experience of motherhood related to her own personality and gifts, to the presence or absence of the baby's father, to the personality and needs of her baby, and to her abundance or lack of resources. Likewise, the joy and challenge of professional leadership is uniquely linked to the community of people, expectations, and support available within a leader's context of service. My intention is not to write a prescriptive guide for every pastor-mother, but to highlight observations with the hope that, for the reader, they may foster reflection and encouragement.

My Story

When I was twelve, I went on a houseboat trip with my church youth group that significantly impacted the course of my life. I experienced the quiet whisper of the Holy Spirit for the first time, inviting me to friendship with the Living God. I found it so compelling that God would desire friendship with me that I responded by reading enormous quantities of Scripture and telling all the other students on the trip about God's desire for friendship with them. People at church began saying things to me like, "You should go into ministry," and offering me speaking opportunities and leadership of various small groups. And, like many women in ministry, I also got this loaded compliment, "You are so gifted in ministry. You should *marry* a pastor."[1] But, marry a pastor, I did not; *become* a pastor, I did.

Six years after graduating from college, I found myself living in New England—three thousand miles from home. I was Director of Student Ministries at a wonderful Christian college and was working on a doctorate at a nearby seminary. The move had been a big risk for me, considering that

I knew not a soul in this faraway land, and hadn't even visited the school until the on-campus interview. It had been a rich adventure in every way, and though I missed home, I was beginning to get settled. Then I received a phone call from a dear friend on the West Coast, saying, "There is a job in Southern California that you need to apply for!" I laughed. But, four months later, I found myself unpacking all of my earthly belongings in a two-bedroom apartment over an alleyway, with a view of palm trees and a California mountain range from the large living room window. The apartment was situated just a few miles from the Christian college that my friend had recommended. I would become the first female that this university had ever hired as a campus pastor and would join one other campus pastor in shepherding 2,700 undergraduate students. My tasks would include regular preaching (with which I had virtually no experience), pastoral care (including counseling and hospital visits), spiritual formation programming (such as retreats, prayer walks, worship nights), and, of course, a host of other responsibilities that go with the title "pastor." In the years to come, the campus would grow from 2,700 to over 5,500 undergraduates (fortunately our pastoral staff would increase as well!), I would encounter students with every possible perspective on women in ministry,[2] and, most significantly, I would learn to pastor.

My leadership role was exciting and challenging. I was able to provide pastoral leadership for a community that newly desired a female pastoral voice, and it was an invigorating experience to serve them in that. However, as wonderful as my ministry life was, I found that building a family (something I desired) was not an easy endeavor for me. After a series of sweet, well-meaning boyfriends, with whom the relationship often ended because of some version of the same problem—"I can't marry a woman who wants to go into ministry," "I need to marry a woman who will submit to my leadership in the home," "Your mom is such a strong leader, I hope you aren't planning to be like that," etc.—I found myself in my early thirties with a doctorate, an intense campus ministry job, an apartment that I lived in alone, a movie collection of all the greatest romantic comedies, a library of books about feminism, an impressive history of exciting adventures I'd taken, a few heartrending breakups in my past, and no romantic prospects on the horizon. I was pretty sure that I had sacrificed a family of my own for a life in ministry. It was a sacrifice I was willing to make, most definitely. However, it was also one that in truth, kept me up at night filled with a sense of loss and gut-wrenching sacrifice. Pridefully, I didn't want to be one of *those women* who could think of nothing else but romantic prospects, so I tried to keep my conversations about hopes and/or loneliness to a minimum. I talked about other things—travel, memories, sermons, my workplace, my family, books, and adventures. I lived an interesting life. And, it was wonderful. Some of my dearest friends still laugh at a conversation we had in which I was bemoaning that I had basically accomplished every other goal on my single-lady dreams list and I said something to the effect of, "Well, I've accomplished every possible thing I can think of . . . I guess I could build another piece of furniture." To these married friends of mine, it sounded preposterous to have had the freedom to pursue so many goals. For me, though, I felt trapped by my inability to change my circumstances. But change was right around the corner.

At age thirty-two, I found myself in the church that my parents were married in thirty-five years before, making vows to love a man—a man I adored—for the rest of my life. My dress was gorgeous and my hair and bouquet turned out exactly as I had hoped. We had a dessert buffet and danced into the night. And, because we had been having too much fun at our reception to eat, we found ourselves shoving cupcakes into our mouths on the rooftop of an airport parking structure before flying to a tropical island for a wonderful week-long honeymoon.

We were in our thirties, and didn't want to waste any time before starting a family. We felt that if we conceived a honeymoon baby, it would be just fine with us. Granted, we would prefer to get the thank you notes written before we got pregnant, but we were so looking forward to having a baby that we would have happily kept the wedding gifts in boxes if it meant more room for a crib and a rocking chair in our tiny home. As it turned out, we finished the thank you notes first.

By our first anniversary we were still not pregnant. We were beginning to feel grief. Well, actually, the accurate thing to say is that my husband experienced a twinge of sadness, overshadowed by deep hopefulness that we would one day conceive. I, on the other hand—the very holy pastor—had convinced myself that God was never going to give us a baby. I went to bed many nights sobbing—truly sobbing—that we were not pregnant. And, as it usually goes, almost all of my friends, and even my sister, announced pregnancies.

Other things in my life weren't going well either. On almost every front there was a source of pain. I felt trapped in my grief. I needed to shake things up. I couldn't just sit around waiting for those few days in the month when I could take a pregnancy test. So, for my husband's birthday, I bought him a puppy—a timid and sweet seven-week-old, fawn-colored pug. Still new, no one knew what a handful he was, so everyone offered to watch him, making it possible for us to take a spontaneous trip to visit dear friends of ours in England. Sometime between the purchase of our puppy and our getaway to England, we conceived a little traveler to take with us on our trip.

Our trip to England was marked with the joy of the pregnancy. Trip memories include taking pictures in front of Big Ben with hands on my still-non-existent baby bump, a mid-morning nap in a pub because I just couldn't stay awake any longer, plate after plate of French fries because it was all that sounded good to my queasy stomach, and lying in bed wide awake with jet lag chatting and dreaming with my husband about our baby.

It was the holiday season, and it was the perfect time for a pregnancy in so many ways. We got to announce our good news to our families at holiday celebrations. Additionally, Advent—the liturgical season of waiting for the fulfillment of God's promise—meant so much to us. And a side bonus was that I was able to eat as many Reese's Christmas trees as I wanted, and when a little baby bump did emerge in January, I imagined that everyone just chalked it up to holiday weight. I could be wrong about that though.

As a campus minister, I was living my life in the public eye. Because we have over five thousand undergraduates at the university, it is often the case that when my husband and I go out to dinner, students recognize me but I won't necessarily recognize them. And, in our worship services, our venue is so large that my face and body are projected onto a giant screen so everyone can see my facial expressions and body (this certainly has its drawbacks). Living in the public eye has never been extremely comfortable for me. I do not share my deepest feelings with large groups of people or total strangers. I am warm and friendly, but somewhat private. Living in a public role while I was pregnant was scary. Many of my friends had suffered miscarriages during their first pregnancies, and I feared that would be my story too. So, even though I shared the news of our pregnancy with friends, students, and coworkers, I didn't mention my pregnancy from the pulpit until I was midway through my pregnancy—at which point it was obvious anyway.

The students were thrilled with the news, and I was blessed by their care and love for me in those months of pregnancy. A few of them decorated my office with blue and pink streamers. When we learned that we would be having a boy, my student leader team threw me a surprise baby shower with all blue foods to celebrate our fun news. And, when I would cross campus, male and female students alike—those I knew and those I didn't know—would yell to me, "Hey, congratulations! How are you feeling?" Even on my end-of-the-year evaluations for the biblical studies class I was teaching, a few students wrote comments like, "Enjoyed the class. So excited about Jamie's baby." I found that most of my pastoral counseling appointments would begin with questions about my pregnancy. And so began the integrated life of motherhood and pastoring, and I found joy in experiencing pregnancy in the context of a loving Christian community.

Ten days before my thirty-fifth birthday, I waddled into an operating room rolling my IV stand along beside me. Two nurses helped me to heave my gigantic body onto the operating table. Thirty minutes later, the C-section would be over and my husband and I would meet our son—our beloved son—for the very first time. Our recovery room would be peaceful with a view of a garden, quiet hymns playing on my iPod, vases of congratulatory flowers around our room, and family members nearby to swoon over our beautiful newborn. In the weeks to come, friends would drop off meals, text messages and emails would convey excitement and prayers for our little family, cards and gifts would arrive in our mailbox, we'd watch a steady stream of the London Olympics, and everyone would give us space to adjust to life together.

The Similar Work of Pastoring and Mothering

I grew up in a church tradition in which pastors were referred to by their first names (not "Pastor Chris" but "Chris"; not "Rev. Sarah" but "Sarah"). However, in recent years, I have developed an appreciation for the titles "Father" or "Mother," which some church traditions use to refer to their priests or pastors. Those titles used to sound extremely formal to me. And though they are still a bit foreign to me, I have come to appreciate the loving and guiding role that is assumed in such a title.

The role of the campus minister is an interesting one. I know that I am not, and do not wish to be, thought of as a mother to my students—that role belongs to someone else. I do believe, however, that there is a strong similarity between the roles of pastor and mother. A minister is one who nurtures souls with the hope of the Gospel and is concerned with the spiritual well-being and development of those to whom God has called her to serve—a spiritual mother for her congregation.

My own mother is a pastor, so for me, the image of pastor and mother are naturally intertwined. Even in the years when she did not hold a professional position as a minister, she was gifted as one and pastored everyone she came across. I saw her use small talk as an opportunity to dive into more substantial conversations about soul care and spiritual formation. Even as a young child, I loved telling her things because she would listen deeply and ask thoughtful questions. She would correct me in a way that no one else could; she could motivate me, make me feel remorseful, speak truths to me, encourage me, and remind me of my true identity in my most vulnerable moments. She had an inspiring collection of books about God and was always sharing their ideas. These roles that I saw in her—teacher, spiritual director, pastoral counselor, and exhorter—are commonly associated with pastoral ministry.

A pastor must be engaged—emotionally, mentally, and spiritually—in order to be effective.

Pastor and theologian Eugene Peterson says,

> The one piece of mail certain to go unread into my wastebasket is the letter addressed to the 'busy pastor.' . . . 'The poor man,' we say, 'He's so devoted to his flock; the work is endless, and he sacrifices himself so unstintingly.' But the word *busy* is the symptom not of commitment but of betrayal. It is not devotion but defection. The adjective *busy* set as a modifier to *pastor* should sound to our ears like *adulterous* to characterize a wife or *embezzling* to describe a banker. It is an outrageous scandal, a blasphemous affront. Hilary of Tours

diagnosed our pastoral busyness as irreligiosa sollicitudo pro Deo, a blasphemous anxiety to do God's work for him.[3]

Author Henri Nouwen says, "Christian leaders cannot simply be persons who have well-informed opinions about the burning issues of our time. Their leadership must be rooted in the permanent, intimate relationship with the incarnate Word, Jesus, and they need to find there the source for their words, advice, and guidance."[4] When I am so rushed that I see my students as an obstacle to bypass en route to a meeting, or when my mind is so occupied with tasks that I miss a large part of what is said in a pastoral counseling session, or when I forget that God is with me and the work is his, I have missed what it means to pastor.

The same is true as a parent. My friend recounts a time when she was nursing her six-month-old daughter, and was checking her emails on her iPhone while she nursed the baby. The baby kept swatting at the phone. As my friend reflects on the experience, she says it was as if the baby was saying, "Put your phone away; pay attention to me." Of course multitasking is a survival skill of parents, and if done well can enable a parent to live an integrated life. However, just as a pastor loses his or her sharpness by being frazzled, burnt out, and half-listening, mothering loses its effectiveness if always done with the glow of a computer screen reflecting off her face or a cell phone attached to her ear, or if the child spends a large part of his or her life in a car seat with nothing but radio top hits attending to the developmental process. Both roles—those of pastor and mother—require maintaining focus and presence of mind and heart, while simultaneously juggling the pressing needs of numerous people.

Subsequently, in the role of pastor, one is trying to guide and nurture a congregation in such a way that they take ownership of their faith, that they don't need to be spoon-fed any longer, but that they will seek out the Lord themselves and serve God willingly rather than out of a sense of obligation. Eugene Peterson states,

> As a pastor, I don't like being viewed as nice but insignificant. I bristle when a high-energy executive leaves the place of worship with the comment, "This was wonderful, Pastor, but now we have to get back

to the real world, don't we?"... Then I remember that I am subversive. My long-term effectiveness depends on my not being recognized for who I really am. If he realized that I actually believe the American way of life is doomed to destruction, and that another kingdom is right now being formed in secret to take its place, he wouldn't be at all pleased. . . . That is why I am a pastor, to introduce people to the real world and train them to live in it.[5]

In motherhood, developing the child's independence is an ongoing objective: give the baby tummy-time so that he can learn to crawl. Let go of the baby while she holds onto the couch so she can practice standing. Entice the baby with his favorite objects so that he will be drawn away from the electrical cords.

In both of these roles, pastor and mother, there is the need to keep directing people away from harm, while encouraging them to grow. In both roles, a sense of ownership needs to be imparted—he cannot be forced to grow in faith, it must be his own idea; she cannot be forced to crawl, it must be her own desire. He cannot be kept away from temptation simply with a word; he must make the decision himself with counsel that affirms his correct choice. She must be kept out of harm's way and focused in another direction until she is mature enough to understand that electrical cords should not be chewed on. In both cases, there is a need for guidance that allows for freedom.

As new parents, my husband and I are just beginning the process of deciding the things that will be important in our family, even if they are countercultural—the kind of language that will be permitted in our home, the frequency with which the television will be on, how we respond to the poor in our world, how we will teach our son to pray, and how we will observe holy days. My campus ministry colleagues and I face the very same questions as we think about nurturing the souls of the students with whom we have been entrusted. Which words and stories will be a part of the language of our Christian community? How much value does our community ascribe to technology and media? How should our community respond to the poor in our world and to cultural norms of consumption? What does prayer look like in our Christian community? How do we celebrate holy days in a way that worships God?

The roles of pastor and mother are similar in that they require pushing back against cultural norms to create a reality that speaks of something else—something deeper, more significant, and more life-giving. All the while, those in our care, who are invited to live within the counterculture we are trying so desperately hard to convey, are often squawking back, "I don't want to do it this way. I want to be like the others. Why do we have to do things differently? Why can't we be like them?" There is a prophetic element to these roles of pastor and mother that is challenging, and enormously important.

As I have fed my baby, I have often thought of the similarity of motherhood and pastoring in the simplicity of the task of feeding others. Jesus says, "Feed my sheep,"[6] and that task makes up a large part of a pastor's work. At the university where I work, students are required to attend a chapel service three times a week. The worship services vary in content, some including messages from popular outside speakers or from beloved in-house faculty, and others with one of our own campus pastors preaching a part of our sermon series. Our pastoral team has sometimes joked that we are "the vegetables" of the chapel meal—we bring the necessary nourishment; we aren't the flashy or exciting ones like some of our outside chapel speakers who are more like "the dessert" of the chapel meal. We are their pastors, the ones who know which vitamins and minerals are needed for a balanced diet because we are with the students day in and day out. We know their weaknesses and fears. We know them, love them, and care about their well-being. So regardless of whether they want what we are serving, we care about them deeply enough to responsibly tend to their nourishment to the best of our ability.

Similarly, for the mother of a newborn baby, nourishing her child is also a great deal of her work. As Barbara Brown Taylor describes in her book, *The Preaching Life*,

> While I was mulling it over, I spent some time with my new god-daughter Madeline. . . . Watching her nurse one day, I saw that her mother was truly her food, the body and blood from which her own flesh had been made and from which she daily accepted her life as a

matter of course. "He who eats my flesh and drinks my blood abides in me, and I in him" (John 6:56).[7]

To nourish these dear ones is a holy task and one central to both roles.

A final observation I will make about the similarity of motherhood and pastoring is that in neither case is there a cookie-cutter model for how the role should look. Some pastors are excellent preachers, but terrible at leading an organization. Other pastors are fantastic at biblical study, but are terrible listeners. Others are great with elderly congregants, but are terrible with middle schoolers. No pastor is exceptional in every category that could potentially fall under the umbrella of "pastoral work." Each pastor has unique ways that God will choose to use her or his gift set.

In the same way, there are a thousand different ways healthy motherhood can look. There is not one lovely model that fits everyone—not even among Christians. Some mothers keep Pinterest stocked with brilliant ideas for creative parenting; other mothers have no time for social media because they are working three jobs in order to keep their children fed. Some mothers come to parenthood while they are still children themselves; other mothers spent decades dreaming of a baby. Some mothers adopt their children. Some mothers sit on the sidelines of a soccer field, while other mothers sit at the side of a hospital bed. Like pastoring, there is not one perfect way that mothering looks. The important thing is nurturing those entrusted to one's care.

Certainly the jobs of motherhood and pastor are not identical to one another—there are significant differences. A mother may not have a faith—the single most important factor of the pastoral life. A pastor may prefer not to be with children—something that is essential for a mother. I am not saying that motherhood and pastoring are identical roles. I am, however, identifying that in my own life, I have a sense of doing similar work in both roles, but for two different families—the family my husband and I are building, and the family of God.

Soul Care for the Caregiver

In the Old Testament of the Bible, Isaiah 40:11 says of God, "He tends his flock like a shepherd: He gathers the lambs in his arms and carries them close to his heart; he gently leads those that have young."[8] This last line is the one that has spoken to me lately: "He gently leads those that have young." I picture a large, haggard sheep, slowly ambling along at the back of the herd, recovering from the work of birth, her new baby close by her side. I picture myself, shortly after my C-section, only able to walk with assistance and at a very slow pace, my baby always in sight. I picture a loving God who knows how to care for a mother, and who gives her special nurturing and care. In fact, in Matthew 23:37, Jesus likens himself to a mother hen: "How often have I desired to gather your children together as a hen gathers her brood under her wings."[9] What joy comes in knowing that God understands the heart of a mother. And yet, many Christian women in the throes of parenting young children place extreme expectations on themselves in every category of life—including the spiritual life. Could it be that what God is looking for from a young mother is different than we imagine? Could it be that God wants to care for the mother *while* she is caring for her young? Perhaps God is not looking for a bifurcated life that separates the ordinary from the holy, the tasks of motherhood from the whisper of the Holy Spirit. As Dallas Willard says, "The secret to a strong, healthy, and fruitful ministerial life lies in how we work *with* God."[10]

It has only been six months since my son left my womb. During his precious first days, I was on maternity leave and he and I were together all day, every day. We spent those days nursing, snuggling, walking, and napping. I was the leading expert on his day-to-day experience. I expected those first days, weeks, months, to be hard—to be horrible. I had heard and seen the horror stories that so many of my beloved friends had endured—colicky babies, postpartum depression, breast infections, babies who wouldn't nurse, babies who wouldn't sleep, and babies who had to stay at the hospital long after the mother was discharged. I assumed this would be my experience as well. But, oddly, when I returned to work and colleagues and friends asked me how my maternity leave had been, I used this descriptor, "It was sabbathy." When I admitted to my staff, upon returning to work two weeks before Thanksgiving, that my fourteen-week maternity leave at the busiest time of our work cycle had been "sabbathy," one of my colleagues, who was also a mother, protectively interjected, "That was NOT my experience, and I don't think that is the experience of most women!" And certainly, she was right; for many women, those months are difficult.

What made my maternity leave so rich was a combination of factors. For one, the pace of my ministry life in the seven preceding years had been extraordinarily intense. A normal week included two to three late nights at work on top of the highly scheduled, very full workday. Because of the fullness and intensity of my workdays, my sermons were planned at night after my husband went to bed or in the dark of the early morning. Most mornings, though, I would wake up and know that I was already behind schedule, there were hundreds—literally hundreds—of unanswered emails in my inbox. There were stacks of papers on my desk that needed attention, a waiting list of people to meet with, and the lingering sense that I wasn't doing enough.

During my maternity leave, there was nothing on my schedule except to give my attention and my love to my child. There was a synchronization of my heart and my time. What I needed to do was also what I wanted to do, which had so often not been the case in my work days—the urgent often eclipsing the important. During my maternity leave, there was little else competing for my time. And I should add here that I guarded my time with my baby like a hawk, knowing the potential for that time to be robbed from us. Once those early days of meal deliveries were over, I only saw a few friends. I delayed writing and speaking projects until well after I went back to work. I said "no" to almost every invitation that came my way—work-related and personal. I counted this time as exceptionally precious and would only fill it with things that would not compete with my deep desire to soak up every sweet moment of my son's presence.

What made these months reminiscent of Sabbath were the quiet and the peace. My soul was full of joy. I was not rushed. In those early months of motherhood, multitasking was not an option. My baby needed my full attention. His body was floppy and he needed to be carefully supported. I needed to be present. I couldn't plan in advance. I had to live in the moment. I couldn't project what my baby would need in a week or two, and I couldn't anticipate my own recovery, emotions, or mothering skills beyond today. For someone who has become accustomed to an academic calendar and can always anticipate events a year in advance, this freedom to live in the moment was a joyful new experience. There was space and time to appreciate the miracle of my son's very existence.

Years ago, I asked a friend of mine who is also a pastor how she juggled her responsibilities as mother and pastor. Her response was stunning to me: "I find that motherhood helps me to be a better pastor." At the time, as a single woman, I couldn't imagine that what she said was true. I had heard the horror stories of motherhood, and her words didn't seem consistent with those stories. I couldn't imagine how much more fatiguing and full life would be with added people in my home.

Before I had a family of my own, I had developed rich habits for soul care. I would begin each morning with Scripture reading over a cup of coffee. I would close each evening in the quiet of my lovely, clean, and feminine bedroom journaling prayers. I had scheduled time each month to take a day at a nearby retreat center to be with God and commit my work to God's care and direction. I would attend campus ministers' conferences with regularity so that I could be refreshed by fellowship and enjoy worshipping with other like-minded colleagues. These rhythms of the soul were ones I greatly enjoyed and looked forward to, and ones that I look forward to resuming in the future. However, for now, new marriage and parenting an infant have altered my soul care rhythms.

Morning no longer begins when the coffee pot chirps and the alarm clock buzzes. Now, the fusses of a hungry baby are my wake-up call, and the appointed time varies from morning to morning. These morning moments are now among the only three hours in which I will be with my baby during the day, and need to be savored. As a pastor, I believe that time with the Lord is essential. Prayer is a central component to all pastoral work. As Henri Nouwen says,

> If there is any focus that the Christian leader of the future will need, it is the discipline of dwelling in the presence of the One who keeps asking us, "Do you love me? Do you love me? Do you love me?" It is the discipline of contemplative prayer. Through contemplative prayer we can keep ourselves from being pulled from one urgent issue to another and from becoming strangers to our own and God's heart.

Contemplative prayer keeps us home, rooted and safe, even when we are on the road, moving from place to place, and often surrounded by sounds of violence and war. Contemplative prayer deepens in us the knowledge that we are already free, that we have already found a place to dwell, that we already belong to God, even though everything and everyone around us keeps suggesting the opposite.[11]

And for now, this looks different than it did before and utilizes a spiritual discipline called "praying the hours." Praying the hours means letting daily routines act as cues for prayer. Adele Ahlberg Calhoun describes praying the hours, or fixed-hour prayer, this way in her *Spiritual Disciplines Handbook*:

Jesus learned to pray in the traditional Hebrew way. In the morning he prayed the Shema: 'Hear O Israel: The Lord our God, the Lord is one' (Deuteronomy 6:4) as well as a series of blessings known as the *tephilla*. In the afternoon the *tephilla* was prayed again. Evening prayer was identical to morning prayer but included private petitions. Like David, who prayed seven times a day (Psalm 119:164), and Daniel, who prayed three times a day (Daniel 6:10), Jesus and the Jews of his day prayed at set hours of the day. It was a devout Jew's habit to go to the temple at the sixth and ninth hour (noon and three o'clock). After Jesus' death, his disciples continued to pray at fixed hours of the day (Acts 3:1; 10:3; 9, 30). This custom of praying at set daily intervals quickly became part of the early church's rhythm of prayer. The Didache, an early manual of Christian practices, encouraged believers to pray the Lord's prayer three times daily (Didache 8.3). Given this history, it is quite understandable how the early church fathers would develop patterns for praying Scripture at fixed hours that integrated rhythms of prayer and work.[12]

In addition to fixed-hour prayer, I have also found that while I am nursing, I have windows of time in my work that I never had before. I have a physical call to soul care. During my work day, even if I want to stay at a meeting, even if a conversation seems essential, my body must withdraw to a quiet place to create food for my baby. And, I have found that in these months of nursing, my work has benefited greatly from the margins of quiet space. In the same way that my baby and I need to be together for a feeding every few hours, so it is with my soul, my need to reconnect with God throughout each day. To come away from my work, from the demands, from the expectations, to sit in a private space where I can quiet my heart and be with God, is a life-giving practice that motherhood has added to my work life. Now it should be mentioned that I do not always use pumping or nursing time to sit in meditation on the Scriptures or in prayer for others. Often I check emails, or pay bills, or make to-do lists, or eat my lunch, but these minutes are protected time. I am alone. There is space there for me to quiet my heart, care for my soul, attend to my own well-being, and attend to things that are important—smack dab in the middle of pastoring and motherhood—if I choose to use it.

Additionally, I have found that because time is more limited in my off-hours than it was before, I need to be more purposeful about my work hours. If I am hungry for Scripture, there are about a hundred opportunities in a day for me not only to nourish my own soul, but also the souls of others. If I am attentive to the cues of my soul, the care I give it may just end up feeding the masses at the same time. As a single person, I was, for the most part, diligent about reading Scripture and praying on my own time, so sometimes I would use meeting times or class times to attend to tasks. But now, I find that I must make the most of the moment I am in, and not save important things for later. If I am feeling hurried, chances are my staff is feeling it as well. If I am feeling overwhelmed with all I have to do, my students are probably having a similar experience. I must use myself as a gauge to monitor the needs of my community. As I like to say to my staff, "Plan an event that you would want to go to" or "Hire a leader that you would want to follow." The same is true with the spiritual life. If I want to have a few moments of contemplative prayer in the middle of the day, I must facilitate that for the group I am with. If I want to read a psalm, then I must read it for the group I am leading. So far, in my short experience of integrating my pastoral life and my mothering life, I am finding that this works. It was the impetus for an afternoon retreat with my staff, in which I got to spend two hours alone with the Lord and an hour praying with beloved colleagues. It was the catalyst for *lectio divina* during a final New Testament class before Holy Week, in which we got to hear the resurrection story read multiple times and reflect on it quietly. It was a secret motivation behind a student event to a favorite service site in Los Angeles, a site in which I got to experience the joy of serving the hungry in my community. As Shawchuck and Heuser say in their book *Leading the Congregation: Caring for Yourself While Serving the People*: "When it comes to forming the congregation in the Spirit of Christ, two things of importance stand out in bold relief: First the pastor must be on the journey; the pastor cannot lead where he or she has never been. Second, the congregation will not journey beyond the pastor; the congregation will not venture where the pastor is not leading."[13] As a spiritual leader, I have the opportunity to take care of my own soul while, at the same time, teaching others to do the same.

So now, just months into the experience of motherhood alongside pastoring, I would wholeheartedly agree with my friend's words; motherhood has made me a better pastor—a pastor who tries to savor the present moment as an opportunity to feed souls, a pastor who tries to be more keenly aware of God's presence in her midst, a pastor who prays the hours and enjoys maternal margins in her day.

Conclusion

I am not a seasoned mother who has years and years of stories to tell. I am figuring it out for the first time. I'm doing things now that I know I won't have the energy for in the long run (like making my own baby food and photographing every sweet moment.) As when my husband and I fell in love, I suddenly developed a host of positive habits energized by new love and a desire to be a better version of myself. Ultimately though, some of the unrealistic—albeit, great—habits faded. Our relationship matured from the initial exuberance to impress one another and became a place of safety in which we could be our true selves, not dependent on pristine habits and routines. As a recent parent, I see myself doing it again—picking up great habits, which will fade as we develop our family culture. My real maternal self will replace my best intentions and noble desires to get it right, and that too will be a gift to my son.

As I write, I write with the optimistic perspective of a new mother and as a veteran campus minister who has settled in and outlived the difficult early years of a new position. My positivity on both counts may be annoying to those who have parented longer than I have or to those who are still facing the uphill battle of trying to fit within a community. I realize that I have an agreeable baby, a husband who is my parenting partner, a ministry context with a theology I can affirm, and colleagues I enjoy—these are unusual gifts and have certainly shaped my experience. Nevertheless, what strikes me most at this point in my journey as a mother and as a campus minister is just how precious time is.

We speak of time—how to balance responsibilities in light of the shortage of time, how to make the most of the lives we have been given, and how not to waste a moment of it. Ash Wednesday whispers, "From dust you have come and to dust you have returned," and my tendency is to yell back, "Dang! I forgot my cell phone. This day is lost!" Ash Wednesday chides, "You are frail, child of God, you are frail." I want to scream, "I'm in control! I've got it all under control!" Ash Wednesday pauses, "You need a Savior!" I want to grumble, "I'm a mother! I'm a pastor! They are depending on me!" But, for the mother who pastors, and for the pastor who mothers, there is time.

As one of my favorite psalms, Psalm 46, testifies, even when time doesn't slow down, when things are falling apart and trouble has come, God is still present. God speaks within the chaos, the disasters, and the battles.[14] While we juggle unhappy babies and heavy grocery bags, as we put final touches on a sermon from the fast lane of the freeway—God is with us. When babies are sick and crisis strikes our community, God is our strength. In our ordinary days, God is Living Water, refreshing us and dwelling within us. From the early morning cry of the baby, God will be our help. When arguments break out with a spouse and conflict ravages our community, God will be our peace. And, *in the midst* of all of the turmoil of life—not separate from it, but right in the middle of it—God invites us to be still. As mothers pastor and pastors mother, both with a commitment to care for those whom God has entrusted to them, God will care for us and unimaginable gifts will be found in the mess of the ordinary, *because* the Lord Almighty is *with* us.

Discussion Questions

1. The author discusses the similarities she has experienced in the leadership roles of mother and pastor; is this comparison a new idea to you? What similarities and differences do you see between these roles? Why don't you think that this parallel is more commonly drawn in evangelical American culture?

2. The writer talks about ways in which the leadership roles of ministry and motherhood have benefited each other in her life. What other advantages do you see that these roles could potentially bring to each other?

3. While comparing the roles of mother and pastor, the author often used the word "mother" instead of "parent" in cases where either might have applied. Why is it particularly significant to use the word "mother" instead of "parent" within this comparison?

4. The author compares her specific roles as minister and mother. Which leadership ideas included in this chapter do you think translate beyond ministry to leadership roles in general?

5. How did this chapter about balancing the leadership roles of ministry and motherhood correspond with what you have experienced or witnessed?

Notes

[1] Sarah Sentilles, *A Church of Her Own: What Happens When a Woman Takes the Pulpit* (Boston: Mariner Books, 2009). In her book, Sentilles says, "We Protestants like to pretend sexism does not exist in our churches, and yet ordained ministry continues to be one of the most male-dominated of all professions. Even though the ministry was one of the first professions to encounter proposals to admit women, it was one of the last actually to do so, and the acceptance of women clergy is far from universal or uncontested today" (4).

[2] Nicola Hoggard Creegan and Christine D. Pohl, *Living on the Boundaries: Evangelical Women, Feminism, and the Theological Academy* (Downers Grove, Illinois: InterVarsity Press, 2005). As Pohl says, "Over the sixteen years of my teaching at Asbury Theological Seminary, I have seen many changes, but each year we also address the same issues again. With a new crop of students annually, with the move of several conservative denominations toward restricting women's leadership roles, and with the impact of the megachurch

movement and its generally conservative views of male and female roles, gender issues remain an important topic" (21). Continuing, Creegan and Pohl say, "Persons trained in theological and biblical studies are responsible for preparing the next generation of Christian thinkers and leaders, and questions of women's authority and legitimacy in the church are substantial" (22).

[3] Eugene Peterson, *The Contemplative Pastor: Returning to the Art of Spiritual Direction* (Grand Rapids: Eerdmans Publishing, 1993), 17–18.

[4] Henri Nouwen, *In the Name of Jesus: Reflections on Christian Leadership* (New York: The Crossroad Publishing Company, 1989), 31.

[5] Peterson, *The Contemplative Pastor*, 27–28.

[6] John 21:17 NRSV.

[7] Barbara Brown Taylor, *The Preaching Life* (Plymouth, United Kingdom: Cowley Publications, 1993), 78.

[8] Isaiah 40:11 NIV.

[9] Matthew 23:37 NRSV.

[10] Dallas Willard, *The Great Omission: Reclaiming Jesus's Essential Teachings on Discipleship* (New York: Harper One, 2006), 123.

[11] Nouwen, *In the Name of Jesus*, 29.

[12] Adele Ahlberg Calhoun, *Spiritual Disciplines Handbook: Practices That Transform Us* (Downers Grove, Illinois: InterVarsity Press, 2005), 224.

[13] Norman Shawchuck and Roger Heuser, *Leading the Congregation: Caring for Yourself While Serving the People* (Nashville: Abingdon Press, 1993), 126.

[14] Psalm 46 TNIV.

9

ESSENTIAL ELEMENTS OF LEADING AND PARENTING

PAMELA M. CHRISTIAN, PhD

"Success is where preparation and opportunity meet."
—Bobby Unser

B lessed with the gift of leadership, my professional leadership experience preceded and informed my parenting. My parental role and my career in higher education have both been extremely fulfilling and rewarding, and eventually the roles became mutually influential and complimentary. This synergy has allowed me to thrive, despite the related stress. In actuality, the stress of maintaining effectiveness in both roles simultaneously may be the cause of my productivity in both areas.

Serving in various institutional settings including public, private, faith-based universities, and community colleges has facilitated my professional, spiritual, and personal growth. The skills that fostered my progression and advancement throughout the past twenty-three years in academia informed my decision to decline a dream job offer I received.

My journey in higher education administration began as an advocate for first-generation, low-income, and underrepresented students within federal Trio Programs—services and programs for disadvantaged students. I transitioned from serving as an educational equity advocate to a student affairs professional when I accepted a position in residence life. With encouragement from my mentors within the academy, I left student affairs for academic affairs. After working seven years for a dean of graduate studies, I assumed a new role as an administrative faculty member working directly for a provost. In that role, I resumed service as an advocate for educational equity, addressing issues in both academic and student affairs. As I grew in the position, the provost reframed the role as an assistant, then associate provost. At the conclusion of seven years in that role, I was offered a provost position at a large urban community college. I was honored and excited by the offer to serve in a capacity that represented the perfect blend of my experience and interests, and an outstanding opportunity to advance my professional career. It prompted me to deeply examine my life, goals, and priorities, and resulted in my thoughtfully considered decision to decline the offer. Four years later, I don't regret my decision that perplexed many of my colleagues. I'm now enjoying my transition from full-time university administration to a full-time faculty position.

This self-initiated descent on the hierarchical ladder provided three benefits representing the most significant and core values in my life: God, family, and the most effective utilization of my gifts and skills. The self-examination process initiated by the dream job offer resulted in an intimate time of dialogue with the Lord as I revisited his purpose and plan for my life. This time of contemplative prayer and reflection was amazing, humbling, and defining. I was amazed by my own testimony of his goodness, humbled by the evidence of his love and grace, and defined again as his servant. My increased availability to my high schooler was a wonderful and welcomed consequence of my decision to say yes to God's timing, and no (or at least not now) to career advancement. Assuming a higher level of leadership and transitioning institutions as my pre-teen navigated middle school in preparation for high school was not in his best interest. As my parental responsibilities superseded my professional aspirations, particularly as a single parent, my transition to a faculty role cultivated a deepened understanding of my academic discipline and proved advantageous for my son's academic advancement.

"A good parent is a better leader, manager and citizen."[1] I've been blessed to enjoy both parenthood and professional leadership. While I don't frequently consider how one informs the other, as I reflect on the interrelated skill sets required to thrive in each, I realize that quality parenting and effective leadership share many characteristics. Most experienced leaders have benefitted from education and training in preparation for various roles and responsibilities. Although many parents don't take advantage of parental training opportunities prior to assuming this lifetime commitment, fully engaging in the role provides on-the-job leadership development. In a discussion of Ann Crittenden's book, *If You've Raised Kids, You Can Manage Anything*, Charles Lauer explains that "anyone who raises kids develops skills that can transfer to the workplace."[2] Crittenden identified four categories of transferable skills including multitasking, interpersonal skills, human capabilities, and habits of integrity. Reflecting on experiences within public and private institutions of higher education, public service organizations, and most importantly, my experience raising my son as a divorced single mother, I concur with Crittenden's list of transferable skills.

In this chapter I will share four characteristics common to professional leadership development programs that parallel skill sets demonstrated by effective parents, mother-leaders in particular. Effective time management, problem solving, crisis management, and communication skills are essential for parents and leaders. This chapter will review these parallel skill sets utilized in leading organizations and in parenting children to emerge as independent adults.

"The increasing numbers of women in leadership positions and women in academia, brought about by dramatic changes in American society, have fueled the scholarly interest in the study of female leaders."[3] It is my hope that this book, and this chapter within the book, will advance the scholarship related to mother-leaders.

Effective Time Management

The varied competing demands and priorities of life create constraints for the finite number of minutes and hours in a day. Various nonprofit organizations and businesses emphasize the incorporation of strategies for effective time management to ensure institutional and individual success. The American Association of Community Colleges (AACC), an association representing "nearly 1,200 two-year, associate degree-granting institutions and more than

13 million students"[4] published a list of six competencies for community college leaders. The second competence focuses on resource management and asserts that effective community college leaders will employ time management skills.[5] The relationship between effective time management and effective leadership is essential as emphasized in several leadership institutes I have attended, including the American Council on Education's Fellows Program, the Harvard Institute for Management and Leadership in Education, the Lakin Institute for Mentored Leadership, and the Oxford Roundtable on Women in Leadership. Each of these professional development opportunities are designed for higher education leaders and are recommended for women aspiring to advance their careers in academe. Time management and other essential skills for effectiveness in leadership are explored.

Researchers have also examined issues related to effective time management strategies. In a study on the "Contextual Influences on Superintendents' Time Usage," Jones and Howley "used allocation of time as a proxy measure of superintendents' attention to certain roles."[6] Their work highlights that leaders function in many capacities simultaneously and must determine how to allocate attention to each. In the case of school superintendents, the functions identified include managerial, educational, and political roles. For parents, mothers in particular, the multifold role, among other titles, includes being a teacher, friend, provider, comforter, disciplinarian, and caregiver. Consider the complexities of time allocation for the professional executive who is also a mother. Cheung and Halpern address the challenges professional working mothers experience in "Women at the Top: Powerful Leaders Define Success as Work + Family in a Culture of Gender." While the authors note that "the choice for highly successful women has been clear: Choose either a baby or a briefcase," they share lessons from women who "refused to make such a choice and succeeded at the top of their professions with children and other family care responsibilities."[7] One characteristic identified by these "dually successful top women leaders" was the propensity to "make more time" by becoming experts in multitasking.

In his bestselling book, *The Seven Habits of Highly Effective People*, Stephen Covey captures the best thinking in the area of time management in a single thought: "Organize and execute around priorities. That phrase represents the evolution of three generations of time management theory, and how to best do it is the focus of a wide variety of approaches and materials."[8] With a plethora of time management resources available, whether physically tangible or electronic, the best tools are those that work for each individual. Some tools actually consume more time than they save because of their intricacy. The greater the intensity demanded by each area of responsibility, the more significant mastery of effective allocation of time or the ability to create more time is required. Regardless of the role, Covey's challenge to organize and execute around priorities ultimately determines success or failure for leaders. Despite the utilization of the best tools available, leaders may be unable to address every matter that requires attention. His concept of addressing what matters most, or keeping "first things first," assures that what may be left undone is not an essential or critical item to the organization or individual. "Effective management is putting first things first. While leadership decides what 'first things' are, it is management that puts them first, day-by-day, moment-by-moment. Management is discipline, carrying it out."[9]

Mothers who also lead in workplace environments tend to master the disciplines of time and self-management. From Crock-Pots to cabinet meetings, homework to human resources, and potty training to performance evaluations, mother-leaders are amazing multitaskers and organizers. Some mothers choose to provide leadership at home until their children attend school, and then engage the workplace. Others utilize childcare resources, which allow them to lead both at home and in an employment situation. We use digital, physical, mental, and human resources to plan, implement, and evaluate. These tools include lists, calendars, smartphones, tablets, personal assistants, nannies, family helpers, and other resources. First Lady Michelle Obama moved her mother to the White House to care for her children during her husband's service as President of the United States. She exemplifies the twenty-first century mother-leader, except that most of us don't enjoy the significant number of assistants available to whom recurrent and special tasks may be delegated. As in professional leadership scenarios, multitasking and creative problem solving are a part of the daily experience of motherhood. Exercising these two essential skills provides noteworthy preparation and training for effective leadership.

Problem Solving

Parents, especially mothers, often serve as the first teachers their children encounter. We provide hands-on instruction for challenging tasks such as tying shoestrings, flossing, and making beds. Additionally, we model inductive and deductive problem-solving strategies to address complex matters such as managing conflicting calendars and limited household budgets for ever-increasing expenses. We also assist with homework assignments and class projects. Customarily without formal training or intentionality, mothers frequently employ strategies that align with theoretical frameworks articulated in academic and management literature. In their seminal work, *Reframing Organizations: Artistry, Choice, and Leadership,* Harvard professor Lee Bolman and University of Southern California retired professor Terrence Deal draw on the social science disciplines of sociology, psychology, anthropology, and political science to "identify ideas that work in practice."[10] Arguably, few experts are as knowledgeable as mothers regarding ideas that work in practice.

Bolman and Deal outline principles of examining effective leadership into four constructs, including the structural, human resource, political, and symbolic frames. The structural frame "demonstrates why organizations—from Harvard University to McDonald's—need different structures in order to be effective in their unique environments."[11] Mother-leaders enact the structural frame as they organize their homes, including their children's bedrooms, study, and play areas, to identify and nurture the natural gifts and abilities inherent within each of their children. Mothers are masters at creating living spaces, as captured by the adage "there's no place like home." Mother-leaders in the workplace bring these transferable skills with them, transforming professional environments into hospitable communities where allowed.

Bolman and Deal's human resource frame describes "how a manager's practices and assumptions about people can lead either to alienation and hostility, or to commitment and high motivation."[12] Mother-leaders who've parented teenagers are particularly adept with this dynamic. The physical and hormonal growth children experience as they transition to adulthood, in a society filled with temptations and all manner of evil, requires that the foundation of trust established in early childhood preserve the relationship between parents and their children. Intimately connected from conception, mothers know exactly how to motivate their children, and keenly adapt and create techniques during each stage of their development. This sagacity fosters an intuitiveness that is often reflected in the sensitivities mother-leaders demonstrate to others in professional environments. John Maxwell articulates this skill as "Informed Intuition" and asserts that "leaders see everything with a leadership bias, and as a result, they instinctively, almost automatically, know what to do. You can see this read-and-react instinct in all great leaders."[13] Although Maxwell provides examples of coaches and quarterbacks enacting this technique, the intuition of mothers is undeniable.

The political frame discussed in the *Reframing Organizations* text describes the processes by which a manager "illustrates basic skills of the constructive politician: diagnosing political realities, setting agendas, building networks, negotiating, and making choices that are both effective and ethical."[14] Anyone familiar with Parent Teacher Association (PTA) interactions with school districts and communities are probably aware of the political nature of the work involved. Oftentimes mothers provide the energy and momentum for PTA initiatives. The organization provides advocacy for all children while individual mothers engage similar activities within the PTA to ensure that their child's best interest is served.

Another example of mother-leaders functioning in the political frame is the 1980 incorporation of Mothers Against Drunk Driving (MADD), a nonprofit organization founded by Candy Lightner. Candy lost her daughter Cari in an accident caused by a drunk driver. By 2011, MADD employed a national staff in regional offices and 1,300 advocates who assisted over 60,000 survivors.[15] The third iteration of the organization's mission statement embodies the effectiveness of mother-leaders operating in the political frame: "Mothers Against Drunk Driving mobilizes victims and their allies to establish the public conviction that impaired driving is unacceptable and criminal, in order to promote corresponding public policies, programs and personal responsibility."[16]

The fourth and final construct in Bolman and Deal's work is the symbolic frame, which articulates how leaders "build a culture that bonds people in pursuit of a shared mission."[17] Among the elements included are the "myths, heroes, metaphors, stories, humor, play, rituals, and ceremonies."[18] These elements are extremely familiar to mothers who spend hours reading, watching, and emphasizing the principles communicated to their children in the cultural symbols provided through various mediums. Mothers use teachable moments facilitated by characters such as Dora the Explorer, Elmo, and the virtuous vegetables in Veggie Tales to teach cultural norms and morality to young children. Other cultural icons are also taught by mothers, such as the meaning of the red hexagon stop signs at crosswalks, and picture signs on the doors of public restrooms. These processes facilitate the acculturation of young people into the families and societies in which they live and learn. Comparably, mother-leaders are assets in organizations committed to a mission and vision based on their proclivity toward collaboration and cohesion, and effortless mastery of instruction.

In addition to utilizing the Four Frames outlined by Bolman and Deal, problem solving is also addressed in terms of employing data-driven frameworks. "Data-driven decision making is not new nor is the quest for using evidence in education to make decisions."[19] Many professions apply data-driven or evidence-based strategies to determine the best course of action for resolving problems. Across the globe, organizations administer Albert S. Humphrey's SWOT analysis in order to determine the Strengths, Weaknesses, Opportunities, and Threats of various potential scenarios. MindTools, an online career consulting service based in the United Kingdom, encourages professionals to apply the SWOT analysis in personal contexts as well to "develop your career in a way that takes best advantage of your talents, abilities and opportunities."[20]

Mothers operationalized the SWOT analysis technique decades before Humphrey's articulation of the concept. Before the Internet provided immediate access to medical reference material, mothers were assessing the symptoms and potential remedies for illnesses. The wisdom of mothers passed down from one generation to the next resolved many ailments with great success and minimal side effects. Mothers continue to engage the SWOT analysis process to decide the best options for purchases and people. Often, mothers will compare products to determine the best household appliances for their family situation. In addition, in protection of their children, mothers will informally apply the SWOT analysis to potential friends of their children, especially as they begin to date.

Steven Covey suggests another strategy for problem solving. He recommends identifying remedies that offer Win-Win solutions.

> Win-Win is a frame of mind and heart that constantly seeks mutual benefit in all human interactions. Win-Win means that agreements or solutions are mutually beneficial, mutually satisfying. With a Win-Win solution, all parties feel good about the decision and feel committed to the action plan. Win-Win sees life as a cooperative, not a competitive arena. [21]

As the mother of two, my mom frequently utilized this method to mediate conflicts between my brother and me when we were growing up. Inevitably, I'd complain to her from the backseat of the car that my brother was bothering me by making faces or touching me. She'd show no favoritism in her discipline as she told him to stop bothering me, with a follow-up directive for me to stop being a tattletale. Since both of us were reprimanded, Mom found a Win-Win. This is a familiar story to mothers with multiple children. It's also a common strategy mother-leaders incorporate in personnel disputes and other negotiations in professional environments. While not always possible, a mother's heart will find the Win-Win solution in any setting, if it exists.

As an admirer of Covey's work, I intentionally merged it with psychologist Gary Chapman's concept of the Five Love Languages to keep peace between my son and me now that he's a teenager. My peacekeeping framework integrates three of Covey's seven habits: Habit 2: Begin with the End in Mind; Habit 4: Think Win-Win; and Habit 5: Seek First to Understand, Then to Be Understood. I consider these alongside the two of Gary Chapman's five love languages that are most applicable to my son: Words of Affirmation, and Gifts. Our challenges seem to occur with more frequency during this season of his transition to manhood, and I'm stretched to exercise more patience than I was aware I possess. When conflict arises, I work diligently to consider my goals for him, attempt to understand his perspective, and determine how best to convey the message I need to give him. I'm mindful of Dr. Chapman's recommendation to parents to treat teens as teens.

The parents' efforts to verbally argue the teenager into submission are in reality pushing the teenager toward rebellion. Without realizing it, the parents are removing the teenager's emotional support system and replacing it with verbal warfare. . . . As parents, our intentions may be good, but the results are definitely bad. Unless we parents change course, we will most certainly end up with a rebellious teenager and often an estranged young adult.[22]

The physical energy required as I parented a very young boy evolved to intense emotional and mental energy parenting an emerging adult.

I experience similar exhaustion working through challenging situations with colleagues. However, I believe that this mental exhaustion is positive, healthy, and worthwhile. As Robert E. Quinn explains in his book, *Deep Change*, "Why, then, would anyone be willing to accept the pain that accompanies acts of transformational leadership? I suspect that such people have discovered that the pain of leadership is exceeded only by the pain of lost potential."[23] I prefer mental exhaustion to the risk of parent-induced rebelliousness in my teenager, or fostering a relationship in which we become estranged during his adult life. As a leader I'm committed to advancing the mission of my institution and department, as well as the cohesion and collaboration of my colleagues. Thus, both at home and in the workplace, I make the necessary efforts to engage problems and people with care.

Crisis Management

Mothers and leaders are required to respond in crisis situations, and rarely do such urgencies occur at opportune times. In his *New York Times* and *Wall Street Journal* bestseller, *The 21 Irrefutable Laws of Leadership*, John Maxwell explains, "the best leaders read and respond."[24] They assess the situation and respond appropriately and on time.

Early in my career in higher education, I served three years as Residence Life Coordinator. Included among my responsibilities were emergency preparedness, discipline, and supervision of paraprofessional staff. I didn't realize at the time that my training and subsequent training of others, particularly pertaining to emergency responsiveness, would remain with me for the remainder of my life. More than fifteen years after leaving Residence Life, I instinctively responded from my training rather than my emotion when I saw my son's bone sticking out of his arm. After I rushed to him from where I sat observing his karate class, I understood that he was seriously injured. I began delegating responsibilities to the staff, never considering that they did not work for me. They responded to my requests without hesitation. I instructed someone to carry him to the car, and someone else to gather his things as I rushed to my car and hurried to transport him to the emergency room. While he was in surgery, my emergency response adrenaline settled, and the emotional mom took control of the trained professional. I'm grateful for the positive impact of my professional training on my parenting, as well as the reciprocal impact of motherhood on my professional leadership accomplishments.

The ability to respond appropriately in a crisis is dependent on adequate preparation and planning before a crisis occurs. Not all crises are related to health and safety, and not all leaders are trained as emergency response professionals. Fortunately, most organizations have strategic plans that frequently include provisions for managing emergencies, and generally providing guidance for dealing with various situations that pose threats to their groups' success. The Association for Strategic Planning surveyed more than one thousand professionals from nonprofit organizations and found that "strategic planning has high impact on overall organizational success."[25]

Leaders generally embody and personify the mission and vision of an organization, and are usually significantly involved in the development and implementation of a strategic plan. The process of developing a strategic plan commonly involves participation from all segments of the organization. "An organization without a plan can be labeled as reactive, shortsighted, and rudderless."[26]

Families are organizations, although not customarily discussed within this context. As the leaders within families, parents frequently have thoroughly considered, although undocumented, strategic plans for themselves and their children. From the moment pregnancy is confirmed, mothers are known to begin planning for the arrival of their newborn. It is not uncommon for the lives of parents to completely change in order to accommodate children. Parental planning may include but is not limited to: changing or modifying residences in order to provide the appropriate structural space and educational opportunities, making provisions for the transportation of the newborn through the various stages of growth, and safety checking and baby-proofing the home environment. The typical, possibly stereotypical, model is for the mother to serve as the primary caretaker of the children while fathers focus on resource allocation and monetary matters. Regardless of the family structure, parents generally engage in planning strategically for the well-being of their children.

My assertion that motherhood provides professional development training is supported by an adage commonly heard in professional arenas describing a project or task assigned to a particular person. There is no ambiguity when an assignment is referred to as "your baby." The connotation suggests that a professional will accept responsibility and total commitment to the successful completion of the task, the way mothers care for their babies. With the wealth of literature and research pertaining to gender equity considerations in the workplace, it would be interesting to study whether this phrase is ascribed to projects assigned to both male and female professionals.

Communication Skills

Another parallel skill set shared by mothers and leaders is effective communication. As explained by three prominent public relations practitioners and scholars, communication is an important tool for leaders in building and sustaining communities and partnerships:

> Although some kind of communication takes place in all walks of life, effective communication doesn't just happen. It is the result of carefully planning the kind of information that needs to be disseminated, the particular audience that is to be reached, and the choice of tools that are best fitted for the job. The job itself is that of bringing about understanding, gaining acceptance, and stimulating supportive action for ideas or proposals.[27]

These competencies are so important to professionals in all careers and disciplines that colleges and universities throughout the world offer degree programs in communications. Opportunities to specialize in the study of communication exist at both the undergraduate and graduate levels. Doctoral degrees in communications are offered at premier universities both within and outside of the United States, including the University of Southern California, Columbia University, and the University of South Africa.

Although mother-leaders may not all possess doctoral degrees in communications, they are generally master communicators. Effective communication is critical to their success at home and in the workplace. The constant interaction with vastly different audiences requires a nuanced savvy that only skilled communicators can engage with excellence. As multilingual professionals, mother-leaders navigate between parental and professional responsibilities communicating appropriately and effectively in both arenas. Although they may speak only one recognized language, such as English, they are conversant in the language and vernacular of their discipline or profession, the subtleties of verbal and non-verbal communication of adults and young people, and the specific individual languages spoken by their supervisors, subordinates, and children.

Mothers are bilingual when their toddlers begin to speak. The primacy of the relationship heightens the mother's awareness and insight regarding matters concerning those they labored to birth. Despite the inability of others to translate the interesting sounds made by these precious little ones, their mothers understand completely. There's an intimacy between mothers and their children that transcends defined language. It's comical that the same pair may seem to forget how to communicate during the child's teenage years. Despite the discombobulating experience caused by growth hormones, mothers generally interpret the spoken and non-verbal languages of their children throughout their lives. Similarly, children understand both the words and heart of the language spoken by their mothers. They can interpret their mother's brand of gestures like the "stink eye."

Dr. Richard Heyman, professor of communication and education at the University of Calgary, outlines five principles of the Communication Ethic as a "foundation for communicating with children."[28] These principles include: 1) be involved, 2) make love the context, 3) listen more than talk, 4) withhold judgment, and 5) never give up. In reality, there are no perfect mothers. I imagine that most of us employ these principles to some extent, and some of them more than others depending on the timing and circumstances.

These principles were based on communication between parents and children; however, I've encountered their application by mother-leaders throughout my lifetime and professional career. While I am aware of many women who embody these characteristics, I will provide two examples from different industries to articulate the alignment of Dr. Heyman's principles of Communication Ethic to the prodigious performance of mother-leaders. These exemplars represent the fields of business and education.

Mrs. Hattie Johnson was my maternal grandmother, who lived from December 25, 1913, until she lost her battle with breast cancer on May 14, 1977. She was a small business owner, minister in a small Baptist church, mother of eleven, and grandmother of twenty-two. In each of these varied roles, she demonstrated the five principles of Communication Ethic to both children and adults: she was involved, made love the context, listened more than she spoke, withheld judgment, and never gave up.

Hattie's involvement in her business, church, and in the life of her family was commendable. The consistency of her character and the skills she modeled in each environment provided a phenomenal case study I had the honor of observing as her eldest granddaughter and persistent shadow. Neither of us realized at the time that she was in essence providing unrecompensed leadership development training. I watched her lovingly demand excellence in every aspect of the soul food café she and my grandfather owned in East Los Angeles. She actively taught the cooks and servers, selected the freshest produce and quality meats, and managed the fiscal affairs of the business. In the same way, she was involved in various church ministries and in the lives of her extremely large family. Despite the irrational requests of certain customers, the irritating recurrent bad habits of personnel (some of whom were her children), inconsistent Christ-like behavior among members of the church, and the drama that is inherent in family life, Hattie was loving, patient, and kind. Even in her anger she was appropriate and caring. If she knew someone, she loved them, and they knew it.

She demonstrated with perfection a concept I later studied while pursuing my master's degree in counseling. It is the phenomenon of unconditional positive regard as postulated by psychologist Carl Rogers.[29] Her business was financially viable because she valued people by listening effectively and with-holding judgment, irrespective of her conservative religious views. Customers, church congregants, and family members felt valued and sought time with her because they knew they would be heard, valued, and loved.

Similarly, Dr. Mary Spangler, the Chancellor of the Houston Community College District from 2007 to 2013, led with compassion and a deep regard for all people. Just as I shadowed and observed Hattie Johnson in her café, church, and home, I accompanied Dr. Spangler to board meetings, campuses within her district, community meetings, and social events. Unequivocally, she is one of the most dynamic leaders I've ever known. She took me under her tutelage as an American Council on Education Fellow, and provided me with an opportunity unlike any other in my career. As Chancellor of Houston Community College, she was responsible for more than 4,700 employees and 72,000 students.

> She has successfully led three of the largest, most diverse and complex urban institutions in the country. She served first as president of Los Angeles City College, the flagship institution of the Los Angeles Community College District, and then as chancellor of Oakland Community College, the largest community college in Michigan.[30]

While the international education community marvels at her professional accomplishments, I am also amazed and appreciative of her character, willingness to mentor, and her commitment to her husband and son.

Dr. Spangler is a master communicator and exemplifies the principles of the Communication Ethic. Shadowing her for a year, I observed her level of engagement and involvement in each of the six colleges within her district, thereby modeling the first principle: to be involved. During my fellowship she visited each campus frequently, and consistently interacted with each of the presidents and the rest of her leadership team, both individually and as a group. She was also very involved with her board of trustees, and available to faculty, staff, students, and community members.

Principle two of the Communication Ethic is to make love the context. Love is not customarily part of the leadership vernacular; however, it is a relevant concept for leaders. Dr. Spangler has a genuine regard for people and demonstrates her care in her approachable and kind demeanor. I admire her ability to be firm and direct without being demeaning, pejorative, or judgmental. She is a skilled listener and problem solver, and her responses to people and problems focus on relevant issues.

As an astute and effective listener, she illustrates the third principle: listen more than talk. While many professionals within and outside of her authority appreciate hearing her speak, she is an adroit listener. Watching her active listening followed by poignant and penetrating observations and solutions was inspiring. Her ability to promote accountability without fostering a community of fear was simply outstanding.

Mrs. Hattie Johnson and Dr. Mary Spangler illustrate transformative characteristics that allow mother-leaders to thrive in varied and multiple environments. Their exemplification of Dr. Heyman's Communication Ethic epitomizes transferrable skills available to all leaders willing to employ each of the five principles.

Leading and Parenting

"Success is where preparation and opportunity meet."[31] While the attention of loving mothers is often solely focused on effectively parenting their children, they are inadvertently participating in superlative leadership development training. The transferable skill sets demonstrated by devoted mothers, including effective time management, problem solving, crisis management, and communication skills, promote their competency as leaders. Mother-leaders benefit both their children and the organizations they lead by promoting their advancement and growth.

Discussion Questions

1. What leadership development training opportunities prepared you for your current professional role? How did they equip you for success?

2. Which of the essential elements of leading and parenting represent an area of strength for you: effective time management, problem solving, crisis management, or communication skills?
3. Which of the essential elements of leading and parenting represent a potential area in which additional training may improve your performance?
4. Consider the mother-leaders you know and identify the characteristics they demonstrate that promote the success of their organizations and children.
5. What, if any, adjustments will you implement to improve your leadership and parenting?

Notes

[1] Charles Lauer, "The Lessons of Parenting," *Modern Healthcare* 34.43 (2004): 36.

[2] Ibid.

[3] Peter G. Northouse, *Leadership Theory and Practice,* 5th ed. (Thousand Oaks, California: Sage Publications, Inc., 2010), 301.

[4] American Association of Community Colleges, "Who We Are," accessed April 2, 2013, http://www.aacc.nche.edu/About/Who/Pages/default.aspx.

[5] "American Association of Community Colleges, "Competencies for Community College Leaders," accessed April 2, 2013, http://www.aacc.nche.edu/Resources/competencies/Documents/compentenciesforleaders.pdf.

[6] Kim Jones and Aimee Howley, "Contextual Influences on Superintendents' Time Usage," *Education Policy Analysis Archives* 17.23 (2009): 2.

[7] Fanny Cheung and Diane Halpern, "Women at the Top: Powerful Leaders Define Success as Work + Family in a Culture of Gender," *American Psychologist* 65.3 (2010): 183.

[8] Stephen R. Covey, *The 7 Habits of Highly Effective People: Powerful Lessons in Personal Change*, 1st Fireside ed. (New York: Fireside, 1990), 149.

[9] Ibid., 148.

[10] Lee Bolman and Terrence Deal, *Reframing Organizations: Artistry, Choice, and Leadership*, 4th ed. (San Francisco: Jossey-Bass, 2008), 14.

[11] Ibid., X.

[12] Ibid.

[13] John C. Maxwell, *The 21 Irrefutable Laws of Leadership* (Nashville: Thomas Nelson Publishers, 1998), 79.

[14] Bolman and Deal, *Reframing Organizations*, xi.

[15] Mothers Against Drunk Driving, "On the Road to a Safer Nation," accessed April 6, 2013, http://www.madd.org/about-us/annual-report/MADD_2011_AnnualReport.pdf., 6.

[16] Mothers Against Drunk Driving, "Mission Statement," accessed April 6, 2013, http://www.madd.org/about-us/mission/.

[17] Bolman and Deal, *Reframing Organizations*, xi.

[18] Ibid.

[19] Ellen B. Mandinach and Sharnell S. Jackson, *Transforming Teaching and Learning through Data-Driven Decision Making* (Thousand Oaks, California: Corwin Press, 2012), 12.

[20] "SWOT Analysis," MindTools, accessed April 6, 2013, http://www.mindtools.com/pages/article/newTMC_05.htm.

[21] Covey, *The 7 Habits of Highly Effective People*, 207.

[22] Gary Chapman, *The Five Love Languages of Teenagers* (Chicago: Northfield Publishing, 2000), 50.

[23] Robert E. Quinn, *Deep Change: Discovering the Leader Within* (San Francisco: Jossey-Bass Inc., 1996), 177.

[24] Maxwell, *The 21 Irrefutable Laws of Leadership*, 77.

[25] Association for Strategic Planning, "Resources," accessed April 8, 2013, http://www.strategyplus.org/resources_articles.shtml.

[26] Bolman and Deal, *Reframing Organizations*, 302.

[27] Edward H. Moore, Donald R. Gallagher, and Don Bagin, *The School and Community* (Upper Saddle River: Pearson, 2012), 70.

[28] Richard Heyman, *How to Say It to Boys* (New York: Prentice Hall Press, 2003), 13.

[29] Carl R. Rogers and Howard Kirschenbaum, *The Carl Rogers Reader* (Boston: Houghton Mifflin, 1989).

[30] Houston Community College, "Dr. Mary S. Spangler, Ed.D.," accessed April 10, 2013, http://www.insidehccs.com/Mary.Spangler/Chevron/SpanglerHiredHCC.pdf.

[31] Bobby Unser, BrainyQuote, accessed October 11, 2013, http://www.brainyquote.com/quotes/quotes/b/bobbyunser126431.html.

EDITORS & CONTRIBUTORS

Editors

Kimberly Battle-Walters Denu, PhD, is the special advisor to the president and provost, a former vice provost for undergraduate programs, and a professor at Azusa Pacific University. Dr. Battle-Walters Denu received her bachelor's degree from Vanguard University of Southern California, her master's degree in social work from Temple University, and her doctorate in sociology, with an emphasis in race and family, from the University of Florida. She has taught graduate courses internationally, was a Fulbright Scholar in South Africa and a presenter at Oxford University, and is an alumna of Harvard University's Institute for Educational Management. Dr. Battle-Walters Denu is also an ordained minister who has done ministry and service on six continents. She served as an associate editor for two academic journals, and published articles on African American issues, women and family matters, and international topics. Her book *Sheila's Shop: Working-Class African American Women Talk about Life, Love, Race, and Hair* (Rowman & Littlefield, 2004) was listed in a Los Angeles newspaper as one of the top ten African American books. She and her husband, Yohannes, are the proud parents of three amazing children—Joshua, Mahlet, and Kylee. She is also the eldest daughter and friend of Janet Walters, the co-editor for this book. A dynamic speaker, Dr. Battle-Walters Denu is passionate about ministry and service, encouraging people around the world.

Janet S. Walters is the vice president of Walters Enterprises and co-owner of Home Video Studio franchise in California. Janet is an ordained minister and enjoys speaking at various church events throughout the United States. She serves on the national advisory council for the United Church of the Living God. Janet is presently working with an Assembly of God church in California and is involved in a number of vibrant ministries. Prior to running her own business with her husband, Janet worked for the Los Angeles County Department of Health Services as human resources director for thirty-eight years. She and her husband, Randall, have been married for over forty years and both enjoy traveling the world and finding new adventures. She is the mother of four daughters and has five lovely grandchildren. Her favorite pastime is nurturing and encouraging women in the faith.

Contributors

Ilene L. Bezjian, DBA, serves as the senior corporate consultant with The Genysys Group, a company assisting organizations and individuals in the midst of deep change. Dr. Bezjian brings a unique perspective, serves on several boards, and is a sought-after speaker. She was the dean of the School of Business and Management for fourteen years and was a professor of marketing for twenty years at a faith-based institution in the Los Angeles area. Prior to her career in higher education, she worked as a consultant in the field of marketing and employee development in the government, aerospace, and entertainment industries, and with small business enterprises. She continues to serve at Newport Church in Santa Ana, California, and is committed to mentoring the millennial generation. She has been married to Dr. Vic Bezjian, Lt. Col., USAF Reserves, for thirty-three years and is the proud mother of two children, James and Laurie.

Pamela M. Christian, PhD, currently serves as a professor of doctoral studies in the Department of Educational Leadership at Azusa Pacific University. Her career in education includes leadership experience within both public and private universities, community college, and in partnership programs with K-12 education. Experienced in leading student groups abroad, she's taught in the state of Alaska and the countries of Ghana, Ethiopia, Egypt, Mexico, South Africa, and the Netherlands. She received the prestigious American Council on Education Fellowship Award, and participated in both the Harvard Institute for Management and Leadership in Education and the Lakin Institute for Mentored Leadership. Dr. Christian formerly served eight years in the Office of the Provost at APU, initially as special assistant for university diversity, as well as assistant provost and associate provost.

Kelly Dickson, MDiv, is the minister of adult ministries at St. Andrew's Presbyterian Church in Newport Beach, California, where she has served in young adult, women, and marriage ministries. She received her master of divinity from Fuller Theological Seminary in 2009 and has been working in full-time ministry for more than ten years. She is passionate about soul care and walking with others as they discover God's presence in their lives. Kelly and her husband, Dustin, have been married ten years, and they have two children, Isaac and Kaelyn.

Doretha A. O'Quinn, PhD, received her master's degree and her doctorate in intercultural education from Biola University, and her bachelor's in theology from Life Pacific College. She is also an ordained Foursquare minister. Dr. O'Quinn is the provost and vice president of academic affairs at Vanguard University. She has served in administrative leadership positions at Biola, Point Loma Nazarene, and Azusa Pacific Universities. She is the author of *Silent Voices, Powerful Messages*, has contributed chapters for several Moody Press books, and has been a recipient of multiple professional and civic awards. She is an international educator and conference speaker in east, west, and southern Africa, as well as in Central America, Asia, and other parts of the world. Her passion is mentoring young women, educational instruction, and preaching the Word. Dr. O'Quinn and her husband, Michael, have been married for forty years, and have four adult children and eight grandchildren.

Irene Neller, MA, is vice president for communications, marketing, and admissions at Fuller Theological Seminary. Irene has served in education, leading marketing programs for Biola University and Fuller. A recognized leader in Christian higher education, she was chair for the Council of Christian Colleges and Universities (CCCU) national committee for communication officers. She earned her bachelor's in communications from Bethany University, and her master's in communications from California State University, Fullerton. She's earned national recognition for advertising campaigns by the American Marketing Association, the Admissions National Reporting Agency, the Council of Advancement in Support of Education, and the Public Relations Society of America. Neller volunteers her time for nonprofit organizations and is committed to mentoring girls and women. She has been married twenty-eight years and has two sons.

Jamie Noling-Auth, DMin, is the university pastor and dean of spiritual life, inclusion, and leadership at George Fox University in Newberg, Oregon. Before her recent move to Oregon, Noling-Auth served as an associate campus pastor and director of discipleship ministries at Azusa Pacific University in Southern California for nine years. She has also taught as an adjunct professor for Azusa Pacific University's School of Theology and Department of Communication Studies. Noling-Auth earned her doctor of ministry degree at Gordon-Conwell Theological Seminary, her master's in theology at Fuller Theological Seminary, and her bachelor's in communication at Pepperdine University. She has worked in Christian higher education for the past fifteen years, including work at Gordon College, Vanguard University, and Westmont College, and she has served on the CCCU Spiritual Life Commission. Noling-Auth and her husband, John, have two little boys, Andrew and Luke.

Carla D. Sanderson, PhD, has a career spanning from critical care nursing and nursing education to higher education leadership as a provost and vice president. Dr. Sanderson has been an actively involved leader by serving on trustee boards and doing national and international presentations on topics such as accreditation, liberal arts education, and leadership development. Her work in accreditation includes workshops for the Kurdish Regional Government in Northern Iraq. In 2014, she retired from Union University after thirty-two years and was named provost emeritus. In her new role with Chamberlain College of Nursing, Dr. Sanderson is giving leadership to the college's growth by ensuring excellence in accreditation and regulation. She is an active leader in her church, and she and her husband are the parents of three adult sons.

Melanie P. Wolf, MA, is the director of discipleship ministries at Point Loma Nazarene University. Before joining the Office of Spiritual Development at PLNU, Melanie worked in discipleship and small group programs at Wheaton College and Azusa Pacific University. Melanie received her master's in educational ministries from Wheaton College after completing her bachelor's in Christian education. In addition to her years working with college students, Melanie worked in youth, family, and children's ministries in local churches. She holds a certificate in leadership coaching and is currently pursuing certification in spiritual direction. Melanie and her husband, Philip, have four children and live in San Diego, California.

BIBLIOGRAPHY

Adams, R. J. Q. "The Women's Part." *Arms and the Wizard: Lloyd George and the Ministry of Munitions 1915–1916.* West Sussex, United Kingdom: Littlehampton Books, 1978.

American Association of Community Colleges. "Competencies for Community College Leaders." Accessed April 2, 2013. http://www.aacc.nche.edu/About/Who/Pages/default. aspx.

_____. "Who We Are." Accessed April 2, 2013. http://www.aacc.nche.edu/About/Who/Pages/default.aspx.

Association for Strategic Planning. "Resources." Accessed April 8, 2013. http://www. strategyplus.org/resources_articles.shtml.

Bardwick, Judith. "Peacetime Management and Wartime Leadership." In *The Leader of the Future,* eds. Frances Hesselbein, Marshall Goldsmith, and Richard Beckchard, 131–39. New York: Jossey-Bass, 1996.

Barnett, Douglas, et al. "Building New Dreams-Supporting Parents' Adaptation to Their Child with Special Needs." *Infant and Young children* 13.3 (2003): 184–200.

Barton, Ruth Haley. *Equal to the Task: Men and Women in Partnership.* Downers Grove: InterVarsity Press, 1998.

Battle-Walters, Kimberly. *Sheila's Shop: Working-Class African American Women Talk about Life, Love, Race, and Hair.* Lanham, Maryland: Rowman & Littlefield, 2004.

Battle-Walters Denu, Kimberly. "For Better or Worse . . . Is Marriage a Good Thing? Christian Women Give Advice to Singles Before They Say 'I Do.'" In *Doing Good, Departing from Evil: Research Findings for the 21st Century.* Ed. Carole J. Lambert. 71–88. New York: Peter Lang, 2009.

_____. "Sheroes: Mothers Make Great Leaders, Naturally." *Women in Higher Education* 18 (2009): 23–24.

Benner, David G. *The Gift of Being Yourself.* Downers Grove, Illinois: InterVarsity Press, 2004.

_____. *Spirituality and the Awakening Self: The Sacred Journey of Transformation.* Grand Rapids: Brazos Press, 2012.

Blair, Sampson L. "Employment, Family, and Perceptions of Marital Quality among Husbands and Wives." *Journal of Family Issues* 14.2 (1993): 189–212.

Bloom, Barbara and Robin Cohen. "Summary Health Statistics for U.S. Children: National Health Interview Survey, 2006." Center for Disease Control and Prevention. Accessed September 10, 2013. http://www.cdc.gov/nchs/data/series/sr_10/sr10_234.pdf.

Bolman, Lee G., and Terrence E. Deal. *Reframing Organizations: Artistry, Choice, and Leadership,* 4th edition. San Francisco: Jossey-Bass, 2008.

Boyer, Ernest. "Creating the New American College," *The Chronicle of Higher Education,* March 9, 1994. Accessed May 27, 2014. http://www.chronicle.com/article/Creating-the%20New-American/93483/.

Bossidy, Larry, Charles Buruck, and Ram Charan. *Execution: The Discipline of Getting Things Done.* New York: Crown Business, 2002.

Brown, Brene. *Daring Greatly: How the Courage to Be Vulnerable Transforms the Way We Live, Love, Parent, and Lead.* New York: Gotham Books, 2012.

Borzelleca, Daniel. "The Male-Female Ratio in College." *Forbes.* February 16, 2012. Accessed May 20, 2014. http://www.forbes.com/sites/ccap/2012/02/16/themale-female-ratio-in-college/.

Brown, Heidi. "U.S. Maternity Leave Benefits Are Still Dismal." Forbes. May 11, 2009. Accessed August 8, 2009. http://sanders.senate.gov/newsroom/news/?id=c840d1fd-d622-4412-a2ca-404c3e48e433.

Brueggemann, Walter. *Spirituality of the Psalms.* Minneapolis: Fortress Press, 2002.

Buechner, Frederick. *Wishful Thinking: A Theological ABC.* New York: Harper & Row, 1973.

Bussey, John. "How Women Can Get Ahead: Advice from Female CEOs." *Wall Street Journal,*
May 18, 2012. Accessed March 30, 2013. http://online.wsj.com/article/SB10001424052702
303879604577410520511235252.html.

Calhoun, Adele Ahlberg. *Spiritual Disciplines Handbook: Practices That Transform Us.*
Downers Grove, Illinois: InterVarsityPress, 2005.

Carter, Erik. "What Matters Most." Presented at The Summer Institute on Theology and
Disability. Chicago, Illinois, July 16–20, 2012.

Center for Disease Control and Prevention. "Autism Spectrum Disorders (ASDs): Data &
Statistics." Accessed September 15, 2013. http://www.cdc.gov/ncbddd/autism/data.html.
_____. "Hearing Loss in Children." Accessed September 5, 2013. http://www.cdc.gov/
ncbddd/hearingloss/data.html.

Center for Reformed Theology and Apologetics. "Westminster Shorter Catechism."
Accessed April 8, 2013. http://www.reformed.org/documents/wsc/index.html.

Chapman, Gary. *The Five Love Languages of Teenagers.* Chicago: Northfield Publishing,
2000.

Cheung, Fanny M., and Diane F. Halpren. "Women at the Top: Powerful Leaders Define
Success as Work + Family in a Culture of Gender." *American Psychologist* 65.3 (2010):
182–93.

Chittenden, Eva H., and Christine S. Ritchie. "Work-Life Balancing: Challenges and
Strategies,"*Journal of Palliative Medicine* 14 (2011): 871–873.

Collins, Jim. *Good to Great.* New York: Harper Collins Publisher, 2001.

Cooper-White, Pamela. "Becoming a Clergy Mother: A Study of How Motherhood Changes
Ministry." *Congregations* 3 (2004): 15.

Covey, Stephen. *First Things First: To Live, to Love, to Learn, to Leave a Legacy.* New York:
Simon & Schuster, 1994.
_____. *The 7 Habits of Highly Effective People.* New York: Free Press, 1989.
_____. *The 7 Habits of Highly Effective People: Powerful Lessons in Personal Change.* 1st
Fireside edition. New York: Fireside, 1990.

Creegan, Nicola Hoggard, and Christine D. Pohl. *Living on the Boundaries: Evangelical
Women, Feminism, and the Theological Academy.* Downers Grove, Illinois: InterVarsity
Press, 2005.

Daft, Richard. *The Leadership Experience,* 3rd ed. Mason, Ohio: Thomson, South Western,
2005.

Dagher, Rada K. "A Longitudinal Analysis of Postpartum Depression among Employed
Women." Doctoral dissertation, University of Minnesota, 2007.

"Depression in Women: Understanding the Gender Gap." Mayo Clinic. January 19, 2013.
Accessed August 24, 2014. http://www.mayoclinic.com/health/depression/MH00035.

Dess, Greory, Thomas Lumpkin, and Marilyn Taylor. *Strategic Management: Creating
Competitive Advantages.* New York: McGraw-Hill, 2004.

DiMari, Christina. *Cultivating Pearls.* Fort Collins, Colorado: Mountain Creations, 2013.
_____. *Ocean Star: You're Designed to Shine, A Memoir.* Carol Stream: Tyndale House,
2006.
_____. *You're Designed to Shine Study Guide.* Loveland, Colorado: Group Publishing,
2011.

Dockery, David S. *Renewing Minds: Serving Church and Society through Christian Higher
Education.* Nashville, Tennessee: B & H Publishing Group, 2008.

Ellison, Katherine. *The Mommy Brain: How Motherhood Makes Us Smarter.* New York:
Basic Books, 2005.

Evans, E. Elrena, and Caroline Grant, *Mama, PhD: Women Write about Motherhood and
Academic Life.* Piscataway, New Jersey: Rutgers University Press, 2008.

Ferrara, Pamela. "Women in the Labor Force." *Oregon Labor Market Information System.*
April, 2008. Accessed August 6, 2008. http://www.qualityinfo.org/olmisj.

Fincher, Jonalyn Grace. *Ruby Slippers: How the Soul of a Woman Brings Her Home.* Grand
Rapids: Zondervan, 2007.

"Forbes, the World's 100 Most Powerful Women." *Forbes*. May 28, 2014. Accessed July 11, 2014. http://www.forbes.com/power-women/.

Forcey, Linda Renny. "Feminist Perspectives on Mothering and Peace." In *Mothering: Ideology, Experience, and Agency* , eds. E. Nakano Glenn, Grace Chang, and Linda Renny Forcey, 355–376. New York: Routledge, 1994.

Foster, Kristin M. "Ministry and Motherhood: A Collision of Callings?" *Theology and Mission* 16 (1989): 99.

Foxworth, Jo. *Boss Lady: An Executive Woman Talks about Making It*. New York: Warner Books, 1978.

Frankel, Lois P. *Nice Girls Don't Get the Corner Office: 101 Unconscious Mistakes Women Make that Sabotage their Careers*. New York: Hachette Book Group, 2004.

Freedman, Brian H., Luther G. Kalb, Benjamin Zablotsky, and Elizabeth A. Stuart. "Relationship Status among Parents of Children with Autism Spectrum Disorders: A Population-Based Study." *Journal of Autism and Developmental Disorders* 42.2 (2012): 539–548. Accessed September 2013. doi:10.1007/s10803-011-1269-y.

Friedan, Betty. *The Feminine Mystique*. New York: Free Press, 1963.

Fuller, Bonnie. "Marissa Mayer Shouldn't Be Criticized for Building an Office Nursery." *The Huffington Post* (February 26, 2013). Accessed May 25, 2014. http://www.huffingtonpost.com/bonnie-fuller/marissa-mayer-office-nursery.

Geisler, Jill. "What Great Bosses Know about Leading Strategically." *Poytner*. January 10, 2010. Accessed May 2014. http://www.poynter.org/how-tos/leadership-management/what-great-bosses-know/100128/what-great-bosses-know-about-leading-strategically/.

Gibbard Cook, Sarah. "Mama, PhD: A Companion for Mothers and Scholars." *Women in Higher Education* 17 (August 2008): 21.

_____. "Research Universities Work to Increase Faculty Flexibility." *Women in Higher Education* 17 (July 2008): 6–7.

Global Down Syndrome Foundation. "FAQ and Facts about Down Syndrome." Accessed September 13, 2013. http://www.globaldownsyndrome.org/about-down-syndrome/facts-about-down-syndrome/.

Green-McCreight, Kathryn. *Darkness Is My Only Companion: A Christian Response to Mental Illness*. Grand Rapids: Brazos Press, 2006.

Greenwald, Maurine W. *Women, War, and Work: The Impact of World War I on Women Workers in the United States*. Ithaca, New York: Cornell University Press, 1990.

Grzelakowski, Maureen. *Mother Leads Best: 50 Women Who Are Changing the Way Organizations Define Leadership*. Chicago: Dearborn Trade Publishing, 2005.

Gutmann, Amy. "Time for More Women to Lead Our Schools." *Washington Post*. February 22, 2013. http://articles.washingtonpost.com/1013-02-22/national37232960_1_higher-education-women-universities.

Halpern, Diane, and Fanny Cheung. *Women at the Top: Powerful Leaders Tell Us How to Combine Work and Family*. Malden, Massachusetts: Wiley-Blackwell, 2008.

Hartley, Sigan L., et al. "The Relative Risk and Timing of Divorce in Families of Children with Autism Spectrum Disorder." *Journal of Family Psychology* 24.4 (August 2010), 449–457. Accessed September 2013, doi:10.1037/a0019847.

Heath, Chip, and Dan Heath. *Decisive: How to Make Better Choices in Life and Work*. New York: Crown Business, 2013.

Heilman, Madeline. "Motherhood: A Potential Source of Bias in Employment." *Journal of Applied Psychology* 93 (2008): 189–198.

Hesselbeck, Frances, Marshall Goldsmith, and Richard Beckhard, editors. *The Leader of the Future*. San Francisco: Jossey-Bass, 1996.

Heyman, Richard. *How to Say It to Boys*. New York: Prentice Hall Press, 2003.

Hill, E. Jeffery, et al. "Exploring the Relationship of Workplace Flexibility, Gender, and Life Stage to Family-to-Work Conflict, and Stress and Burnout," *Community, Work & Family* 11 (2008): 165–181.

Hitt, Michael A., and Duane Ireland. "The Essence of Strategic Leadership: Managing Human and Social Capital." *Journal of Leadership and Organizational Studies* 9 (2002): 3–14.

Hoddap, Robert M., and Richard C. Urbano. "Divorce in Families of Children with Down Syndrome: A Population Based Study." *American Journal of Mental Retardation* 112 (2007): 261–274. Accessed July 12, 2014. dsagsl.org/storage/forms-for-news-posts/DivorceDownSyndrome.pdf.

Houston Community College. "Dr. Mary S. Spangler, Ed.D." Accessed April 10, 2013, http://www.insidehccs.com/Mary.Spangler/Chevron/SpanglerHiredHCC.pdf.

Hughes, Richard, and Katherine Beatty. "Five Steps to Leading Strategically." *Training + Development* 59 (2005): 46. Accessed July 12, 2014. www.ccl.org/Leadership/pdf/news/TDCCLStrategicLeadership.pdf.

Jakes, T. D. "Maximize the Moment." *Time Life Video Series*. Alexandria,Virginia, 2001.

Jarrett, Valerie. "Women's History Month Proclamation." *Council on Women and Girls*. March 1, 2012. Accessed May 14, 2014. http://www.whitehouse.gov/blog/2012/03/01/womens-history-month-proclamation.

John Wiley & Sons. "How to Manage Time by Prioritizing Daily Tasks." 2013. Accessed August 6, 2013, http://www.dummies.com/how-to/content/how-to-manage-time-by.

Jones, Kim, and Aimee Howley. "Contextual Influences on Superintendents' Time Usage." *Education Policy Analysis Archives* 17.23 (2009): 2.

Josefowitz, Natasha. *Paths to Power.* Philippines: Addison-Wesley, 1982. "The Juggle Struggle: Strategies for Balancing Work and Family." Knowledge@ Wharton. University of Pennsylvania. December 2010. http://knowledge.wharton.upenn. edu/10000women/article/cfm.2010.

Kaplan, Robert, and David Norton. "The Balanced Scorecard-Measures That Drive Performance." *Harvard Business Review* (Jan.–Feb. 1992): 71–79.

Kidd, Sue Monk. *When the Heart Waits.* New York: Harper Collins, 1990.

Kokemuller, Neil. "The Importance of Timing in Leadership." *Chron.com*. Accessed October 5, 2013. smallbusiness.chron.com/importance-timing-leadership-51987.html.

Kouzes, James, and Barry Z. Posner. "Seven Lessons for Leading the Voyage to the Future." In *The Leader of the Future*, eds. Frances Hesselbein, Marshall Goldsmith, and Richard Beckhard, 99–110. San Francisco: Jossey-Bass, 1996.

Kramer, Vicki W., Alison M. Konrad, and Sumru Erkut. "Critical Mass on Corporate Boards: Why Three or More Women Enhance Governance." Wellesley Centers for Women's Publications, 2006. Accessed July 26, 2011. http://www.wcwonline.org.

Kristof, Nicholas, and Sheryl WuDunn. *Half the Sky*. New York: Vintage Books, 2009.

Labich, Kenneth. "Take Control of Your Career." *Fortune* (November 18, 1991): 89. Accessed July 12, 2014. http://archive.fortune.com/magazines/fortune/fortune_archive/1991/11/18/75761/index.htm.

Lafair, Sylvia. *Don't Bring It to Work: Breaking the Family Patterns That Limit Success.* San Francisco: Jossey-Bass, 2009.

Lauer, Charles. "The Lessons of Parenting." *Modern Healthcare* 34 (2004): 36.

Licona, Thomas. *Educating for Character: How Our Schools Can Teach Respect and Responsibility*. New York: Bantam Doubleday Dell Publishing, 1991.

Lindgergh, Anne Morrow. *Gift from the Sea*. New York: Pantheon Books, 1955.

Longman, Karen, ed. *Thriving in Leadership: Strategies for Making a Difference in Christian Higher Education.* Abilene, Texas: Abilene Christian University Press, 2012.

MacDonald, Gordon. *Ordering Your Private World,* 3rd ed. Nashville: Thomas Nelson, 2003.

Mandinach, Ellen, B., and Sarnell S. Jackson. *Transforming Teaching and Learning through Data-Driven Decision Making.* Thousand Oaks: Corwin Press, 2012.

Manktelow, James, and Amy Carlson. "To Do List: The Key to Efficiency." *MindTools*. Accessed August 6, 2013. http://www.mindtools.com/pages/article.

Maxwell, John, C. *The 21 Irrefutable Laws of Leadership*. Nashville: Thomas Nelson Publishers, 1998.

McKinnon, Gina. *What Would Grace Do? How to Live a Life like the Princess of Hollywood.* New York: Penguin Group, 2012.

Miller, William R., and Kathleen A. Jackson. *Practical Psychology for Pastors.* New Jersey: Prentice Hall, 1995.

Moore, Edward H., Donald R. Gallagher, and Don Bagin. *The School and Community.* Upper Saddle River, New Jersey: Pearson, 2012.

Morris, Betsy. "Is Your Family Wrecking Your Career? (And Vice Versa)." *Fortune* 135 (1997): 70-76. Accessed July 13, 2014. Archive.fortune.com/magazines/fortune/fortune_archive/1997/03/17/223313/index.htm.

Mothers Against Drunk Driving. "Mission Statement." Accessed April 6, 2013. http://www.madd.org/about-us/mission/.

_____. "On the Road to a Safer Nation." Accessed April 6, 2013. http://www.madd.org/about-us/annual-report/MADD_2011_AnnualReport.pdf.6.

National Women's Law Center. "The Reality of the Workforce: Mothers Are Working Outside the Home." February 2008. Accessed August 6, 2008. http://www.nwlc.org.

Northouse, Peter G. *Leadership Theory and Practice,* 5th ed. Thousand Oaks, California: Sage Publications, 2010.

Nouwen, Henri. *In the Name of Jesus: Reflections on Christian Leadership.* New York: The Crossroad Publishing Company, 1989.

_____. *Life of the Beloved.* New York: The Crossroad Publishing Company, 1992.

_____. *The Wounded Healer: Ministry in Contemporary Society.* New York: Crown Publishing, 1972.

Nugent, Georgia. "Can We Stop Talking about the Glass Ceiling?" *The Washington Post.* February 22, 2013. Accessed February 22, 2013. http://articles.washingtonpost.com/2013-02-22/national/37232957_1_female-leaders-first-female-president-higher-education.

Oasis @ MAAP. "Asperger Syndrome." Accessed September 15, 2013. http:/ / www.aspergersyndrome.org/ Articles / kelley.aspx.

Oates, Kim, Elizabeth Hall, and Tamara Anderson. "Pursuing Multiple Callings: The Implication of Balancing Career and Motherhood for Women and the Church." *Journal of Psychology and Christianity* 27.3 (2005): 227–237.

Oates, Kim, Elizabeth Hall, Tamera Anderson, and Michelle Willingham. "Calling and Conflict: The Sanctification of Work in Working Mothers." *Psychology of Religion and Spirituality* 4.1 (February 2012): 71–83.

Oden, Thomas. *Pastoral Theology: Essentials of Ministry.* San Francisco: Harper and Row, 1983.

Palpant, Andrea. "Suburbia Needs Jesus, Too." *Christianity Today (*May 21, 2013): 2–3. Accessed October 25, 2013. http://www.christianitytoday.com/women/2013/may/suburbia-needs-jesus-too.html.

Parks-Stamm, Elizabeth. "Motivated to Penalize: Women's Strategic Rejection of Successful Women." *Personality and Social Psychology Bulletin* 34 (2008): 237–47.

Peterson, Eugene. *The Contemplative Pastor: Returning to the Art of Spiritual Direction.* Grand Rapids: Eerdmans Publishing, 1993.

Quinn, Robert E. *Deep Change Discovering the Leader Within.* San Francisco: Jossey-Bass, 1996.

Ries, Eric. *The Lean Startup: How Today's Entrepreneurs Use Continuous Innovation to Create Radically Successful Businesses.* New York: Crown Business, 2011.

Rima, Samuel. *Leading from the Inside Out.* Grand Rapids: Baker Books, 2000.

Roberts, Robin. *From the Heart: Seven Rules to Live By.* New York: Hyperion, 2007.

Rogers, Carl R., and Howard Kirschenbaum. *The Carl Rogers Reader.* Boston: Houghton Mifflin, 1989.

Roosevelt, Eleanor. *BrainyQuote.* Accessed July 13, 2014. http://www.brainyquote.com/quotes/authors/e/eleanor_roosevelt.

Saad, Lydia. "Despite Less Time and Rest, Working Moms Managing Well." *Gallop Well-Being.* May 7, 2010. Accessed July 13, 2014. *http://www.gallup.com/poll/127745/despite-less-time-rest-working-moms-managing.aspx.*

Sandberg, Sheryl. *Lean In: Women, Work, and the Will to Lead.* New York: Alfred A. Knopf, 2013.

Sansone, Kathryn. *Women First, Family Always: Real-Life Wisdom from a Mother of Ten.* Des Moines, Iowa: Meredith Books, 2006.

Schoemaker, Paul, Samantha Howland, and Steve Krupp. "Strategic Leadership: The Essential Skills." *Harvard Business Review* (January-February 2013): 2–5.

Schwartz, Felice. "Management Women and the New Facts of Life." *Harvard Business Review* 89.1 (January 1989): 65–76.

Scott, Kesho Yvonne. *The Habit of Surviving: Black Women's Strategies for Life.* New Brunswick, New Jersey: Rutgers University Press, 1991.

Sentilles, Sarah. *A Church of Her Own: What Happens When A Woman Takes the Pulpit.* Boston: Mariner Books, 2009.

Shawchuck, Norman, and Roger Heuser. *Leading the Congregation: Caring for Yourself While Serving the People.* Nashville: Abingdon Press, 1993.

Slawinski, Natalie. "Strategic Leadership." In *Cases in Leadership*, eds. W. Glenn Rowe and Laura Guerrero, 297–99. Los Angeles: Sage Publications, 2010.

Smith, Gordon T. *Courage and Calling.* Downers Grove, Illinois: InterVarsity Press, 1999.

"Sonia Sotomayor: From Bronx Housing Projects to the U.S. Supreme Court." Interview by Katie Couric. *The Katie Show.* February 8, 2013. http://katiecouric.com/videos/sonia-sotomayor-from-bronx-housing-projects-to-the-u-s-supreme-court/.

Sotamayor, Sonia. *My Beloved World.* New York: Alfred A. Knopf, 2013.

Spar, Deborah. "Why Our Brightest Female Graduates Are Still at a Disadvantage." *The Washington Post.* February 2013. Accessed February 27, 2013. http://www.washingtonpost.com/national/on-leadership/why-our-brightest-female-graduates-are-still-at-a-disadvantage/2013/02/21/68cb192a-7c5a-11e2-82e8-61a46c2cde3d_story.html.

Starling, Kelly. "Power Moms." *Ebony* (July 1999): 52–58.

Stevenson, Jeanne. *In Her Own Time: Women and Developmental Issues in Pastoral Care.* Minneapolis: Augsburg Fortress, 2000.

Stout, Kristie Lu. "Chinese Women Fight to Shake Off 'Leftover' Label," *CNN,* August 21, 2013. Accessed May 27, 2014, www.cnn.com/2013/08/21/world/asoa/cjoma-women-lu-stout/.

Strickland, Alonzo, and Arthur Thompson. *Strategic Management: Concepts and Cases*, 13th edition. New York: McGraw-Hill/Irwin. 2003.

Strong, Bryan, and Christine DeVault. *The Marriage and Family Experience,* 6th edition. St. Paul, Minnesota: West Publshing Group, 1995.

Strong, Bryan, and Theodore F. Cohen. *The Marriage and Family Experience: Intimate Relationships in a Changing Society,* 12th edition. Belmont, California: Cengage Learning, 2014.

Sweet, Stephen, and Phyllis Moen. "Integrating Educational Careers in Work and Family: Women's Return to School and Family Life Quality." *Community, Work and Family* 10 (2007): 231–250.

"SWOT Analysis. Discover New Opportunities. Manage and Eliminate Threats." MindTools. Accessed April 6, 2013. http://www.mindtools.com/pages/article/newTMC_05.htm.

Taylor, Barbara Brown. *The Preaching Life.* Plymouth, UK: Cowley Publications, 1993.

Thomas, Joyce King. "Joyce King Thomas Offers Tips on Getting Ahead." *Advertising Age,* September 24, 2012. Accessed May 16, 2014. http://adage.com/article/special-report-100-most-influential-women-in-advertising/joyce-king-thomas-offers-tips-ahead/237304.

Torabi, Farnoosh. *When She Makes More: 10 Rules for Breadwinning Women.* New York: Hudson Street Press, 2014.

Unser, Bobby. BrainyQuote, Accessed October 11, 2013, http://www.brainyquote.com/quotes/quotes/b/bobbyunser126431.html.

U.S. Bureau of Labor Statistics, *Occupational Outlook Handbook, 1990–1991*. Washington, DC. Accessed July 13, 2014. http://www.bls.gov/ooh/.

U.S. Census Bureau. American FactFinder. "Selected Social Characteristics in the United States: 2005–2007." Accessed July 17, 2009. http://factfinder.census.gov/servlet/ADPTable?_bm=y&-geo_id=01000US&-qr_name=AC.U.S. Census Bureau, "Fertility of American Women: 2008" Accessed August 6, 2009. http://www.census.gov/population/www/socdemo/fertility/mer-fert-slides.htm.

U.S. Department of Labor: Bureau of Labor Statistics. "Women in the Labor Force: A Data Book, Report 1011." December 2008. Accessed July 16, 2009. http://www.bls.gov/cps/wlf-table7-2008.pdf.

_____. *2008* "Annual Averages—Household Data—Tables from Employment and Earnings." Accessed May 27, 2014. http://www.bls.gov/cps_aa2008.hm.

Van Ogtrop, Kristin. *Just Let Me Lie Down: Necessary Terms for the Half-Insane Working Mom*. New York: Little, Brown and Company, 2010.

Vandeley Design. "7 Tips for Prioritizing Tasks Effectively." April 21, 2011. Accessed August 6, 2013. http://www.vandelaydesign.com/blog/business/how-to-prioritize-tasks/.

Vanier, Jean. *From Brokenness to Community*. Mahwah: Paulist Press, 1992.

Waite, Linda, and Maggie Gallagher. *The Case for Marriage: Why Married People Are Happier, Healthier, and Better Off Financially*. New York: Doubleday, 2000.

Walcutt, Diana. "Birth Order and Personality." American Psychological Association's Psychological Central. Accessed May 26, 2014. http://psychcentral.com/blog/archives/2009/07/22/birth-order-and-personality/.

Wallace, William Ross. "What Rules the World." In J. K. Hoyt's Cyclopedia of Practical Quotations, 402. New York: Funk & Wagnalls, 1896.

Warren, Rick. "What Drives You?" *Oprah's Lifeclass* on the OWN Network. February 24, 2013. Accessed May 19, 2014. www.oprah.com/oprah-lifeclass/Partor-Rick-Warren.

White House Council on Women and Girls. "Women in America: Indicators of Social and Economic Well Being." Report. U.S. Department of Commerce Economics and Statistics Administration. Accessed March 30, 2013. http://www.whitehouse.gov/administration/eop/cwg/data-on-women.

Willard, Dallas. *The Great Omission: Reclaiming Jesus' Essential Teachings on Discipleship*. New York: Harper One, 2006.

Willcoxson, Leslie. "Leading Strategically." *International Journal of Organizational Behavior* 2.2 (2002): 30–36.

Williams, Alex. "The New Math on Campus." *New York Times*. February 5, 2010. Accessed May 20, 2014. http://www.nytimes.com/2010/02/07/fashion/07campus.html.

Wilson, Robin. "Gettysburg College Takes Work-Life Balance Seriously." *The Chronicle of Higher Education* (July 10, 2009): B-8.

_____. "Is Having More than 2 Children an Unspoken Taboo?" *The Chronicle of Higher Education* (July 10, 2009): B-16–19.

Wolf, Erik. "10 Tips for Time Management." *FranklinCoveyReview.com*. Accessed August 7, 2013. http://franklincoveyreview.com/featured/10-tips-for-time-management.

Womack, S. "Careers Put Family Life under Huge Strain." *The Telegraph*. July 17, 2007. Accessed April 2008. http://www.telegraph.co.uk/news. "Women in the Workplace: A Research Roundup." *Harvard Business Review* (2013). Accessed September 10, 2013. http://hbr.org/2013/09/women-in-the-workplace-a-research-roundup/ar/1.

Wymbs, Brian T., et al. "Rate of Predictors of Divorce among Parents of Youth with ADHD." *Journal of Consult Clinical Psychology* (2008): 735–44. Accessed September 2013. http://www.ncbi.nlm.nih.gov/pmc/articles/PMC2631569/.

www.ingramcontent.com/pod-product-compliance
Lightning Source LLC
Chambersburg PA
CBHW032134020426
42334CB00016B/1157